1995

Dreams of Darkness

DREAMS OF DARKNESS

Fantasy and the Films of Val Lewton

J. P. TELOTTE

UNIVERSITY OF ILLINOIS PRESS

Urbana and Chicago

Publication of this work was supported in part by a grant from the Andrew W. Mellon Foundation.

An earlier version of chapter 4 was originally published as "Formulas and Labyrinths: Tracking *The Leopard Man*," in *New Orleans Review* 8 (1981).

This book is printed on acid-free paper

Library of Congress Cataloging in Publication Data

Telotte, J. P., 1949 –
  Saving the dark.

  Bibliography: p.
  Includes index.
  1. Lewton, Val.   2. Horror films—United States—History and criticism.   I. Title.
PN1998.A3L488   1985   791.43′0232′0924   84-6619
ISBN 0-252-01154-6

Contents

1 Seeing in the Dark

The cinema comes to life with dark—like Dracula.

—David Thomson
America in the Dark

An abiding paradox of the movies is that they are made possible by darkness, by the theater's ability to shut out the light, while at the same time they must dispel that darkness by their nature as figurations of light. It is a curious situation that, quite naturally, little troubles us as moviegoers. That light needs darkness, that for the movies to exist the two must work symbiotically, seems of far less moment to our lives than the stories this minor paradox allows us to view. As David Thomson[1] implies however, this phenomenon affords an interesting trope for the working of certain popular film forms. The fantasy genre specifically, populated as it is with figures of night—vampires, werewolves, and all manner of alien presences—draws fundamentally on a realm of darkness and psychic imagery for its existence. Such films typically evoke a dreamlike environment or nightworld in which, as if it were our own sleep, we can pleasurably and profitably immerse ourselves. This pleasure and profit, however, imply more than simply our delight in being scared or amazed as these presences rise up in the dark, and more too than the box office receipts that fantasy films, particularly in recent years, have amassed. Rather, I wish to call attention to their ability to reveal how we also might come "to life with dark," finding an important, even life-enhancing meaning in the fantastic's dream realm. The fantasy film finds its purpose in its capacity to suggest—almost as a paradigm of the movie experience itself—how much our own lives depend on the dark, even as in our waking lives and outside the theater's confines we deny its substance and defy its pull.

The ability of fantasy to rework or refocus our perspective—to let us "see" the dark in the light—has frequently been described.

Tzvetan Todorov, for instance, defines the fantastic in precisely these terms, as a form which evokes an "indirect vision" that transcends or "transgresses" normal perception, as we willingly open our eyes to a world of possibilities usually repressed by the self or denied by custom and culture.[2] Following this lead, Eric Rabkin allows that "the fantastic does more than extend experience; the fantastic contradicts perspectives," and Rosemary Jackson describes how the form "problematizes vision."[3] These opinions can "problematize" our thinking as well, however, leading us to view the genre simply as a response to the everyday world, compensation for some social or personal lack due to cultural or psychic repression. As Jackson succinctly puts it, the fantastic "is never 'free'"[4]; subordinated to the material world and its constraints, fantasy's dark realm has typically been seen as the shadow cast by our world of common day, on which it is totally dependent and in which we find its sole meaning. Thus we are urged to mine and analyze the fantastic in order to understand and, it is hoped, eliminate our individual and cultural pathologies.

Because of film's grounding in the physical world through its representational function and realistic bias, our thinking about cinematic fantasy inevitably shows the trace of this problem. While we readily allow that film, as Siegfried Kracauer has suggested, accomplishes a "redemption of physical reality,"[5] of the material world in all its discernible substance, we hesitate to ascribe to cinematic fantasy a corresponding salvation of our dreams and unconscious desires. In his account of the genre, therefore, Mark Nash concentrates on physical structures, describing a linking of the seen and the unseen, embodied in a characteristic dialectic between "impersonal shots" and "point of view structures"; and he views this formal stylistic as subversive, undermining our normal perspective to help us view reality more clearly.[6] Of course, the many forms of film fantasy have always suffered much critical condescension, because they contravene a perspective rooted in the physical, as they seemingly evoke a dreamlike, even nightmarish world, one apparently far removed from the realm of truth that, by implication, an art grounded in a mechanism and tradition of mimesis should make available. Consequently, these films are often seen as fundamentally seductive, offering audiences not a better understanding of the world they inhabit, but an escape from its pressing—and often depressing—reality.

Certainly, this is the attitude commonly taken toward the horror film, arguably the major form which cinematic fantasy has taken. When *King Kong* first appeared, for instance, what negative comment it drew derived precisely from this realistic bias; thus one critic complained about its "straining our powers of credulity and perhaps also one or two fundamental laws of nature."[7] Later, the film became largely a cultural symbol, a sign of social unease, as Andrew Bergman offers, of the nation's "concern over social and economic chaos and incipient collapse."[8] I do not mean to suggest that this materialist bias is the only approach taken to the horror film, for in light of the persistence of its figures of darkness in the public consciousness, we are increasingly reluctant to hold their fantastic existence hostage to the physical world and its laws. As audience reactions show, even in the case of traditional horror films, such as the monster series produced by Universal Studios in the 1930s and 1940s, we often become, almost in spite of all expectations, completely bound up in the being and fate of those figures of otherness, entranced beyond all cultural relevance with what one critic rightly terms their obviously "absurd presence."[9] Of course, confronted by a society that seems devoted to denying difference and leveling out all values, we may simply find in them a mirror of our individual need for differentiation. But more than merely representing such alienation, these cinematically real presences add an unsettling sense of human incompletion. While film's photographic basis implies that all we see has a model in reality, the horror film confronts us with "copies" which, we would normally hope, have no originals, no correspondence to the real world. Yet we derive a strange satisfaction from their life in the dark, even as they question the whole pattern our perceptions of the world have heretofore fashioned. This fundamental attraction suggests that the horror film does something more than bring our dreams and fears into the light of day where they might be explained away; it also calls attention to a human need, possibly of an archetypal nature, for that realm of darkness and its "absurd" forms of life.

We would do well, therefore, to see in these fantastic images more than a stimulating experience of the strange, a sign of the known world's boundaries, or a symbol of our personal and social discontents. Such applications to the real world, after all, only emerge from a prior contradiction of that realm, such as the horror film's pointed transgression of all that our world is thought to contain and be. Thus a normally safe environment can, in this genre, suddenly seem full of dangers—monsters, ghouls, or vampires; a matrix of civilized human relationships may inexplicably give way to the primal law of survival of the strongest; and stable personalities—like our own—can unexpectedly become protean, unpredictable, and uncontrollable, as in the case of Jekyll and Hyde. Such films, however, draw us back, as if we were acting out a larger, archetypal pattern of return and finding in their transgressions satisfaction for some need. What cinematic fantasy formulates is a *union* of real and imaginary relations—of light and dark—momentarily bound together in an unsettling manner typical of the human psyche and its dreamwork. What its recurrent threats signify, then, is not an abiding fear of the world, others, or even the self's disturbing components which, in the daylight and outside the theater, we usually repress by the massed strength of culture and reason. Cinematic fantasy reflects a desire or need to gain access to an archetypal experience, one of myth and mythic patterns, where we might confront the dreamself we daily turn from and save the dark side of our self and our world from a strictly material perspective.

For this very reason we find the horror film such a paradoxically pleasurable experience. It appeals not simply because it permits us to vanquish demons, dispel mystery, or encode the irrational and aberrant in reason, as many critics would have it; in fact, film often has the opposite effect—starting more fears than it stops, evoking images to haunt us long after we have left the theater, even long after we have forgotten the particular movie in which they first emerged from the dark. Rather, as a fantasy form, the horror film offers an important psychological experience, although one whose significance most viewers remain unconscious of, just as they do their dreams. Psychologist James Hillman describes the "human adventure" as "a wandering through the vale of the world for the sake of making soul," and he describes our "fantasy images" as the very "stuff and values of soul," the necessary material for its creation. By the term "soul," however, he intends something more than our commonplace notions of spiritual substance; it designates "a perspective rather than a substance, a viewpoint toward things rather than a thing itself. This perspective is reflective."[10] The term thus indicates a special way of seeing ourselves, especially our place in a world of other people and substances. It is a viewpoint that comes not fully blown and automatically, but in the course of a lifetime as the result of our individual journeys into the dark or vesperal regions of the psyche through the process of dreaming and fantasizing.[11] By confronting us with images that defy our normal viewpoint and force us to grant reality to things that seemingly lack any correspondence to the world of common day, the horror film experience can cater to this creation. Viewed in this vesperal light, the terrors and preternatural forces we encounter in such films are neither gratuitous nor merely cathartic in effect; they insinuate another sense of the world we inhabit and, more important, another sense of the self. At their best such films massage the psyche, stimulating its growth and development in order that it might better see itself and find its place in the larger scheme of life and death, in the fullness of human reality.

The horror film has long been dominated by the sort of monsters, ghouls, and aberrances that might easily be read as embodiments of our repressed urges and instinctual fears. Frankenstein's monster, the wolfman, the vampire, and Dr. Jekyll/Mr. Hyde have spawned numerous progeny that, in turn, have been subjected to psychological and cultural analysis, as we try to understand the anxieties which their deviations from the normal seem to signal, and thereby banish their disturbing specters from our dreams. The persistence of such images and their basic absurd similarity—their half-human, half-monster aspect—however, continue to trouble our analytical efforts and have led to efforts to deny or reduce their power. Our critical unease with these figures is mirrored by the trivializing process they underwent in the hands of popular filmmakers themselves. During its long life at Universal Studios, the Frankenstein monster, for instance, degenerated from the status of a Promethean myth (*Frankenstein*, 1931), to a malevolent creature, tenuously kept under human control (*Son of Frankenstein*, 1939), to one of a group of nearly interchangeable physical threats to mankind (*House of Frankenstein*, 1944), before becoming the ultimate "straight man" in a comedy routine (*Abbott and Costello Meet Frankenstein*, 1948). Despite such distortions and denials of its true nature, the Frankenstein monster maintained a tenacious hold on our imaginations, as its rejuvenation for a later generation by Hammer Films testifies. While this imaginative persistence suggests that such figures are indeed possessed of a special life of their own, which calls for a different sort of understanding than our normal perspective allows, it also seems clear that their very otherness can undermine that discernment by leading us to seek some compromise between their realm of night and our own world of day.

One group of horror/fantasy films, specifically conceived as an alternative to the works produced by Universal Studios, managed to demonstrate how this compromise might be avoided—by exploiting the archetypal or vesperal potential of the fantasy formula. In the early 1940s RKO Pictures established its own horror unit, headed by producer/writer Val Lewton. Faced with a world war that delivered a much more real and impregnable horror than film could ever conjure, and lacking the rights to any of the cinema's well-known and photogenic fantasy figures other than King Kong, Lewton and his collaborators were forced to take a different path, one simultaneously more real and more truly fantastic. While far more concerned with the texture of reality than their predecessors, the Lewton unit employed this context to lure audiences back into a dark, almost mythic realm, where our lives find their fundamental purpose. Although devoid of the traditional monstrous figures of cinematic horror, their films explore the very source of those well-known images—an internal activity by which the human psyche sets about fully creating itself, gaining its necessary perspective, "making" its "soul." Unlike any other body of fantasy films, the Lewton productions permit us to see precisely what goes on in the dark, where both film and fantasy always carry out their most vital activity.

The Lewton unit came into being in 1942 not because its head had any background in or even a special fondness for the horror genre. In fact, in his usual self-deprecating way, Lewton claims that he was brought in to direct this group because of a misunderstanding: "I write novels for a living, and when RKO was looking for producers, someone told them I had written horrible novels. They mistook the work *horrible* for *horror* and I got the job."[12] Despite this negative assessment of his own talents, Lewton possessed a solid background as a writer and, more important, a keen instinct for a good story. He had published nine novels, one of which—*No Bed of Her Own* (1932)—went through numerous printings and translations before being adapted into a successful movie with a slightly less provocative title, *No Man of Her Own*. Probably more significant is the fact that Lewton could range across a number of different formulas; besides the urban naturalism of *No Bed of Her Own*, he turned his hand to the tale of detection with *The Fateful Star Murder* (1931), the heroic adventure story, *Rape of Glory* (1926), and romantic melodrama, *This Fool Passion* (1934), among other genres. And he seemed to handle each with equal facility and a fine feel for the conventions of the respective formulas. This ability to understand and tap the basic conventions and appeals of a genre was coupled with a capacity for recognizing the cinematic potential inherent in a story. While working as a story editor for David O. Selznick from 1933 to 1942, for example, Lewton is credited with securing the movie rights to a great number of classic tales then in the public domain. The Selznick list of such reserved properties included works like *Julius Caesar* and *A Tale of Two Cities*; and under Lewton's direction it grew to become, in the estimation of friend and fellow producer John Houseman, "the envy of the trade."[13]

That titles such as the two mentioned above were eventually made into successful films suggests an important point about Lewton's talent, which may help us to understand his curious combination of a fondness for the great classics and a tendency to write novels of the most sensationalistic sort, works with titles like *Rape of Glory* and *Where the Cobra Sings*. Apparently he had an almost unerring cinematic sense, a way of knowing what would work on the screen, even though he never directed a single film himself. Contributing to this insight was a deep understanding of formulas and mythic structures that enabled Lewton to discern in the great and the generic alike the presence of important archetypal patterns. What some would term Lewton's genius lay in his grasp of those formulas that we not only commonly employ, but also even *need* to give some order to and communicate our human experience. When hired to organize and run the new B-film unit at RKO, he brought as his major contribution his understanding of the subtle patterns we all dream or fantasize—and which both the best and the merely popular writers have consistently tapped—in the process of making our psyches whole, as Hillman would explain it. Jacques Tourneur, director of the first three films produced by the Lewton unit, appropriately describes his collaborator's work in precisely this context, terming him "the dreamer" of the team, whom he constantly had to bring back to a sense of the real world.[14]

Fortunately, RKO had a history of providing opportunities for such cinematic dreamers and their dreams. Willis O'Brien and Merian Cooper, for instance, a decade earlier had convinced the studio to gamble on an expensive and time-consuming experiment in stop-action animation and fantasy. The result was *King Kong*, an immediate popular success and a picture that, as Tim Onosko explains, "established the type of image that RKO wanted—fantastic, fascinating, and totally original . . . a symbol of the movies themselves."[15] Later, when the studio's prestige and financial stability began to falter, another dreamer was imported and allowed to try his hand; this time it was Orson Welles, fresh from his infamous "War of the Worlds" broadcast, another phenomenally successful excursion into the realm of fantasy. He was given an almost unprecedented free hand to craft the kind of films he wished—the sort which, the front office hoped, might help bail out the troubled studio. Despite the disappointment with which Welles's first efforts, *Citizen Kane* and *Magnificent Ambersons,* were received by studio heads and the general public, the potential for a certain creative freedom apparently lingered at RKO, and the Lewton team benefited from it. Of course, its work was on a much smaller scale; the unit's shooting time, for instance, typically ran just under four weeks, as compared to *King Kong*'s year-long production schedule, and their budgets were minuscule, so whatever financial risk they represented was minimal. Within the bounds of a general directive to produce "chillers" that might run on double bills, therefore, there were few real restrictions. Joel Siegel sums up the situation facing Lewton when he first formed this film unit: "his production unit would make only horror movies with budgets limited to $150,000 per picture. The films were to be 'programmers,' slated for placement on double features in less than key theatres, with a running time not to exceed 75 minutes. [Production Chief Charles] Koerner's office was to dictate the titles of these films, based upon a system of market pre-testing."[16]

Starting with those assigned, usually rather lurid titles, Lewton normally composed a rough story or adapted a property to be filmed. It is at this initial stage of conception that he could draw on his highly developed sense of formula and of the manner in which structure and convention could be manipulated for best effect. Tourneur, in fact, calls attention to this aspect of Lewton's input, particularly remarking on his characteristic concern with "structure, construction, progression of high points, low points" in the narrative.[17] If Lewton subsequently made few appearances on the set during the actual shooting, it was essentially because, as director Mark Robson suggests, he had already "thought everything out" in such detail that little of what he was concerned with had been left to chance.[18]

This summary of Lewton's uncharacteristically creative contributions for a Hollywood producer does not necessarily mean that he was—as we typically think of Welles, for example—the sole creative force behind these films. Even given that, as Lewton's secretary Jessie Ponitz relates, for each screenplay "the last draft was always his,"[19] we should remember that the realization of any script demands a great deal of interpretation, just as the transformation from one medium into another always entails significant change. More obvious, in order to cope adequately with the unit's extreme restrictions on time, money, and resources, all of its members had to be involved in the planning of the films; in effect, an extensive amount of cooperation and perhaps even co-authorship was necessary. Fortunately, the Lewton unit became the home of a number of highly talented and creative individuals who could work well together: writers like DeWitt Bodeen, Curt Siodmak, and Ardel Wray; art director Albert D'Agostino; cinematographer Nicholas Musuraca; and directors Tourneur, Robson, and Robert Wise. Almost all of these talents had some share in the shaping of the films, contributing their own visions to the larger design Lewton tried to set out before them.[20] Bodeen, writer on three of the films, has described the typical preproduction procedure that resulted in a collective sense of what each film was to be. After receiving the front office's audience-tested title, Lewton would devise a general framework for the story—usually out of whole cloth—and that outline was then fleshed out in conference with the writer and director. For a film like *Cat People,* their first effort, Bodeen next sketched out a rough scenario in the form of "a long short story . . . keeping in mind all the story points . . . discussed and feeling free to invent new sequences."[21] Afterward the entire production group met to analyze, evaluate, and revise this story, and from this later conference the first full draft of the screenplay emerged. After several refinements, the shooting script would go to Lewton for his final touches before being passed on to the director, whose task it was to interpret this collective product. A major result of this process was, as Wise describes it, the creation of the sense of a "kind of community of creators, a meeting of the minds between

Lewton, his directors, his writers and sometimes art directors. . . . It was very stimulating, very exciting."[22]

Because of this collaborative process, any evaluation of these films solely from a single auteurist vantage could be misleading, perhaps even quite wrongheaded. Lewton, after all, did not direct any of the eleven films he produced at RKO, and in only two cases—*The Body Snatcher* (1945) and *Bedlam* (1946)—did he even take screen credit for his contributions as writer.[23] Since the purpose of this study is not simply to survey the Lewton films, but to mark off a significant and distinct textual field of the fantasy film, however, the question of authorship becomes a secondary and almost irrelevant consideration.[24] Of more concern is a certain unity of conception and accomplishment that marks these films and redounds to the credit of the entire Lewton unit—the producer, directors, writers, actors, and other co-workers. In fact, a conclusive argument either for or against Lewton's status as the auteur in this case may even prove impossible, as Paul Willemen demonstrates in his assessment of Tourneur's directorial career: "No conceivable auteur analysis of Lewton's work would be able to dispel at least a suspicion that the producer was merely trying to recapture and recreate the successful elements of the films Tourneur had directed for him. Obviously this argument could equally be applied to Tourneur, who could be seen to have spent the rest of his career elaborating on the work of Lewton."[25] To focus attention all the more clearly on the films themselves, therefore, we might think of the Lewton unit as representative of a particular achievement in cinematic discourse and of the films this group produced as demonstrative of a singular development in film fantasy.

Within this textual field we have identified, we find a body of films that clearly share significant characteristics—ones important for the study of the fantasy impulse and, what is at least equally important, for a proper understanding of the way in which film addresses this genre. In slightly more than three years the Lewton unit produced eleven films, nine of which can be classed within the large area of fantasy in light of their concern with myth, folk beliefs, mysterious and murderous events, and our basic fears of the unknown.[26] It is with this body of work that Lewton earned the popular sobriquet of "Chillmaster." The chills these films consistently evoked, however, owed not simply to the typical threatening presences, monsters, or ghouls lurking about; rather, they derived largely from what we do not see, both because it lacks normal substance, and because it is essentially something within the self, defiant of the normal, externally directed perspective. On the occasion of Lewton's death at the age of forty-six, Manny Farber singled out this quality in the body of work he left, remarking especially on how he "hid much more of his story than any other filmmaker, and forced his crew to create drama almost abstractly with symbolic sounds, textures, and the like."[27]

Of course, we traditionally think of film as drawing its greatest capital from photographing what we *do see*, as the dominant realistic theories of cinema testify. We typically accept that its raison d'être is, as André Bazin argues, to reconstruct "a perfect illusion of the outside world."[28] By capturing the essence of reality on celluloid, we presume, film frees it from time and the conditions of its being, frees it so that we might observe its tangible presence all the more clearly. In spite of their sensationalistic titles, which prime certain viewer expectations, however, films like *Cat People*, *I Walked with a Zombie*, and *The Leopard Man* are most marked by a lack—of monsters, of gruesome presences, and even of concrete evidence of a malevolent force at work in the human environment. In fact, "lack" in its broadest sense—as an absence in our lives and environments, something that can never quite be captured on film—seems to constitute the substance of these movies and of the reality they most often reproduce.

There is, admittedly, a substantial sense of the everyday captured here, especially in the modern, urban settings that form the backdrop for a number of the films. Whether set in the streets of New York, on islands in the Caribbean or Mediterranean, or in nineteenth-century Edinburgh, the films scrupulously detail the texture of daily life, as the Lewton unit went to great lengths to achieve a verisimilitude, carefully copying architecture, costumes, and the general look of a time and place; as Robson explains, each production was preceded by an elaborate research process that was quite unusual for such genre films: "Before filming, we looked endlessly at books and books of paintings. This came out of Val's training with David Selznick. If there was a sunset, we looked at hundreds of paintings and photographs of sunsets. We looked at modern art and at 18th Century art to find the light and shadow of a painting."[29] This procedure probably shows to best effect in *Bedlam,* which employed William Hogarth's illustrations as transitional devices and as the basis for several shot compositions. Besides this stress on context, the Lewton films emphasize characters who can be identified by their station in life or occupation, and who thus seem like a natural part of this texture of the commonplace. Bodeen makes special note of the fact that Lewton "always insisted that all his characters have occupations or professions and be shown working in their jobs."[30] Precisely because of this texture, of a visible and even substantial reality in which these people live their lives, the emergence of the abnormal, mysterious, or irrational—as if through the cracks in that veneer of normalcy—becomes all the more unsettling and conspicuous in these films. In effect, it serves to cast into relief our usual sense of reality and to make us mindful of the normally unnoticed fissures in its seemingly solid façade. What results is a subtle dialectic between substance and lack, presence and absence, replacing that of the more traditional horror film, wherein the self, as the audience's surrogate, is opposed by a threatening otherness in the shape of a monster or murderous apparition. The tension that typically results in the Lewton films is therefore no less, though it has a different source and is more disturbingly lodged in the individual and the way in which he perceives and conceives of his world.

If, on close examination, we find none of the zombies or leopard men the titles promise, and nothing as visually satisfying or iconic as Universal's Frankenstein monster or wolfman, the Lewton films are no less unsettling and visually haunting. Films that emphasize an external threat to our normal way of life attempt to expose our human weaknesses and fears, reminding us almost therapeutically of our natural vulnerability to the abnormal. By vacating that otherness, though, the RKO films could reveal that, in essence, we are "they," that the otherness we fear actually resides within, although it goes denied or unperceived in the welter of daily life. Our real fears, consequently, are shown to be of this hidden portion of the self that threatens the "normal" being which we show to the world in our efforts to remain in harmony with its formidable appearance of normalcy. The portentous shadows, strange sounds, and eerie low-key lighting that characterize these films add an ominous coloring that helps to undercut their sense of the commonplace and marks a path which leads back within—in that vesperal motion described by Hillman—to the darker regions of the self.

One technique which these films share and for which they are probably best known illustrates the way that approach helps to map out the human psyche and its fantasizing impulse. The bus technique, as it is termed, was used first in *Cat People* and then in various forms throughout the RKO series to manipulate audience expectations and undermine any feelings of complacency. In *Cat People* this shock effect grows out of a woman's lonely walk through the dark streets of New York, while she is being stalked by someone or something—she knows not what. When tension has reached its height through alternating shots of darkness and light, and as an attack from the surrounding blackness seems imminent, a city bus suddenly intrudes into the frame, the sound of its brakes and of the door opening serving to startle viewers every bit as much as would the eruption of violence they have been primed to expect by every detail of the scene. Robson, who developed this effect while working as an editor for the unit, explains that "the sharpness of that cutting" was designed to "knock people out of their seats in a theatre."[31] The basic mechanism of the technique is fairly obvious. Following a series of events which lead us to expect some dread occurrence, we react predictably, projecting our fears "out there," in the direction of what initially seems a threatening arrival, only to find that what we recoil almost instinctively from is quite harmless, an element of the commonplace. Whether employing a bus, train, or even a fluttering bird, this technique effectively startles, but, more important, it reveals our tendency to anthropomorphize in a most disconcerting way: that is, we invest our surroundings with a darkness we carry within us, corresponding in part to a fear we commonly have of an inability to close the self and the human world within a secure realm of light and knowledge.

Such "horror spots," as Lewton terms them, are carefully spaced throughout each of the films and are frequently followed or preceded by scenes that have quite the opposite tone, scenes designed "to give the audience relief by going to something very beautiful, lyrical if possible."[32] This visual sequencing especially underscores the attention given to narrative structure and an understanding of film's inevitable emphasis on sequentiality which mark these works. The sequence of shots immediately preceding the first bus in *Cat People* clearly illustrates this attention to the effects of cinematic structure. Cut in parallel, several tracking shots show a woman walking hurriedly along the dimly lit city streets, moving from darkness to a pool of light and then into the dark again; all the while she is being followed by another woman, stalking her through the same dark-light-dark patches. This parallel movement is complemented by the dissonant clacking of the women's high heels on the city sidewalks—an insistent noise which adds a note of tension and intensity to this simple sequential pattern. Three nearly identical shots emphasize this pattern and establish a rhythm of expectation, although our sense of expectancy is then undercut when the pursuer's footsteps are no longer heard and she fails to emerge from the darkness into the pool of light her quarry has just vacated. Consequently, the focus held on an unexpectedly empty frame generates a most disturbing atmosphere, as the shift from expected presence to absence hints at a transformation in the landscape of normalcy, a sudden and disconcerting gap in the larger picture we have formed of this world. Although again we have essentially *seen nothing*, that lack, primed by a particular structural repetition, points up how much we contribute to the delineation of that frightening environment, how much our fantasizing draws its structures from within the self. As Lewton explained, such effects reveal the viewer's participation in that which he sees, showing that under the appropriate conditions man himself "will populate the darkness with more horrors than all the horror writers in Hollywood could think of."[33]

This human tendency to inform with our fantasizing that which we see or the realm we inhabit shows up as well on the narrative level in the films that came from the Lewton unit. The dialectic between absence and presence, for example, operates as a structural principle at all levels in *Cat People*, while in the two films which followed, *I Walked with a Zombie* and *The Leopard Man*, both directed by Tourneur, that absence translates into an unsettling openness in narrative style, a gap of unknowing in the act of narration, on the one hand, and its generic structure, on the other. Robson's first directorial effort in the series, *The Seventh Victim*, returns to the repetition mechanisms of *Cat People* but develops them into a primary focus by emphasizing the archetypal patterns of life and death which repetition can signify. The next works in the series, Robson's *The Ghost Ship* and Wise's first contribution, *Curse of the Cat People*, are more conventional initiation stories, focusing on the nature of innocence, of that unknowing which can often pose an important challenge to our usually assured and complacent perspective on the world. In the last three films under consideration, *Isle of the Dead*, *The Body Snatcher*, and *Bedlam*, a complex questioning of our scientific and rational attitude occurs, in the first through a reemergence of powerfully mythic forces, and in the latter two by way of a transformation of the powers of reason and order into that which their very being seems intended to deny, the irrational and chaotic. In these last three films it is the fundamental fabric of modern society which, at a safe geographic and temporal remove from contemporary America, is shown to bear the mark of an inherent and troubling human absence and sorely to need an infusion of the archetypal patterns our culture continues to deny.

What these nine films share is a disturbingly revelatory pattern that we might see in terms of a process of phenomenological bracketing. Each narrative attempts to isolate an element of the commonplace—the city streets, the telling of a story, a generic pattern, the images of innocence, or our *supposed proofs* of reason and sanity—in order ultimately to discern its underlying nature and "give it a different value"—it might be supposed, a more human one.[34] Through this process the films call attention to the manner in which we normally perceive our world, conceive of its nature, and see our own place in its makeup. In sum, they reveal how much we share in shaping these phenomena, in giving to them, by turns, a pleasant, neutral, or even threatening aspect, and at the same time, how great a role they play, especially on the psychic level, in revealing the meaning of our lives.

In this light we should recall what Todorov describes as a major characteristic of the fantastic, that "indirect vision" by which the genre allows us to see the "mysteries" usually blocked from view by our experience of the "ordinary world."[35] If we include in this sense of mystery our human nature, then the notion of an indirect vision well describes the effect of the Lewton films. It explains as well why an ironic mode pervades these works, constantly suggesting the disparity between what we expect or normally perceive and that which is actually the case. The greatest threats that emerge from the Lewton films, after all, typically prove to be the most logical or rational of people—especially the doctors, professors, and other authority figures who appear so frequently here— who simply interpret their world and others wrongly or harshly. The sudden revelations that this approach almost inevitably entails, so that it seems practically a thematic equivalent of the bus technique described earlier, may indeed frighten or disconcert viewers in the most unexpected ways; however, they also leave a beneficial bequest: reflexively, those revelations reassert our narrative-bound limitations, our inability to see beyond a certain plot movement or to perceive the menace in the most commonplace occurrences. Analogously, they also recall our inability to see beyond the light of common day—or outside the privileged darkness of the theater and our dreams—and they thereby emphasize the need for a more comprehensive vision of ourselves, our world, and our place therein.

When examined carefully, the strategy of the Lewton films should bring us to reconsider the manner in which we think about the function and appeal of cinematic fantasy. Accustomed to figures defined by paradox or a peculiar illogic—such as the zombie or "living dead"—we might see in the traditional horror film an effort to seize upon these figures' illogic and explain it away, or—often as part of the same process—to destroy them and thereby preserve both the physical safety and rational coherence of our world. Thus we typically interpret such films in a light conditioned by the traditional activity of psychoanalysis, which generally sees its task as one of distilling and reinterpreting the dream residue of our waking life, bringing our dreamwork into the light of common day where we might slay our personal and cultural demons. Robin Wood's description of the horror genre as a vehicle for visualizing "our collective nightmares" so that we might cope with common, if subconscious fears "in more radical ways than our consciousness can countenance"[36] exemplifies this conventional psychoanalytic approach.

A major distinction of the Lewton films is that they make such a perspective, one bound to the material world and its analytical light, far less effective. Their lure, in fact, derives from the path they follow back within the psyche as part of a fundamental creative process. To Carl Jung we owe the notion that fantasy actually—and even necessarily—precedes our normal sense of reality; as he explained, "The psyche creates reality every day. The only expression I can use for this activity is fantasy."[37] According to Hillman, the fantasizing process draws the materials for this creation from deep within the self, where the human spirit "is ceaselessly talking about itself in ever-recurring motifs in ever-new variations, like music."[38] The language of this internal conversation consists of primal, archetypal images and patterns which defy our rationalizations and analyses, and which teach us not how to interpret our lives and actions, but how *to be*. Through the images of fantasy, we participate in a most fundamental and individual act of construction, even when they conjure up those disturbing visions of death, the underworld, and an enigmatic darkness that especially mark the horror film. Because those images correspond to a disturbing lack which the dreamself or fantasizing mind senses, they remind us that there is "always a concealment within, . . . a lost bit" of the psyche that can be located nowhere within our dayworld and its usual interpretations.[39] By turning our attention back to the dark, then, they effectively frighten us into wholeness. Adopting this fantasy approach, which seeks not simply to explain away or vanquish our anxieties, but to return us to a sense of mystery and incompletion, the Lewton films reveal a distinctive dreamlike potential of the genre. They take viewers on a necessary journey into the regions of the psyche, especially to its mythic substratum, where a most basic and profitable kind of regeneration may occur—and where another, frequently disregarded level of reality may be "redeemed."

When queried about his formula for this sort of effective cinematic fantasy, Lewton explained, "If you make the screen dark enough, the mind's eye will read anything into it you want! We're great ones for dark patches."[40] What those "dark patches" signal is something innate, a dark region of the self which we typically overlook, deny, or try to disguise with the press of commonplace presences or activities. Plato employed approximately the same formula in *The Sophist* to describe both the imagery of dreams and the shadows of our waking life, seeing them as resulting "when dark patches interrupt the light," but thereby "yielding a perception that is the reverse of the ordinary direct view" we have of our world.[41] It is just such an epistemological reversal that these films accomplish, as they all, Ariadne-like, provide threads we might follow into the labyrinth of the self, there to confront the most disconcerting and formidable—because inherently human—of horrors: a dark and unfathomable realm at the center of the human experience. This movement within, a dreamlike initiation into the dark reaches of the human psyche, represents the key function of the Lewton films, and it is what marks them off so distinctly from the more traditional efforts of cinematic fantasy. For these reasons they both deserve and reward a more detailed investigation than our criticism has previously managed to provide.

Such an examination should shed important light on the nature and appeal of film fantasy as well as on the Lewton productions themselves. Our critical thinking still largely situates film narrative, regardless of its genre or function, within an identifiably real world and defines it in terms of its reproduction of reality. Meanwhile, the fantastic, whatever its medium, has always sought to delineate and challenge the boundaries of the real. This possible conflict usually goes unnoticed in discussions of cinematic fantasy, although it is an oversight that may simply indicate the lack of rigor with which such films are often approached. What a rigorous examination of a body of fantasy films, like those produced by the Lewton unit at RKO, should make clear are the only terms by which the fullness of reality can truly be measured, and thus a key to this seeming contradiction. The Lewton films insist on the problematic nature of perspective—for their characters and the moviegoers as well—and they dramatize how perspective ultimately shapes our sense of reality. Those dark patches which Lewton found so effective and evocative draw upon usually indiscernible structures and contexts, absences rather than disturbing presences, but they engage our vision in a way that makes us reexamine our normal preoccupation with the surfaces and objects we typically label real. In effect, they remind us of our participation in the substance of reality, help to broaden our sense of that realm, and thereby achieve a far more extensive redemption than most film theories allow us to acknowledge—one which extends to the world of day *and* the world of night, to the self and those shadows without which it could not fully come to life.

2 Structures of Absence: *Cat People*

From seeing the bars, his seeing is so exhausted
That it no longer holds anything anymore.
To him the world is bars, a hundred thousand
Bars, and behind the bars, nothing.
—Rainer Maria Rilke
"The Panther"

While Val Lewton, like few other producers in Hollywood, generally wielded a free and creative hand in crafting his unit's films, his first production, *Cat People* (1942), demonstrated the typical studio distrust of any tampering with traditional and box-office–proven formulas. Alarmed by his unconventional approach to what was seen as a simple horror "programmer," and especially the substitution of little more than shadow and suggestion in place of the usual monstrous presences of the genre, the RKO front office demanded that the film be tailored to look more like the successful competition at Universal Studios; thus added footage of a menacing panther was inserted in several scenes. Although that interference was mitigated and little affected the final film, it points up the salient difference between the work of the Lewton unit and the typical horror vehicles of the era. As Curtis Harrington summarizes, Lewton "observed that the power of the camera as an instrument to generate suspense in an audience lies not in its power to reveal but its power to suggest; that what takes place just off screen in the audience's imagination, the terror of *waiting* for the final revelation, not the seeing of it, is the most powerful dramatic stimulus toward tension and fright."[1] This commentary recalls Lewton's personal dislike for the "mask-like faces hardly human, with gnashing teeth and hair standing on end,"[2] that were common to the genre. At the same time, though, it might also seem to imply that he produced simply stylish, *frisson*-evoking vehicles, master texts in the mechanism of horror with little substance at their core. The absence of the traditional and highly visual threats that characterizes *Cat People* and the Lewton unit's subsequent films implies more than a concern with the machinery of suspense or horror, more too than a simple admission of the imagination's power. In these works absence takes on substance, forming the cornerstone of their distinctive fantasy aesthetic.

What a film like *Cat People* especially demonstrates is how well Lewton and his production team—particularly director Jacques Tourneur—understood the fundamental relation between our perceptions of the world and our conceptions of its nature. Certainly, the limitations of time, money, and material necessitated that less concern be given to fashioning elaborate spectacles than to making audiences believe they had seen something unusual or nightmarish. Lewton from the first realized that monsters and what we today term special effects were quite dispensable, even in films targeted at a far from sophisticated wartime audience mainly looking to the movies for distraction, hence his comment on the use of shadows or "dark patches" into which "the mind's eye will read anything." Consequently, the ominous and ubiquitous dark patches, which became a stylistic signature of these films, shoulder a heavy structural and thematic weight. They generate a pervasive dreamlike atmosphere, that of a world in which the individual seems to have little autonomy, and they are the surest sign of our participation in this world; as James Hillman reminds, "Dreams are made by the persons in them, the personified complexes within each of us; these persons come out most freely in the night."[3] While engaging our imaginative participation, the absence marked by those dark patches speaks of a fundamental—and disturbing—relationship between man and his world: it signals a black hole or vacant meaning in the physical realm which, in spite of man's natural desire to fill it with consciousness and significance, persistently and troublingly remains open. This sense of absence, therefore, not only supplements the presence of the many quotidian, even banal elements abounding in a film like *Cat People,* but also points up the main problem facing both the audience and this film world's inhabitants, both of whom struggle to account for the unknown, to explain away the ambiguities with which the human realm is plagued.

To be sure, absence serves a fundamental rhetorical purpose, akin to the literary convention of apostrophe, since, like the gaze of Rilke's panther, it signals something not even present. In studying what he terms "the marriage between speech and Being," Jacques Derrida observes that we typically "represent the presence in its absence" whenever "we cannot take hold of or show the thing, let us say the present, the being-present, when the present does not present itself"; we might think of absence, then, as "a deferred presence."[4] But of what? It must be something that stubbornly resists signification, that we often defer from consciousness, perhaps to consign to dreams and the night. Joel Siegel simply describes this aspect of the Lewton films as the "symbolic displacement" of "drives and desires presumably too dreadful to be shown directly."[5] However, such "drives and desires," especially Irena Dubrovna's fear of possession by an evil spirit and her growing sense that, like Rilke's panther, she is trapped in a barred-off realm, are precisely what *Cat People*'s rhetoric foregrounds. Certainly it is what the film's characters have on their minds and are constantly discussing. In fact, one of the key concerns here, at least superficially, is whether Irena is lying about those anxieties she confides to her husband and which soon become general knowledge. A greater concern of the film is our inability to make satisfying sense of such admitted impulses. More than simply investing the environment with a threatening aspect, then, those shadows which abound in the Lewton unit's films, those black holes in the fabric of the commonplace which seem to intrude into every frame, warn of an absence lodged at the center of the self, one which we strive to defer and project onto the world we inhabit. What we fear in those disconcerting absences are, after a fashion, truly monstrous presences, but are they those of our own creation, modeled on a most disturbing anxiety—absence of meaning, of order, of any discernible difference between man and that dark, enigmatic realm in which he must live.

That sense of absence shapes *Cat People*'s world both thematically and structurally, while it also qualifies how we perceive its characters. Irena's Serbian origins and her enduring and insistent folk beliefs show up this absence most clearly, for her untold personal history, her life as an immigrant living in the New World mecca, New York, seems simply swallowed whole by her Old World cultural background, especially the medieval legends of her homeland concerning King John and the Mamelukes, which she recounts to Oliver Reed. In effect, it is as if she has no personal history, hardly any past beyond her first encounter with Oliver. Yet those deep cultural roots which cloak her absent personal past— or render its detailing irrelevant—not only suggest a mysterious depth in her character, but also underscore a significant absence in the Americans here who seem quite divorced from history. Ironically, Irena's residence is the only one shown; it is a personalized place of her own into which Oliver moves when they are married. Not only do the other players lack such characterizing locales, but their very homelessness seems emphasized. Dr. Louis Judd, the psychiatrist, is an international traveler with no permanent home; Alice tells how she first met him on a yacht, and when in New York he stays in a hotel. Alice apparently lives in a YWCA, and, while we never see her room, only the building's lobby and basement swimming pool, the insecurity of her place is underscored by the panther attack which occurs there. Neither do we know anything about Oliver's residence, and he apparently takes his meals at a diner near his work. Consequently, the immigrant in many ways seems least rootless here, as her situation accentuates an unexamined rootlessness typifying the Americans around her.

In contrast to Irena's history-haunted psyche, Oliver Reed seems unconscious of any cultural past, and his lack of awareness, once revealed, actually becomes as troubling as Irena's accumulation of folk beliefs. He clearly knows nothing about Serbia; he has never been in love before; and he simply sees himself as "quite a nice fellow." Oliver's limited experience and understanding speak of a personal and even cultural absence that has been deferred or banished, as if to the shadows or dark patches which frequently frame the screen or fill its depths, hinting at some discomfiting presence which lingers just out of view. Besides evoking a sense of the unknown or unseen, therefore, those ubiquitous shadows suggest how much in these people's lives remains unconscious, unformulated, and unquestioned. The darkness surrounding the pool into which Alice jumps to escape attack—from she knows not what—clearly echoes this absence, as the water, casting its eerie and shifting shadows on the oppressively low basement ceiling, recalls the archetype of the unconscious, whose fears have formed a reservoir here which, once tapped, readily floods the darkness with unnameable horrors. Whether they truly exist "out there" or only arise from our own absence-haunted psyches to fill the void is never made clear.

The recurrence of such shadow imagery, like the repetition of the water/unconscious motif, renders the sense of absence in a way that, as one critic notes, practically "constitutes a dramatisation of the structure of phantasy itself."[6] That structuring begins in the film's opening sequence when Oliver walks Irena home from the zoo where they have met and remarks on her lodgings, "I never cease to marvel at what lies behind a brownstone front." His comment not only introduces the darkly elaborate interior of Irena's apartment building, dominated by an immense winding staircase—originally constructed for Orson Welles's *Magnificent Ambersons*—which seems to thread labyrinthinely only to Irena's apartment, but also suggests a significant disjunction between immediate appearances and the fullness of reality that comes to characterize this world. In addition, their entrance into the brownstone's foyer starts a recurring pattern of entry, a motif of thresholds waiting to be crossed, of doors which wait open—or mysteriously fail to open—onto some unknown, often foreboding presence. The simple act of entrance thus becomes a traumatic, anxiety-laden event, as we see with the Cooper Building's revolving door, which several times seems to move by itself, Oliver's office door, which mysteriously closes to suggest Irena's threatening presence, and the elevator door in the same building, half-open at one point, as if waiting for Oliver and Alice, but strangely shutting when they take the stairs. These doors hint, too, at the threshold between Irena's conscious and unconscious mind, crossed tentatively under Dr. Judd's hypnotic trance and definitively in a later dream sequence, but suggested by the locked door with which Irena separates herself from Oliver on their wedding night. That door she cannot open to her husband, Robin Wood interprets, is in turn "paralleled by the cage which separates her from the panther: divided between two worlds, she is barred from access to either."[7] Unlike those other doors, though, the one in the zoo seems to mark a greater danger that lurks within, not a desire to control Irena's most dangerous impulses but a compulsion to release them; according to Dr. Judd, it represents her unconscious but insistent "psychic need to loose evil upon the world," and thus points to a dialectical struggle deep within her personality.

The most obvious structural use of absence, though, shows up in the film's visual styling, for instance, in the long tracking shots which serve less as transitions from one locale to another than as a means of emphasizing the shadowy world these characters are passing through. *Cat People*'s most effective sequence in this regard, as outlined in the previous chapter, depicts Irena, apparently transformed by her jealousy, stalking Oliver's friend Alice as she walks home after a late-night meeting with him. Parallel tracking shots of the two women traversing the dark city streets give way to a series of static shots which emphasize the patterns of light and shadows, as each girl enters and exits from the field of view. In repeating these compositions the narrative creates a pattern of expectation which primes us for the most discomfiting anxieties, not through the appearance of what we have imagined lurking beyond our view, but simply through the disruption of this pattern of presences, as happens when one woman fails to appear as expected. Confronted by an absence—really nothing at all—we draw on the surrounding shadows for some explanation, a substance to fill the sudden gap, some means of securely closing what now seems a disturbingly open world. Such an encounter leads us back within, in a preliminary vesperal motion, there to glimpse our own frailty.

What makes the sudden encounter with absence all the more effective is that it typically goes masked in images of normalcy or even banality, such as recur in the Lewton films—and for which they have at times been criticized. One such carefully calculated injection of the normal in *Cat People* is the precise detailing of occupation for every character. As Siegel notes, during initial script conferences the Lewton team would spend some time assigning occupations to the film's key characters and determining how each might "be shown at work during the course of the movie."[8] Following this formula, *Cat People* quickly establishes that Irena sketches fashion designs, that Oliver is a draughtsman for the Cooper Ship and Barge Construction Company, and that his best friends—Alice, Doc, and the Commodore—all hold positions with the same firm. The details surrounding these characters then flesh out this sense of the quotidian, decisively distancing them from any hint of the fantastic. Oliver we first see drinking a bottle of soda pop at the zoo, where he calls Irena's attention to an anti-littering sign and, displaying his best baseball form, tosses the drawing she has discarded into a receptacle. An additional touch to this characterization is that Oliver seems to order apple pie whenever he goes to the local diner. He is, in short and by his own admission, "a good plain Americano," having simple pleasures and holding down a steady job. Despite her foreign accent Irena, too, gives every indication of normalcy; she likes to visit the zoo, lives in one of those anonymous brownstone apartment houses which abound in New York, and innocently offers Oliver a cup of tea when he escorts her home. Her rival for his affections, Alice, seems more the typical female buddy of the type popularized by Howard Hawks in this period than a romantic predator and is described simply as a "good egg" by Oliver. Even the film's minor characters are woven into this fabric of the commonplace, as we learn of the cleaning lady's matchbook collection, the zookeeper's absentmindedness, and Millie the waitress's concern with pushing the chicken gumbo on her customers. Rather than a distraction, the development of this texture provides an effective prelude to the aberrant, the strange, the lack of normalcy which people like these typically try to gloss over with details that make them seem like ordinary people. Oliver's impulsive marriage to Irena works in this way, although when she fears consummating the marriage and it begins to sour, another effect of this texture of normalcy surfaces. As Irena tells Oliver, she envies every woman she sees because "they're happy; they make their husbands happy; they lead normal, happy lives." The seemingly universal and rather formidable appearance of normalcy also suggests its opposite, breeding the most debilitating anxieties in a person who must confront the absence of such a norm in her own life.

This phenomenon of absence, though, is a necessary supplement for its opposite, the presence with which consciousness is typically concerned, so that in a film like *Cat People* we see absence and presence contributing to a dialectic which informs the human world. In fact, this film derives much of its unsettling effect from a series of conflicts or oppositions which echo this absence/presence matrix: between Oliver's Americanness and Irena's foreign background; between his scientific concerns and her artistic ones; between the inanimate, nonthreatening world of modern-day New York and the frighteningly animate environment in which Irena sees herself trapped; and between the different explanations offered for her anxieties, the psychological/Freudian interpretations of Dr. Judd and Irena's folk belief that she is possessed by some evil spirit. What we learn is that neither side, no single element in the dialectic adequately explains these problems. Moreover, our attention is continually called to the fact of absence as an unsettling supplement that defies systematization, articulation, and explanation. In this way the problems of understanding which always plague the human consciousness come into more immediate focus.

The most obvious element in *Cat People*'s system of oppositions is its meeting of American and Serbian cultures, which provides the springboard for much of the film's action. In fact, Oliver's at-homeness and Irena's foreignness are played up immediately to emphasize their character differences. Both are at the zoo as the film opens, Oliver surrounded by others as he eats and drinks at a sidewalk vendor's stand, and Irena alone in the frame, isolated by her thoughts as she sketches a panther in its cage. As we later see, Oliver tends to surround himself with friends, all "good plain" types like himself; they do things together and know each other's business. Irena, on the other hand, has made no friends since coming to America, and her isolation is hardly accidental; as she confesses to Oliver, "I've stayed away from people; I've lived alone." Later, she admits that she "never wanted" to fall in love because she was afraid of the effects any commitment might have, especially the consequences due to her foreign birth and a curse that she fears follows from it. In essence, each person suggests the other side, the absence in his opposite's life: Oliver offers the love Irena has denied and fled from, while she, in her morbid fears, brings dark, unimagined possibilities into his simple, everyday existence. Oliver confesses to Alice afterward that he has "never been unhappy before. Things have always gone swell for me," and for this reason his troubled marriage is all the more perplexing: "That's why I don't know what to do about all this. I've just never been unhappy." Even as they complement each other, Oliver and Irena also reveal a lack in their lives: their equal inability to cope with an absence shown to be at the core of their being.

Their basic characteristics also suggest much of what has been omitted. Oliver is, after all, a ship designer, someone interested in figures, forms, measurements—he even seizes upon a T-square to ward off Irena when she has apparently been transformed into a menacing panther at one point. And Alice can tell when something is troubling him by his mathematical miscalculations: "That's the third wrong figure you've given me," she notes just before he confides his marital problems to her. His abiding interest in ships, extending to the models he brings into Irena's apartment after they are married and those he admires in the museum scene, subtly combines with the film's recurrent water imagery—most often associated with Irena—to sketch out the place of the unconscious in his everyday life. Oliver's concern, like that of his friends, is with vehicles enabling one to float over and thus avoid any dangerous immersion in that unconscious realm where unknown and potentially threatening forces contend. In contrast to his scientific and rational perspective, Irena takes the artist's outlook. She views reality through her imagination rather than conforming the imagination to a hard and fast reality as Oliver does. Her introduction clearly emphasizes this trait, as we see her sketching a panther in the zoo but repeatedly ripping up her attempts, not because they fail to capture her subject, but because they do not express what she feels inside, which is some deep, unarticulated impulse from her cultural past. As we see, Irena is not simply tracing out the cat's appearance, but depicting it, as if a dream image, transfixed with a large knife. In her distinctly imaginative way she responds to a recurrent threat stirring within her; figuratively she tries to kill off that haunting force. In keeping with this introduction Irena proves prone to dreams, visitations from the unconscious which Oliver little comprehends, as we see in his mocking response to her fears of the cat people legend of her birthplace: "Oh Irena, you crazy kid." Her very constitution dramatically distances her from his supremely practical, commonsense world. It is not just her deep-rooted fears or even the drawings and paintings which decorate and personalize her apartment, but her perfume, her singing, her great fondness for the night ("I like the dark; it's friendly," she tells Oliver), and the pleasure she finds in the screams of the cats in the nearby zoo ("To me it's the way the sound of the sea is to others, natural and soothing. I like it," she notes) that distinguish her personality and underscore its immersion in everything that Oliver's lacks.

Because of this difference in their personalities, yet another disjunction seems so marked, that between the largely inanimate view of the world which Oliver, Alice, and Dr. Judd maintain and Irena's animate vision. Her world seems fully alive, filled as it is with flowers, animals, and wild sounds; its ruling deity could easily be the cat goddess Bubastis, shown juxtaposed to Irena as she stands on a museum staircase. This animate perspective lets her see the world as much more threatening than it seems to Oliver.

Val Lewton (far right) with director Mark Robson (left) and cast of *Youth Runs Wild*.

Director Mark Robson (center) in discussion with Boris Karloff and Val Lewton on the set of *Bedlam*.

Irena (Simone Simon) tells Oliver (Kent Smith) of her fears.

Cat People's love triangle: Oliver, Irena, and "other woman" Alice (Jane Randolph).

The umbrella forms a dark cloud over Oliver and Irena as they examine her new canary.

The cat and the canary: Irena and Alice—note bird pin on Alice's lapel.

Irena's double, a fellow Serbian who "looks like a cat."

Oliver and co-workers—the Commodore (Jack Holt), Carver (Alan Napier), and Alice—at ship design firm.

Irena immersed in her world of art and imagination.

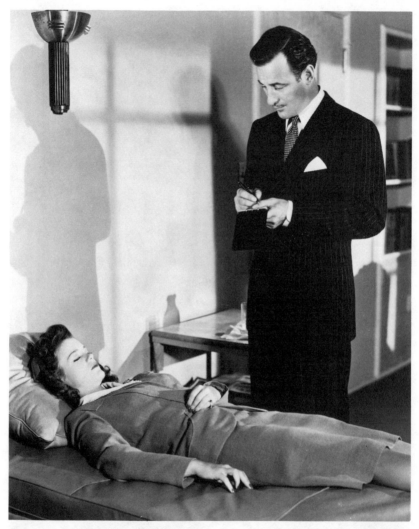

Dr. Judd (Tom Conway) probes Irena's fears and dreams.

Surprise and anxiety attend every entrance and exit in *Cat People*.

Driven by her instincts, Irena visits the zoo at feeding time.

Alice returns from swimming to find her robe ripped to shreds.

The unexpectedly fierce reaction of a pet kitten to Irena and a canary that dies of fright when she tries to play with it both hint at a menacing, almost predatory aspect in her and signal a blurring of distinction between the human and animal. Her folk belief in a race of cat people, who are inexplicably turned into murderous felines when their emotions are aroused, naturally accords with this animistic view. Oliver, however, has no such dreams to haunt his nights, so he simply terms Irena's notions "nonsense." In his experience everything can be "got at"—measured, studied, or manipulated—and fears of the unknown are considered the stuff of "fairy tales," as he says, or products of mental problems that should be dealt with by the proper medical authorities.

In fact, Oliver and several other characters here, like proper denizens of the modern, rational world, readily defer to the experts, in this case, the psychiatrist Dr. Judd—first of a long line of wrong-headed, even dangerous doctors in the Lewton films—whom Alice suggests could help Irena. And his involvement underscores a related dialectic at work in *Cat People*, that between modern psychology and Irena's folk belief in evil possession. Oliver admits his own inability to solve Irena's problems and offers a suggestion that directly reflects his quite limited perspective: "There's something wrong and we have to face it in an intelligent way. We don't need a King John with fire and sword. We need someone who can find the reason for your belief and cure it. That's what we need—a psychiatrist." In his simplistic, almost ludicrous response, reflecting Oliver's naive faith in the world of science, we glimpse the popularized notion that psychology's primary purpose, as Hillman explains, is to interpret dreams, "to bring them over into the dayworld, shall we say rescuing or 'reclaiming' (Freud's own metaphor) the dream from its underworld madness."[9] In response to Irena's plea for help and her "feeling there's something evil in me," however, Judd with his clearly Freudian perspective can only suggest that her troubles may stem from some early, half-remembered experience: "These childhood tragedies are inclined to corrode the soul, to leave a canker in the mind. We'll try to repair the damage." While she recognizes that dark, ineffable force within and realizes that "whatever is in me is kept in, is harmless, when I'm happy," Judd and Oliver both presume that there is no real absence, no depth in the personality that cannot be plumbed and brought to light. To them it is simply a case of uncovering the truth or finding the right events in the past which have fostered Irena's present neurosis. In short, they see her dis-ease as no more than a disease awaiting cure.

As in many of the films produced by the Lewton unit, however, that dis-ease seems lodged in a human history that the individual attempts to deny in vain. In this instance, Irena readily admits that the legend of the cat people remains a living reality for her people in Serbia, that it "haunts the village where I was born"; and her chance meeting in a Serbian restaurant with a woman who "looks like a cat" only demonstrates how completely she feels bound by that cultural heritage. It is an intangible bond, not al-ways present to her consciousness, as we several times note when she attempts to go routinely about her daily activities. Subtly, though, it influences her every action—her sketches, home deco-rations, pets, and her relationships with Oliver and Judd espe-cially. Judd's solution, like Oliver's, is simply to annihilate that troubling past: "You keep going back to the mad legends of your birthplace. Forget them. You surround yourself with cat objects, pictures. Get rid of them. Lead a normal life," he tells Irena. And after a fashion he is right, that Irena's history-haunted psyche pre-vents her from living in the present, but his own view, shared by Oliver, that history should simply be denied existence, that myths have no substantial hold on us, and that absence cannot affect the present if we choose to gainsay its influence is itself shortsighted and signals a failure to understand the depths of the human psyche. Presence clearly has a time component, that of the pres-ent, but so does absence, which bears upon the past and future, both of which should help to cast a more comprehensive and re-vealing light on the immediate situation. For a person can live neither in a constant present nor in another time than his own; the human world, marked as it is by memories, hopes, and present concerns, demands that we merge these various time schemes to live our lives.

Neither this time relationship nor the other dialectical structures in the narrative are reconciled, however. The potential for happiness promised in the wedding of Oliver to Irena—of the complacent American to the mysterious foreigner—vanishes as their marriage goes unconsummated; Oliver turns to Alice—almost his mirror image—for affection; and Irena fully abandons herself to her fears of cat possession and attacks Oliver, Alice, and finally Judd. The possible combination of the scientific and the artistic, the rational and the imaginative, issues not in a kind of humanism, a happy combination of two complementary ways of seeing and understanding the world, but in a fundamental struggle, as each seeks to deny the validity of the other. Dr. Judd's treatment of his patient predictably brings no cure, not even a proper understanding of her problem; if anything, his treatment only exacerbates Irena's trouble and precipitates the film's tragic conclusion. Even Irena recognizes why Judd's approach to her problem is of no avail: "You're very wise; you know a great deal. Yet when you speak of the soul, you mean the mind, and it is not my mind that is troubled." Meanwhile he sees in her fears "hallucinations" that "approach insanity," nothing less than "a deterioration of the mind, an escape into fantasy—and it's dangerous." Finally, the inanimate and animate views of the world meet not in a more coherent perspective, not in a mythic view of man and his place in the world, such as the Lewton unit fashioned in their later *Isle of the Dead*, but in an anthropomorphism gone wrong, a tendency to project our fears and anxieties into the absence felt around us. As the bus technique, which made its debut in this film, demonstrates, it is often because of such anxieties that our world grows so dark, objects begin to assume menacing shapes, shadows take on dangerous substance. At the same time ignorance of those dark possibilities or the belief that they are simply "bad dreams" that need to be brought into the light of day and rational understanding can be every bit as dangerous and debilitating and can certainly prevent one from ever truly understanding himself, much less others. It is the tension between these vying powers that creates the main threat here and generates a sign of that absence which the psyche typically and stubbornly seeks to deny.

Unable to locate a counterbalance, that tension is effectively subsumed within the individual as a self-destructive force, a maelstrom drawing him—though almost with a kind of relief, *Cat People* suggests—to oblivion. When faced, like Rilke's panther, with a world that seems totally barred from her, Irena plunges further into her primitive cat people belief and its realm of evil, as she fears that if she "were to fall in love and if a lover were to kiss her, take her into his embrace, she would be driven by her own evil to kill him." This fear, despite what Carlos Clarens and others suggest, represents not a "repressed lesbianism" at work,[10] but an unconscious fear of the self's opposite. Neither is it an attraction for mirror images of the self—as her more than physical recoil from the Serbian woman who calls Irena "my sister" demonstrates—as much as an anxiety at what happens when a psyche surrenders itself wholly to that opposite. Of course, as Irena's statue of King John with his sword impaling a cat and the sword cane with which Judd later stabs her imply, male sexuality does at times seem threatening; yet Irena does not find it totally frightening, or so the drawing she makes in the first scene suggests. Indeed, she seems to long for that sexuality, for absence to assume a masculine and authoritative shape. Her dream of Judd as a modern-day knight in armor, bearing before him a long, drawn sword, explicitly emphasizes this point. Through that symbolized sexuality, if she could only embrace it, Irena might vanquish the fears which beset her.

The only forms that opposite takes, however, are Oliver and Judd, the one too immature for a proper sexuality, the other too detached and self-concerned to perceive its full importance for his patient. When his marriage fails to meet his naive expectations, Oliver can only turn to Alice—who shares his commonsense, day-world view of things—for an almost motherly consolation and admit, "I don't know what love really is." In contrast, Judd's growing sexual attraction to Irena eventually comes to stand in the way of his diagnostic and therapeutic roles, while his coldly rational attitude precludes any real sympathy for her. As he readily admits, he has "never believed" any of her stories. In this way he serves as a comment on the extremes of Freudian psychology, particularly its manner of explaining the sense of absence which haunts all human consciousness. As Hillman explains, the basic thrust of the Freudian project is "interpretation," a drive "to take the *via regia* of the dream *out* of the nightworld," its proper place.[11] The film's opening epigraph—"even as fog continues to lie in the valleys, so does ancient sin cling to the low places, the depressions in the world consciousness"—is attributed to Judd himself and his fictive book *The Anatomy of Atavism,* but it seems almost a paraphrase of Freud, particularly his *Civilization and Its Discontents.*[12] And his initial approch to Irena's troubles suggests the classic manner of Freudian analysis, as Judd seeks to tap the id through hypnosis and dream interpretation to determine the source of her problem, which he identifies not with her folk beliefs but with her libido and the sexual dysfunction in her marriage. The folklore he interprets as a disguise for some deep secret, a trauma resulting from her father's mysterious death in the forest when Irena was a child or some other childhood experience too long repressed by the superego. That libidinal cause, he is certain, can be located, examined, and treated to permit her to function sexually and thus save her marriage. When his attempts to determine that cause fail, he responds with his own sexuality, embracing and kissing her, only to evoke the very cat-persona his theories have denied, liberating that violent impulse he has simply seen as an instance of sexual repression. To what he determines to be a biological problem, he reacts biologically himself, with a peculiar but undeniably biological revenge the result—Irena's transformation into the panther which mauls and kills him, despite the protection afforded by his phallic sword cane. In this mutually destructive encounter we might see a dramatization of what Jung was to describe as the fundamental limitation of the Freudian approach: it "is limited to the task of making conscious the shadow-side and the evil within us. It simply brings into action the civil war that was latent, and lets it go at that."[13]

In its manifest inability to cope with Irena's terror, Judd's perspective only underscores the persistence and power of certain archetypal forces, what Hillman terms "underworld images," which provide an alternative account of human consciousness. The cat imagery is obviously pervasive here, extending even to the tiger lilies employed in one scene and the claw-shaped feet on Irena's bathtub; that animal motif, we might recall, "is usually symbolic of man's primitive and instinctual nature," its constant appearances normally signaling "that an instinct has been split off from the consciousness and ought to be (or is trying to be) readmitted and integrated into life."[14] In Jungian terms this imagery suggests the shadow element of the psyche, the dark element in human nature which must find a proper balance with the persona and anima if one is to live happily, without a disabling dread of that dark realm within. In Irena's case that integration is denied by her husband, her psychoanalyst, and even society—all refusing to acknowledge what they cannot see. The general attitude is that cats are only animals, to be kept in boxes at the pet store or cages in the local zoo, to be used as pets, mousers, or visual attractions, and they have no business running free; in such situations they might well be run over by a car, as indeed happens at the film's end when Irena frees the zoo's panther. Modern society, rational and ordered as it is, free from anxieties about the unknown and the superstitions of folklore, clearly allots no place for shadows in its makeup.[15]

As Jung was to remind, however, there are undeniable "deeper spiritual needs" in man[16] which psychology, at least of the kind practiced by Judd, can never touch, a depth of human nature upon which the scientific perspective casts no light. A final dialectic, measured by the film's opening epigraph and its closing title, underscores this mystery. The former, as we previously suggested, simply dismisses anxiety as an atavism, a residue of man's religious taboos, and thus a dream of humanity in general from which we must be awakened. It is an explanation, however, which seems most ironic in light of Judd's failure and death. In contrast, the closing epigram is poetry of an emphatically spiritual sort, a quote from one of John Donne's Holy Sonnets: "But black sin hath betrayed to endless night / My world, both parts, and both parts must die." While the two passages similarly speak of "sin" and of the "night" and "fog" which shroud humanity, their implications are quite different. For Judd, "sin" is simply a primitive sensation which unnecessarily haunts those who will not emerge from the "low places" of their cultural past and cast a modern, rational light on their anxieties. For Donne, in contrast, the very word "sin" bears an almost archetypal meaning and deeply moral value, as it refers to a primordial Fall that still casts its dark shadow over man, reminding him of his frailty and inevitable end. It affords a sobering yet necessary perspective, since it admits the tragic nature of the human story, though in acknowledging the absence with which man must live, it opens onto a more truthful vision and holds out the possibility for some meaning.

If there is truly sin, if there is a "sickness unto death" such as Kierkegaard suggested in describing the most fundamental human sense of absence—absence of the divine presence—then there also exists the hope of coming to oneself. Kierkegaard posited that the very "possibility of this sickness is man's advantage over the beast, and this advantage distinguishes him far more essentially than the erect posture, for it implies the infinite erectness or loftiness of being spirit."[17] In effect, a sense of absence, of this human "sickness," is what differentiates man from animal, keeps him from becoming no more than a violent cat person. In the shift from the opening epigram to the film's last statement, then, we can glimpse the revision of human perspective which is at work in this story. It is one that, the film's makers may have felt, modern America particularly needed. At the same time, creating such a new perspective is the fundamental process in "soul making," as Hillman describes it. Seen in such contexts, the notion of a "cat people" seems especially suggestive, implying a threat that haunts man as a direct result of his Fallenness. The film's final shot, of an empty panther cage in the background and Irena's lifeless body

in the foreground, emphasizes this point, for it hints at the imprisoning nature of life, as well as the one sure release from it—death.
For Oliver and Alice who view this spectacle and note that Irena
"never lied to us," it also serves a cautionary purpose, like a collective dream from which they have simultaneously awakened. It
reminds them of the otherness they originally dismissed as the
product of her "overworked imagination," while it also reaffirms
both the existence and unseen power of absence.

Cat People affords a prototype of the world which the Lewton
films consistently evoked. It is a perfectly open, if not openly perfect realm which its characters inhabit, that is, its bounds are
unmarked, its depth unmeasured, though largely because it is a
human world, distinguished by the same troubling ambiguity, the
same property of absence as is man himself. The Lewton films
draw their structure and imagery from this fundamental substance.
They indeed offer mainly shadows, dark patches, half-opened
doorways—all threatening absences somehow bracketed on film
by the most mundane of presences; however, as Derrida cautions,
"the absence of an object" should hardly be seen as indicating
"the absence of meaning."[18] In fact, the opposite occurs as those
enigmatic elements evoke common human lacunae, dark patches
from within the self.

The studio heads did force an element of presence on *Cat People*
in the form of insert shots of a real panther to supplement the
shadows and suggestion which originally distinguished the film.
As Tourneur notes with some satisfaction, though, despite orders
to reshoot one scene, "I shot it so that you couldn't really be sure
what you were seeing. That's the only way to do it. In the swimming pool sequence, the cat was my fist. We had a diffused spot-
light and I used my fist to make shadows against the wall."[19] This
bit of directorial trickery only amplifies the suitably knotted interworkings of presence and absence in this and the subsequent Lewton films, as absence not only stands in for a presence—shadows
evoking a cat—but even masquerades as itself, through the sil-
houettes cast by the director's hand, which make us guess at the
substance of what we have seen. The resulting *mise en abîme*, as

contemporary critics would term it, an abyss of ambiguity, pervades the subsequent films and injects that degree of complexity which distinguishes them from other narratives in the genre. In short, it represents the very structure of what we have termed a vesperal film. The discomfiting twists and turns, the dark patches that mark the meeting of presence with absence, as *Cat People* effectively demonstrates, dwell in man's psyche and, consequently, always inscribe their ambiguous patterns on the stories we tell of it. What the Lewton unit sought to do was to map those dark patches where possible and to put us on that track of the cat which leads within.

3 Narration and Incarnation: *I Walked with a Zombie*

> If . . . reality is psychological and spiritual, by which I
> mean ideational, religious, imagined, fantastic . . . then
> affecting reality requires instruments for moving ideas,
> beliefs, feelings, images, and fantasies. Then rhetoric,
> persuasion, holds major importance. Through words we
> can alter reality; we can bring into being and remove from
> being; we can shape and change the very structure and
> essence of what is real. The art of speech becomes the
> primary mode of moving reality.
>
> James Hillman
> *Facing the Gods*

While fantasy seems devoted to examining our limitations of vision, understanding, even belief, it does so bearing its own burden of restriction, that which attends any attempt to speak the ineffable or structure the unstructured. Rosemary Jackson hints of this difficulty in her comment on the problem facing the fantasy artist: "Objects are not readily appropriated through the look: things slide away from the powerful eye/I which seeks to possess them, thus becoming distorted, disintegrated, partial and lapsing into invisibility."[1] While her observation clearly addresses the difficulty of *depicting* the elements of fantasy, of rendering them believably—a task compounded in the case of film because of its mimetic grounding—it also hints at the trouble involved in fitting the phantoms of fantasy within a narrative framework or coherent perspective, for they tend to "lapse" into absence, as our examination of *Cat People* demonstrated, and disappear from a narrative field defined by such conventional devices as a voice-over narrator or subjective camera. An added problem is that a narrative intelligence, deprived of a source in the visible world and a tangible reality of its own, can itself seem to disintegrate. A truly omniscient and detached narrator of fantasy, for instance, will also seem like a fantasy creation—or simply the voice of the fantasist, wrestling with the difficulty of depicting his creations. As many contemporary novelists have shown, one solution to this problem is to acknowledge it, making the difficult act of narration or depiction a central feature of the fiction. Employed in the service of fantasy, such an approach can afford yet another avenue for the vesperal, open an additional path leading to the perspective which is the goal of the fantasy experience. The extent to which Lewton and his associates understood this principle shows up most vividly in their second production, *I Walked with a Zombie* (1943), the most complexly structured of their films.

RKO Pictures had established a modest reputation for ingenuity and artistic innovation. In fact, because the studio was always pressed for finances and lacked the dominant stars for whom movies had to be especially tailored, it of necessity "put a premium on ingenuity," as James Naremore explains.[2] Within budgetary limits its filmmakers were often allowed a freer hand than was normal in the studio system, even a chance to experiment with narration and structure, particularly if such experiments might save money. Thus Orson Welles, despite his inexperience, not only had the opportunity to make films, but also—in the case of *Citizen Kane* at least—to do so in a manner unique to cinematic narrative. Due to the presence of such Welles alumni as Robert Wise and Mark Robson, as well as the financial and material limitations imposed by their B-film formula, the Lewton unit paid similar attention to the shaping of their narratives by way of economically yet effectively evoking audience response. Joel Siegel hints at this approach when he describes the typically "fragmented, mosaic-like structure" of the films, with their dependence on a "series of tiny, precise vignettes which do not so much tell the story as sketch in its borders and possibilities."[3] In Robin Wood's reference to the often illogical "poetic structure" of these films,[4] we find yet another suggestion of their stylistic distinction. In general, the early Lewton films display a narrative style which recalls Jean-Paul Sartre's prescription for fantasy storytelling: "In order to achieve the fantastic, it is neither necessary nor sufficient to portray extraordinary things. The strangest event will enter into the order of the universe if it is alone in a world governed by laws."[5] The Lewton films do not simply strip the world they depict of those laws which Sartre describes, as do many horror films; rather, they manipulate the context within which even the most commonplace actions are perceived. By maneuvering that "eye/I" which Jackson identifies—the vision of both audience and film characters—these films gradually draw viewers, as they do their protagonists, into a deceptively quotidian world and thus suggest a more unsettling misgovernance in what we typically perceive as the ordinary.

Considered by most critics to be the masterwork of the RKO series, *I Walked with a Zombie* employs a familiar narrative device, the voice-over, in a way that at first resembles the first-person narration of the film's purported source, *Jane Eyre*. As that narration unfolds, however, its atypical development suggests the influence of the studio's pacesetter in narrative experimentation, *Citizen Kane*. Just as Welles employed a variety of narrative voices, speaking consecutively and often contradictorily, to fashion his enigmatic portrait of Charles Foster Kane, so does *Zombie* display a succession of voices and perspectives—of I's and eyes— to construct its world. And as in *Kane*, those voices work to reveal just how "partial" and "distorted" a single perspective can be.

The film's focus, however, is not so much the multiplicity of viewpoints available, as the stance those narrative voices imply. As Bruce Kawin reminds, in the fictional film a voice-over narration typically indicates an "interpretive response" to events.[6] In that capacity it not only introduces and frames what we see but also appends a sense of detachment, as the voice narrates or comments upon actions, standing psychologically outside of them, even while being involved in all that transpires. With this distance there comes as well a suggestion of control or interpretation, as the speaker's words direct access to this world and exercise certain rights over it, even the prerogative of dishonesty in narrating, of lying about what we are permitted to see, as Alfred Hitchcock demonstrated in his *Stage Fright*. In all the Lewton unit's fantasy productions we find a concern with our human tendency to distance the self from anything discomfiting, especially the fantastic, and, in reaction, to assert steadfastly the controlling power of our rational faculties and of those laws which we believe govern our world. In *Zombie* Lewton and his associates fashioned a narrative structure that speaks directly to these concerns by focusing attention on the manner in which we perceive and make judgments about that mysterious and often threatening realm in which the fantastic conventionally places us.

Given a sensationalistic title leading viewers to expect little more than grotesquery and standard chills, Lewton's unit could justifiably have employed a conventional horror formula, like Universal's, in *Zombie*. Simply plunging viewers into a world threatened by monsters and eventually releasing them from that dire grip by vanquishing the threat would have offered audiences a comforting and not yet trite allegory for the world struggle in which they were involved. *Zombie*'s narrative mechanism, however, pointedly works against such a pattern and the dayworld perspective it implies in favor of a more challenging movement into the vesperal regions of the psyche. Thus the film opens with a voice-over that evokes our normal desire to know and explain away whatever we find disturbing in our world. Betsy, a Canadian nurse who comes to the Caribbean island of Saint Sebastian to tend the invalid wife of a sugar planter, introduces the story by laughing at its very premise: "I walked with a zombie. . . . Heh, heh. It does seem an odd thing to say. If anyone said that to me a year ago, I'm not at all sure I would have known what a zombie was." Her calm, detached voice promises an amusing anecdote, something that we can laugh at, by way of explaining her initial intriguing statement and dispelling any anxiety latent in the term zombie. The ensuing narrative, combining Betsy's voice with various scenes of her new home, hardly fulfills that promise, though; instead it simply demonstrates a naiveté she has brought to this world. Subsequently, another voice intrudes to add a different, previously withheld view of things; the song of a calypso singer lets us glimpse the dark and complex human motivations operating just beneath the idyllic surface which Betsy initially describes. While hardly a traditional voice-over, the singer's narration, from off-screen at first, complements Betsy's commentary by offering an insight into the tensions and suspicions surrounding the household in which she must work and by imparting a far different, darker tone to all that follows. What this commentary reveals is the rivalry between the half-brothers Paul Holland and Wesley Rand and their love for the same woman, Paul's wife Jessica, Betsy's patient. When this intrigue breeds disaster, with Jessica being killed by Wesley who then drowns, yet another voice-over intrudes to offer a coda for the entire narrative: "O Lord God most holy. Deliver them from the bitter pain of eternal death. The woman was a wicked woman, and she was dead in her own life. Yea, Lord, dead in the selfishness of her spirit. And the man followed her. Her steps led him down to evil. Her feet took hold on death. Forgive him, O Lord, who knowest the secret of all hearts. Yea, Lord, pity them who are dead and give peace and happiness to the living." This final solemn "say" comes from a mysterious, never identified speaker, although it seems clearly a native voice, one far removed from the cheerful, quite civilized commentary with which the film began. The distance between these two bracketing voices, however, measures how far we have been brought into this world and its mysteries, while it also reaffirms how little of it can ever be satisfyingly explained; it leaves us simply with a recognition of the terrible paths human nature frequently takes and an admission of the force that darkness wields.

Obviously, bracketing the story with such varied voices violates the usual voice-over approach which, drawing on literature and oral storytelling traditions, relies on a single narrator to present or comment upon the events depicted and thus serves as a filtering and moralizing agent for all that we see. By violating these expectations, however, the film produces an element of complexity seldom met with either in genre programmers or in more traditional film forms. Kawin significantly reminds us that "the question of voice becomes, finally, the question of mind, and both are inseparable from the question of meaning."[7] The many consciousnesses here, like the numerous voices which paint the ambiguous portrait of "Citizen" Kane, inevitably reflect upon our own capacity to sift meaning from events, to stand apart from and judge our world. This is the proper aim of fantasy, as James Hillman explains; it should challenge our normal "literal perspective, its identity with material life," since that perspective is usually "stuck in coagulations of physical realities. This perspective of reality needs to break down and fall apart, to be skinned alive and sensitized, or blackened by melancholic frustration."[8] Just such a breaking, sensitizing, or even blackening of normal perspective is precisely *Zombie*'s thrust, for its various voices are less satisfying than frustrating, leading us from a promise of explanation or rationalization to an admission of human limitation. However, it is this movement that enables the film to work its most effective variation on the familiar matters of its genre.

What *Zombie*'s unconventional narration calls to mind is the unfolding of a pattern that has been doubled and redoubled, folded so neatly and compactly that its true shape and significance have effectively been hidden from sight, reduced to absence. That "folding," however, suggests the human psyche at work, attempting to order and arrange events and reality according to its particular perceptions, to enclose any ambiguities or troubling uncertainties within a securely bound volume of knowledge. The varied perspectives which these shifting voices embody, however, reveal how vain the attempt is, as each reads a slightly different story in the text, unfolds its leaves to display another, more complex pattern therein. As J. Hillis Miller notes, this result characterizes all discourse, for "the coherence of the monological has all along been undermined by the presence within it, inextricably intertwined in any of its expressions, of that other non-system, the 'instance' of fragmentation and the absence of unifying authority."[9] By underscoring the "instance of fragmentation," however, the film raises a narrative ghost of sorts, the absence of "authority," to haunt its tale, to make it speak of those complexities narration typically tries to order, and thus to carry out more effectively the function of fantastic discourse as a fundamental mode of knowing—perhaps the only truly reliable one we have.[10] The message that *Zombie*'s voices whisper, then, is distinctly discomfiting on various levels, as they speak of how unformulable, unnarratable, even fantastic our most involving experiences always tend to be.

That untroubled voice which introduces the film—Betsy describing the events leading to her employment at Fort Hudson—tries to still the anxieties we almost automatically bring to the horror film. Her detached voice suggests a frame and closure for the ensuing events, within which they can all, no matter how fantastic, be explained and rendered rational. The only ominous note Betsy relates is from her job interview, a query on whether she believes in witchcraft, and it is quickly dispelled by the promise that she will spend much of her time in the Caribbean "sitting under a palm tree, swimming, taking sunbaths." Those words color her subsequent thoughts, for on the boat to Saint Sebastian her voice-over becomes a present-tense revery on the idyllic beauty of the tropical sunset and the sea. Her thoughts, though, are interrupted by someone speaking from off-screen, another narrative voice of sorts, challenging her unspoken interpretation of this world. That sobering voice is embodied or made incarnate when Paul Holland enters the frame and continues his explanation, noting that "everything seems beautiful because you don't understand. Those flying fish—they're not leaping for joy; they're jumping in terror. Bigger fish want to eat them. That luminous water—it takes its gleam from millions of dead bodies, the glitter of putresence. There's no beauty here, only death and putresence. Everything good dies here, even the stars," and a falling star at that point flashes across the skies. Paul's commentary quickly establishes a pattern of dark possibility and disillusionment to complement the impulse for explanation, while it also suggests the potential for other voices ready to challenge the authority of Betsy's narration. Her limited perspective may well prove incapable of providing a coherent understanding of this world, in part because of the romantic notions she brings to and attempts to impose on her new environment, but also because of the narrative distance implied by her voice-over, a distance underscored by the process

of incarnation that Paul, first as voice-over, then as presence, acts
out for us.

What *Zombie*'s opening affirms is the possibility for various perspectives or depths of knowledge, as well as the need for a gradual
initiation or immersion in this world's complexity. The initial ship-
board shots of Paul and Betsy confirm the disparity in perspective
suggested by their voices. We first glimpse Paul in long shot,
framed aginst the evening sky and open sea in the background,
while a group of native sailors chant an eerie and indistinguishable
song in the foreground; in contrast to this composition in depth,
Betsy appears in an almost claustrophobic and strangely lit medium shot, one in which she is completely framed by the rope
ladder on whose rung she leans. These compositions underscore
the disparity in the knowledge that each bears: the one signals a
dark, yet almost limitless depth of possibility; the other, an unnaturally bright and strictly limited vision. Betsy, although trained in
observation by her nursing profession, as she proudly points out,
too quickly seizes upon appearances, too heavily relies upon that
limited ability. She well understands disease symptoms and dos-
ages, which her scientific training has brought her to respect, but
she is hard put to go beyond perceived reality and understand that
for which there may be no remedy or treatment.

When she arrives in Saint Sebastian, a native cab driver recounts the island's slave heritage and describes Ti Misery, the fig-
urehead of an old slave ship that symbolizes the black man's
sorrowful introduction to this island and his fall from the happiness
of his homeland. Following his narration, Betsy simply gazes at
the flowers and greenery around them and offers a judgment that
points up her tendency to judge on appearance, as she notes that
at least the slavers "brought you to a beautiful place, didn't they?"
The rhetorical nature of her comment, implying the truth she expects the driver to echo, suggests that she will not notice his ironic
response to her cultural myopia—"If you say, miss, if you say"—
much less the implication that there are indeed other possible interpretations. As Betsy's voice-over then relates her first impressions of Fort Hudson, this sense of limitation recurs as she

describes the "strangely dreamlike" world she saw through the plantation's gates. The accompanying subjective shot through the bars of the gate reinforces the impression of her alienation from this world and establishes a recurring visual pattern of barriers, suggesting just how barred off Betsy is from all she surveys, especially from all that might be termed fantastic. This motif is replicated by the bar shadows which suffuse her room and the lattices on her window, through which she first glimpses her patient, Jessica, wandering like a sleepwalker through the garden outside. This visual pattern then issues in a particularly telling encounter, as the nurse emerges from her room to follow Jessica, only to find that her patient has a frightening, deathly look about her—which prompts Betsy to scream for help when Jessica approaches menacingly. After gaining some distance on this unsettling encounter, through a night's sleep, Betsy can laugh at her reaction—as she did in the film's opening—but only by first bracketing it within a familiar context, by creating a narrative of sorts in which her patient is described as nothing more than a "mental case." Paul's overly eager agreement with her diagnosis, however, hints at his own weakness, undercuts Betsy's assurance, and evokes a doubt that lingers for the rest of the narrative.

From this encounter a series of explanations by various characters follows, functioning essentially as embedded authorial or narrative voices, as several people attempt to furnish Betsy with an overview of this world or to explicate its mysteries for her. Paul initiates this pattern by explaining why Betsy heard a mysterious crying in the night. Because "for generations they found life a burden," the servants "still weep when a child is born and make merry at a burial"; so that crying, he suggests, is simply their mysterious and mythic way of marking a recent birth into this world of misery. Dr. Maxwell, in charge of Betsy's patient, next recounts Jessica's medical history to explain how she became "a sleepwalker who can never be awakened—feeling nothing, knowing nothing." Her condition results, he believes, from a tropical fever which "burned out" portions of the spinal cord. Halfjokingly, though, he also suggests another possibility, remarking that Jessica "makes a beautiful zombie." Since that term leaves Betsy puzzled, he then defines it: a zombie is "a ghost, the living dead. It's also a drink." His double definition, like his divergent diagnoses, bespeaks both the native intelligence, which employs its voodoo system to explain the mysteries of the world, and the detached, scientific perspective of modern medicine, that which even Paul ultimately prefers to believe in. This epistemological duality hints as well at the complex situation facing these characters, a complexity which is but thinly disguised by Maxwell's subsequent musing that when faced with a condition like Jessica's, "sometimes it's better for a doctor to laugh than to pull a long face." Despite the explanations of her husband, doctor, and maid (who offers, "She was very sick and then she went mindless"), then, Jessica's condition and the circumstances precipitating it remain cloaked in mystery; and if Betsy, "the nurse who's afraid of the dark," as Paul significantly styles her, seems little troubled by these ambiguities, it is because she persists in seeing this world as essentially knowable and narratable, open to her familiar perspective.

The narrative voice which subsequently—and unpredictably—intrudes on these events seems a direct response to this attitude. When Betsy spends her day off at an outdoor cafe with Wesley, she hears a calypso song describing for the first time the vicious love triangle which led to Jessica's current condition. Even before the off-screen voice is incarnated as a street singer, apparently singing a story well known to the local populace, Wesley defensively responds to this narrative with another, raising his voice to recount a humorous story of the plantation. This attempt to drown out one narrative voice by overlaying it with another, much as the larger structure of *Zombie* does, though, is frustrated by Betsy's curiosity, which mirrors our own concern with this new information. With these dark revelations, the earlier conversation's light tone gives way to a dim and menacing climate; we literally enter a vesperal atmosphere, as night comes on and Wesley, prodded by too much rum, joins in the pattern of explanation and revelation, offering the disconcerting view that Paul is not what he seems: "He's playing the noble husband for you." Even after he drinks himself into a stupor and thus silences his own voice, the discomfiting revelations continue, as the singer reappears, not only to conclude his story of the two brothers' tragic conflict, but also to implicate Betsy, who still sees herself as an outsider, uninvolved in these events and distanced from their implications. In the song's conclusion that "the brothers are lonely and the nurse is young," Betsy finds herself drawn into this dark world, transformed from the distanced narrator to the subject of narration, even a substitute for Jessica in a reenactment of the original romantic intrigue. The threatening implications of this unexpected involvement are underscored in the shift from a bright and cheery daylight, full of holiday promise, to the disturbing darkness in which the calypso singer holds forth, approaching Betsy in the same ambiguously menacing manner as the "zombie" Jessica earlier had. His appearance also repeats the pattern established by Paul and Betsy, whereby an off-screen voice is incarnated as an on-screen figure— a narrative pattern which subtly points up that motif of increasing involvement by promising to prove every commentator, every detached voice, a participant in these actions, in fact, to emphasize that such involvement in this dark world is the mark of the human. The appearance of this second narrative voice thus points up an ongoing process of revelation and incarnation, one plunging Betsy deeper into the mysteries of this world, into depths her initially distanced narration seems ever less likely to be able to illuminate. At the same time, the singer's intrusion points up the audience's similarly increasing immersion in the film's fantasy context, for we have been dislodged from our initial perspective and cast into a world where nothing is quite as we had originally expected, no appearance totally reliable.

When Betsy's voice briefly resumes the narration, it is appropriate to speak of her involvement in these affairs and the new level of knowledge she has gained. Against a dark background of waves crashing on jagged rocks, suggesting the inner turmoil she feels and recalling the similar background from which the calypso singer emerged, Betsy vows to try to set things right, to do whatever she can to restore Jessica's sanity, though primarily because, despite Wesley's comments, she finds herself in love with Paul. Just how incommensurate with this world her perspective remains and thus how slight her chance of restoring any normalcy is, however, show up in the two radically different solutions she seizes upon. Betsy first convinces Dr. Maxwell to try a new and still dangerously experimental medical technique on their patient—insulin shock therapy. When it fails and she must face the inadequacy of the scientific approach, Betsy turns in an opposite extreme to native voodoo. The long set piece which follows, wherein she takes Jessica on a midnight walk through the sugar cane fields to the voodoo houmfort, encountering along the way various emblems of death and decay, as well as the giant guardian of the crossroads, Carrefour, is easily the film's eeriest scene; it is not, however, as Siegel asserts, one which exists solely "for the sake of its own grace of movement."[11] Marking the mid-point in the film, this dreamlike scene metaphorically summarizes our own and Betsy's slow and deliberate journey ever deeper into this dark and menacing world, seeking to narrate its complexities, to find at its center some explanation for the mysteries it holds. Once at the houmfort, Betsy again listens to an off-screen voice, that of the houngan or witch doctor, whose task it is to "speak to Laba and Dumbala," the native gods, about Jessica. When this voice is incarnated, though, it proves to be that of Mrs. Rand, who ironically earlier warned Betsy to disregard the natives' voodoo "nonsense." It is a disturbing and, for Betsy at least, a disappointing revelation, yielding none of the answers she had hoped for, only other mysteries and the unsatisfactory explanation that these sinister ceremonies simply mask a kind of primitive yet practical psychology. This encounter, following Betsy's trek into the "heart of darkness," underscores the Chinese-box nature of this world and repeats the pattern of explanations—increasingly unsatisfying ones—which has begun to dominate the film. By this point, though, one of the directing forces behind that explanatory impulse, Betsy's narrating voice, has completely disappeared, or, as Sylvie Pierre suggests, has "exploded" into a myriad of possible voices.[12] With the loss of the monological coherence initially promised by her narration, we are left with no special key to these mysteries, no comforting distance, only the inexplicable phenomena themselves, mocking our desire for explanation, for intellectual distance—much as our dreams often seem to do—by their insistent yet almost insubstantial presence.

Through her growing involvement in these events, Betsy reveals the simple principle informing the film's narrative style: that nothing here is as it initially seems. Like the brioche which the maid brings Betsy for breakfast on her first day—puff pastry which looks like "too much" until one pokes it with a fork and deflates it—or the sea as Paul describes it in the opening scenes, all appearances are deceptive, at least for the untrained perspective. And this principle governs the audience's perspective on events as well, for in scene after scene the low-key lighting and strategically placed shadows work upon our generic expectations to *suggest* some threat which never materializes. Our participation is thereby fueled, our anxieties stirred, but never to be fully allayed. In retrospect, even the highly atmospheric walk through the cane fields seems almost an exercise in deception, since we are led to believe, by Betsy's loss of the "voodoo badge" needed to pass by Carrefour, by the recurring images of death and decay, and by the eerie sound effects, that this journey is indeed hazard filled; however, nothing happens. In the middle of that forbidding realm we find only an old woman who claims to be trying to help these primitive people in a way that they will understand. If Mrs. Rand's explanation of her presence is unsatisfying—as even Betsy comments, "This still doesn't explain why you're here"—it is because the narrative has at every level fostered skepticism, revealed its own inherent mystery by demonstrating how much remains inexplicable, even as we seem to approach nearer some determination. The repeated undercutting of expectation makes those many attempts at explanation seem far less adequate, as if they too were simply façades which a civilized society, with its great store of rationalizations and great stock in their power, might impose on whatever it finds disconcerting or inconsistent with its normal, nonfantasy perspective.

Betsy (Frances Dee) arrives at Fort Hudson.

The elaborate voodoo ceremony at the Houmfort.

The voodoo Sabreur "calls" Jessica Holland to the Houmfort.

The rational and the irrational: Betsy and Mrs. Rand (Edith Barrett) observe the drunken Wesley (James Ellison).

A torchlight procession brings the bodies of Wesley and Jessica, united in death, back to Fort Hudson.

Pursued by death, Wesley carries Jessica (Christine Gordon) into the sea.

The film's conclusion effectively dramatizes the collision of these varied and equally unsatisfactory explanations, analogues for the conflicting narrative voices which direct our perspective. The local police commissioner decides to conduct "a legal investigation" of the circumstances surrounding Jessica's condition—a task undertaken merely to quell curiosity. Appropriately, his inquiry only discloses contradictory versions of the events leading to Jessica's illness: one recounted by Mrs. Rand, who now claims deliberately to have turned her daughter-in-law into a zombie in revenge for tearing her family apart; the other by Dr. Maxwell, who believes his patient is simply the victim of "a fever with a long Latin name and a reputation for its aftereffects." Reason momentarily holds sway again, as both Paul and the doctor remark that, even if someone could be turned into a zombie, the person would first have to be dead, and Jessica was not. Soon after this logic is asserted, however, it too is undercut, as Paul and Wesley reveal another bit of privileged information, that Jessica had indeed lapsed into a deathlike coma—which suggests to Wesley that she could well have been transformed into a zombie as his mother claims. Their argument over this point prompts another reassertion of the rationalizing impulse which dominates so much of the narrative, with Paul claiming that he has "heard nothing that would convince a sober man." In their irreconcilable viewpoints the two brothers evoke the rational and emotional forces which contend so near the surface in this film and whose archetypal antagonism the Lewton films continually explored. In this instance neither form of understanding seems able to account adequately for the present situation—or to determine if Jessica is a zombie. This unsettling inability to distinguish even the most fundamental characteristics—such as life or death—combines with the disharmony of these perspectives to suggest the sort of partial vision we inevitably have of our world. It is a fragmented perspective which, Miller believes, informs every act of narration, every attempt to explain the mysteries of the human situation.

Because it is a *fantasy* narrative, however, *Zombie* is concerned not simply with an inability to narrate or explain reality—like so many other modern narratives—but also with the consequences of this inability, especially of our failure to understand and bear with it. This incapacity is essentially the source of the horror with which the Lewton fantasy formulations were always concerned, and it provides the impetus for the dread events with which *Zombie* concludes. Afraid of what experiments the natives might try to perform on Jessica if she is allowed to roam free, Paul keeps his wife locked within Fort Hudson, whose high walls and iron gate speak not only of his desire to protect her but also of his unspoken fear of the unbounded, unpredictable forces which operate just outside this fragile enclave. Fort Hudson becomes, in effect, a fortress of the rational, imprisoning its inhabitants within the "sober" perspective to which Paul now clings and attempting to shut out the vesperal. In fact, we might see this compound as an additional image of the film's narrative impulse—a mute testimony to the result of all such attempts to explicate this mystifying world. Faced with its basic limitations, the rational perspective turns within itself, becomes a conservative force which shuts out, as a way of denying existence to, that with which it cannot adequately deal.

Paul's final explanation, that the native voodoo is simply "nonsense" which functions by making one think "just as they want you to think," finds neither substantiation nor refutation in the film's last scenes. *Zombie* culminates in a wordless sequence of events about which we are to draw our own conclusions, although one of them must be a sense of how inadequate language is for understanding the full range of reality. Apparently moved by the voodoo drums and his conviction that Jessica is already dead, Wesley frees her from Fort Hudson and follows with a shaft pulled from Ti Misery, the arrow-studded emblem of human suffering which serves as a fountain centerpiece in the estate's garden. A cross-cut montage then parallels a voodoo ceremony wherein a doll is stabbed with a pin to a beach scene which finds Wesley standing over Jessica, the arrow with which he has apparently dispatched her still in his hand. Whether he was impelled by enchantment or was simply the victim of his own dark imaginings upon abandoning the rational world, we never learn; instead, we undergo the moment of "hesitation experienced by a person who knows only the laws of nature, confronting an apparently supernatural act"[13]—as Tzvetan Todorov defines fantasy—as Wesley also dies after walking into the sea, the recurrent emblem of the unconscious and its power in the Lewton films. The many unanswered questions have been rendered practically irrelevant by the stark facts of tragedy and death which dominate our attention.

At this point the final narrative voice takes over, but it offers little more satisfaction or consolation.[14] A native voice now supplants Betsy's, apparently bringing to these events a greater familiarity with human tragedy. In its commentary we can discern a combination of both pagan and Christian perspectives, drawn together in this instance to acknowledge and lament the human limitations which the narrative has described. "The secret of all hearts," it reminds us, remains beyond our normal vision, beyond too the capacity of this narration. Yet this last voice does more than simply unsettle our expectations for a satisfactory closure or frustrate our desire for narrative consistency. It also speaks of itself, of the limits on any single perspective, and thus reminds us, with its final supplication for the Lord's "pity," of why man continually seeks for, and finally requires, some kind of faith.

While this last voice remains off-screen, disembodied and unidentified, it clearly recalls the previous voices by the water imagery from which, in effect, it emerges. Like Betsy's opening narration as she walks along the seashore, the calypso singer's as he emerges from a dark and turbulent seascape in the background to sing of the Holland-Rand family, and Betsy's as she muses on her feelings for Paul while perched above the crashing waves of the coast, this last narration comes from the sea, beginning as native fishermen wade through shallow waters and discover the bodies of Wesley and Jessica, and ending as the camera tracks in to a final close-up on the fountain and Ti Misery in the Holland garden. Both sea and fountain are complex images with which to end the film, since they archetypally suggest birth, life, and eternity, and at the same time the unconscious and an omnipresence of "death and putresence." They remind us of the islanders' original fall, their introduction from across the sea to this death-surrounded land via the slave ship decorated with Ti Misery, and they recall as well the most fundamental of human mysteries—a life which leads inexorably to death, the central motif of several subsequent Lewton productions. As the water plays upon the head and chest of that fountain, it seems to suggest tears, as if in unspoken comment upon the sorrows and sufferings of all these people. It is fitting, then, that the various narrative voices lead to this single recurring image of the film, the "silent" narrator Ti Misery, whose enigmatic presence evokes those same mysteries and quietly underscores how little of the human predicament can be verbally narrated or spoken apart from the language of fantasy.

Certainly this emblem of death and suffering—of Saint Sebastian's martyrdom—in the middle of a beautiful tropical garden stirs mythic resonances, and it provides the pattern for similar subtexts exploring the myth of man's Fall in later Lewton films. At the same time, though, its mysterious presence reminds us how enigmatic the mythic always seems to our normal perspective. Modern man, it seems, ever desires to raise mystery and dream to the conscious level, there to deal with them in a rational manner and thus exorcise their more disturbing portents. The self-consciousness of the various narrative voices here comments upon that capacity for explicating and understanding the world in this way. As Kawin reminds, we must associate such narration "not with the inability to function in the given world, but with the attempt to know the world and self more deeply and thus to function in a way that would otherwise be impossible."[15] If we see *I Walked with a Zombie* essentially as a flashback story, a reminiscence of Betsy's traumatic initiation into a world where nothing is as it seems or as she expected it to be, where the forces of life and death, love and murder are arrayed in contention just beneath an idyllic surface, then the other narrating voices which ultimately seem to take over the tale emerge as lingering spirits that always haunt her recollections. They continually revisit the consciousness with a reminder of how irreconcilable the dark forces it has encountered and how inexplicable the world it inhabits will always be. The upset in our own narrative expectations which this medley of voices brings approximates the radical upset in perspective which Betsy did and, in fact, still does experience. It is, though, the sort of upset we might need to experience, the vesperal "walk" we must take "to function" properly in this complex human world.

A fantasy narrative like *Zombie*, Todorov suggests, "implies an integration of the reader into the world of the characters," a world "defined by the reader's own ambiguous perception of the events narrated."[16] In horror films such engagement is generally achieved visually, through an atmospheric setting or abnormal presences; and *Zombie* in part follows this tradition, especially with its effective compositions in depth and layering of shadows to locate barriers or mysterious dark areas between the audience and the actions depicted. Such compositional effects delineate the very structure of the fantastic, as they point to the absence of full knowledge which is available in this realm. Like the film's narrative structure, these stylistic components serve to ensure our engagement in the fantasy context, subtly to draw us into what Michel Foucault would term a "geneology of knowledge" here,[17] as we explore the disjunctions between the various possible interpretations of events. What results from this marriage of generic convention to the complex narrative model of a film like *Citizen Kane* is a more intricate fantasy context, which subtly subverts the monological, but only to draw us into a more involving, vesperal vision of our world.

When Paul learns that Betsy has turned to voodoo for help, he worriedly notes, "There's no telling what you may have started with this insanity." His reaction well demonstrates the sort of fear sparked by any challenge to the normal, but especially to a rational order which obstinately clings to its narrow, dayworld interpretations of its surroundings. This fear is not just of other explanations, though, but of the very potential of multiplicity, which brings with it the possibility that there could exist many, perhaps an infinite number of voices, speaking versions of reality whose full range we might never grasp. That way, it may well seem, lies madness—or at least the world of the fantastic; that way, in any case, leads to a profound confrontation with the psyche and its depths. All that we can be certain of at the end of *Zombie* is how very fragile our normal environment is and how inadequate to experience our rationalizations remain. While the film may lack in monsters and such frights, then, it draws from that absence, as did *Cat People*, its own effective type of horror—one born from knowledge, which arises, paradoxically, from the experience of unknowing. Through Betsy, we learn of our incarnation or humanness, which implies as well our fundamental inability to stand outside of and delineate the complex world in which we dwell and which colors all that we usually think and feel. Such a knowledge results from an experience of limits and in this instance arises from the indeterminate style of narrative which flourished, contrary to most expectations, at RKO. *Zombie*'s particular development of that style draws us into a singularly challenging fantasy realm, which can effectively speak to an audience that too often prefers its truths distanced from significant experience, narrated rather than made incarnate.

Formulas and Labyrinths: Tracking *The Leopard Man*

> I know of one Greek labyrinth which is a single straight
> line. Along that line so many philosophers have lost
> themselves that a mere detective might well do so, too.
>
> —Jorge Luis Borges
> "Death and the Compass"

While *Cat People* and *I Walked with a Zombie* were both
critically and financially successful, the Lewton unit's
third production, *The Leopard Man* (1943), met with far
less favor. With the exception of its cinematographer, Robert de
Grasse, the film was crafted by essentially the same team responsible for the previous works, as Lewton again employed Jacques
Tourneur as director, Mark Robson as editor, and Albert D'Agostino and Walter E. Keller as art directors. This time, however,
their collaboration resulted in what was perceived to be a loose
and confusing narrative. Bosley Crowther, for instance, described
The Leopard Man as a "half-baked" effort "to frighten and shock
the audience with a few exercises in mayhem."[1] With few excep-
tions recent revaluations of the film have followed this lead. Carlos
Clarens derides the "mechanical repetition" of the film's plot, and
Joel Siegel, while praising much of the production, judges it to be
"uncertain in structure," as it unfolds "in a curious, fragmented
fashion" that is "not wholly successful."[2] In retrospect, even Tourneur admits to some dissatisfaction with the structure of this, his
last film for the Lewton unit: "It's episodic, a series of vignettes.
It got very confusing."[3] In marked contrast, though, Manny Farber, often a dissenting voice, sees *The Leopard Man* as best evidence of its producer's skills in storytelling, an "early peak
example" of his ability "to tell a story about people that isn't dominated by the activity, weight, size, and pace of the human fig-

ure."[4] When viewed in light of *I Walked with a Zombie*'s complex structure, this disagreement regarding the film's narrative form becomes quite telling and argues for a reexamination of the later film's strategy. Its labyrinthine style, marked by formula-defiant twists, unexpected revelations, and a disconcertingly open ending, may well represent an additional and complementary structural development of the vesperal narrative form developed in the earlier Lewton films.

Rosemary Jackson believes that the fantastic impulse as frequently depends on structural form as it does on unnatural figures and contexts; "by presenting discrete elements which are juxtaposed and then reassembled in unexpected, apparently impossible combinations," she observes, a fantasy "draws explicit attention to the *process* of representation. It moves towards an 'anarchic discourse' by combining units in new relations."[5] In film this "anarchic" element defines itself against the form provided by what is usually termed "classical narrative," the traditional pattern of storytelling which relies upon "cause-effect logic and narrative parallelism" operating "through psychologically defined, goal oriented characters."[6] It is this structuring formula which long dominated the American cinema in general and the genre film in particular and which created in moviegoers definite patterns of narrative expectation. The horror film, for instance, typically conjured up the extraordinary image—that of a monster or some aberration—and placed it within a preternatural setting. In this genre the possibility of using complex narrative structures to evoke the fantastic was little explored, in part because of audience expectations, but also because of the natural resistance of any established pattern to change. In fact, films that violated either their generic formula or the patterns of classical narrative would most likely be seen as incoherent, structurally flawed, or at least ineffectual attempts at a traditional form.

Audiences usually associate meaning or significance, as J. Hillis Miller explains, "whether in a narrative, in a life, or in a word," with "continuity, in a homogeneous sequence making an unbroken line."[7] At the same time, though, the unique nature and true interest of a particular narrative—its personality, as it were—derive typically from digression, repetition, or deviation from expectations and causal connections. Miller suggests, in fact, that every narrative harbors a measure of this labyrinthine potential, even the most commonplace tale containing a tendency to the anarchic or fantastic, simply "by becoming 'complex'—knotted, repetitive, doubled, broken, phantasmal."[8] In classic American cinema this complexity usually went undeveloped, the narrative's potential for the unexpected and anarchic untapped. With the influence of European filmmakers on the postwar cinema, the hold of this classical pattern finally began to give way, resulting in what David Bordwell describes as the "art film," wherein "ambiguity is the dominant principle of intelligibility" and a "broken teleology" replaces the conventional linear development toward a sharply defined goal or specific statement.[9] In that "broken teleology"— echoed in Todorov's description of the "certain hesitation" of fantasy wherein we question the "laws of nature"[10]—we might recognize an expansion of the complexity which characterizes all narrative and carries a distinctly discomfiting message of its own. As such a narrative twists or turns back on itself, makes a sudden revelation or plunges us further into the enigmatic, a clear goal or resolution usually disappears from sight; as a result, the tale tends to speak more and more of the ambiguity which has become its informing principle. Such a discordant structure clearly offers certain advantages for speaking of the chaotic welter which often seems to characterize modern life. Properly directed and emphasized, though, it can also prove a fitting complement to various disconcerting themes, especially those of the fantasy forms in which the Lewton unit usually worked.

At first glance, *The Leopard Man* indeed looks like a narrative at odds with itself and its generic roots. Its broadest outlines suggest a classical narrative formula of the type found in the detective or mystery stories so popular at the time. In contrast to the previous Lewton films, which were largely the product of their creators' fertile imaginations, *The Leopard Man* is an adaptation, drawing on Cornell Woolrich's conventional murder mystery *Black Alibi*, and the plot distilled from it clearly retains much of the novel's generic trappings. As the film's title suggests, though, with its clear echo of *Cat People*'s fantastic amalgam of man and animal, that mystery formula is here married to the horror concerns of the other Lewton films. As a result, the narrative repeatedly veers off from the expectations we bring to the thriller; it never follows one character's actions long enough for us to identify with him, and its various murder sequences initially appear almost incidentally linked to a single plot line. This mixed style probably accounts for the critical consternation which first greeted the film, since that is what most distinguishes it from the typical genre programmers of its day. At the same time, its unconventional structure firmly links it to *I Walked with a Zombie*'s atypical voice-over narration and similarly helps to infuse it with an ambiguity and complexity—even a sense of the modern, in anticipation of postwar narrative developments—which are hallmarks of the vesperal form developed by the Lewton unit.

Instead of the dark patterns of the human mind explored in the earlier firms, *The Leopard Man* initially seems concerned with the brute force of nature, a naturalistic darkness symbolized in a leopard accidentally unleashed on a small New Mexico town as the result of a publicity stunt that backfired. In an almost predictable pattern the narrative then describes the series of apparently random murders which ensues, and it follows the investigation into those deaths as it finds not only the leopard but also a man who, imitating the cat's pattern, proves responsible for two of the killings. We are thus initially plunged into a threatened but seemingly *known*—or knowable—world, and through the detective work of Jerry Manning, the publicity agent responsible for the leopard's escape, this threatening force is apparently vanquished. On this melodramatic level, then, the narrative seems essentially consistent with the classical form, even if its material is more unsettling than usual.

The narrative also initially seems to affirm a cause-effect logic, which usually characterizes the detective tale. Much of the story describes the three parallel murders of young women, the episodes all sharing a common tone, atmosphere, and structure. However, the narrative repetition ultimately has a subversive effect on our perspective; because of it, we assume, as do the film's characters, that the killings are all the leopard's work. To further this misconstruction, the narrative withholds visual corroboration of this suspicion, cutting away just prior to the murder in each instance. However, it does hint at an alternate possibility through another element of repetition, by interspersing the death sequences with scenes of the two parallel investigations into the murders: one, the formal police inquiry conducted by Sheriff Robles, who assumes from all appearances that the leopard is the sole danger to his normally quiet community; the other, Jerry Manning's personal investigation, as he follows his hunch that a demented person, one of those "men with kinks in their brains" of the type more common to the horror film, is using the leopard's escape as an alibi to disguise his own pathological assaults. This pattern of parallel investigations also establishes a link to the classical detective formula, for, as in films like *The Maltese Falcon, Murder My Sweet,* and *The Big Sleep,* the official investigation here stumbles along in a fruitless search for "facts," while the private operator, working outside the sanction of the law—and unbound by its limited perspective— effectively becomes an extension of the justice which his society, because of its limitations, is incapable of administering.[11] Predictably, though, this thematic parallel is undercut by the problematic nature of the justice which results.

Within this generic structure, *The Leopard Man* evidences a pattern of psychological motivation which also recalls that of classical narrative. Since Jerry and his girlfriend Kiki Walker are responsible for the leopard's escape, they naturally feel guilty for the death of Teresa Delgado, the first victim, and both secretly give money to the girl's family to pay for her funeral. Raoul Belmonte, the second victim's fiancé, feels similarly responsible, since Consuelo was killed in the cemetery where they had arranged a tryst. And even Charlie How-Cum, owner of the leopard, when told that in a drunken stupor he might have murdered one of the girls, readily accepts the burden of guilt, asking Robles to lock him in jail if that is the case because "if I do things like that, I want to be put away. I don't want to hurt nobody." Guilt becomes a pervasive feeling here, spurring various people to try to expiate this sense and to assist in ridding the community of its menace.

Beyond such a simple, melodramatic line of reasoning and motivation, however, the narrative ultimately establishes multiple layers of motivation, many causes for every effect, all working together to determine, in a way that they can never quite comprehend, the characters' every action. What results from this complexity of forces at work is, at first glance, a thoroughly naturalistic narrative, reminiscent of Lewton's novel *No Bed of Her Own* in its detailing of the economic, environmental, and psychological impulses which drive the self. An economic determinant is clearly enunciated in the first murder sequence, when Teresa Delgado's mother forces her to go to the grocery for corn meal, lest the neighbors think they are too poor to provide the usual tortillas for her father's dinner. When she asks the grocer for credit, he tells Teresa to pay him "the next time" she comes, and that he trusts her because "the poor don't cheat one another. They're all poor together." Although the second murdered girl, Consuelo Contreras, is rich, her boyfriend is not, so she must meet him secretly to avoid her family's disapproval. In this case the clandestine assignation in the cemetery leads to the girl's death. Similar economic pressures determine the very life-style of Clo-Clo, a nightclub dancer and the third victim. She admits to being a "gold digger," and "why not," she asks, since she must support her mother, brother, and sister in whatever way she can. Her one dream is to meet a rich man who might support her, even if she must forget about the poor clerk she loves. After all, as she says, feelings do not matter, for "feelings don't buy houses and pay for rent and help bring up kids and buy clothes for them." This attitude indirectly leads to her death, though, for she is killed while looking for a $100 bill given to her by a sympathetic wealthy man. It is a situation like the others, as an economic imperative directly contributes to the tragic consequences which ensue.

In a slightly more subtle fashion the environment also comes to

seem a controlling force in these events. The frequently employed
bus technique of the Lewton films underscores this impression, as
the dominant night setting makes almost every encounter—with a
tumbleweed, a passing train, and even a noisy car—suggest a
threatening world, an environment filled with bestial forces like
the leopard, ever ready to prey on mankind. In fact, the environment seems essentially coterminous with the mazelike cemetery
where Consuelo is accidentally imprisoned and murdered, the desert arroyos and stark city streets just as lifeless and potentially
menacing.

The leopard itself symbolically links this threatening, almost
naturalistic environment to an uncharted psychological realm,
thereby hinting at an unrecognized bestial influence within man
which is the film's true concern. In the introductory sequence Kiki
announces that when she makes her nightclub debut with the leopard on a leash, she intends to wear her black evening dress, so
that "I'll be just like him." She is unable to control that leopard,
the shadow element of her persona, though, because of its great
strength and the fact that, as the museum curator Galbraith explains, such animals "are unpredictable; they're like frustrated
human beings." In its obvious mirroring of man and his most irrational actions, then, the cat becomes a means of exploring equally
dark elements of the human psyche: when under leash it resembles
man repressing his most violent antisocial impulses; once loosed,
it is like a man such as Galbraith, moved by a savage, inexplicable
instinct and free to strike out in dangerously unpredictable ways.
When he finally confesses to murdering Consuelo and Clo-Clo,
Galbraith points up how uncontrollable those psychological forces
can be, even in a scientist and supposedly rational person like
himself: "You don't know what it means to be tormented this way.
I didn't want to kill, but I had to," he protests, trying to explain
the invisible—and ineffable—powers that move within.

Explanations or rationales for human action typically occur in
the Lewton films, just as they do in most horror films, as attempts
to debunk the mysterious or supernatural forces which man encounters and which disturbingly challenge his normal world view.

The Lewton works, however, always undercut those accounts, by way of demonstrating how insufficient they are for explaining human experience. In *The Leopard Man*, to be sure, causes seem to abound for every action, but their very multiplicity ultimately makes them seem bewildering and unsatisfactory and suggests a maze of motivation which promises that it will never be adequately explored or understood. In their superfluity, then, these many causes represent a dissent from the classical orthodoxy of motivation and cause-effect behavior, and thus a subtle subversion of the pattern of classical narrative.

The film's opening, on close inspection, demonstrates that this sense of multiplicity and indeterminacy of human impulses are complementary. A moving camera introduces three women, as it tracks down the dark hallways of the nightclub where they all work. This unsettlingly mobile perspective takes us into a harshly lit background, where we see the dancer Clo-Clo reflected in a mirror; as the camera approaches, she dances into and then out of our view—as if hinting at the limitations of our perspective— while practicing her act before that most revealing of audiences. Suddenly shifting to the right, the camera tracks along another dark hall toward an adjacent dressing room in which Kiki Walker and the club's cigarette girl also gaze into mirrors, similarly concerned with the appearances they present to the public. This irregular camera movement immediately thrusts us into a shadowy labyrinth, a confusing nighttime world that recalls the dark streets and confusing interiors of the previous Lewton films. The characters we encounter here show a marked concern with the images they project to the world, with those appearances which inevitably mask all human motivations, and whose maintenance can lead to tragedy. In dealing with such a geographic and psychological maze, the film's narrative style, employing the fluidly tracking camera almost randomly to encounter and introduce new characters or to shift with equal suddenness from one line of action to another, seems most appropriate. The leopard's first victim is singled out, for instance, by the same tracking technique, as the camera follows Clo-Clo from the nightclub and along the dark city streets until she passes the home of Teresa Delgado, who happens to be looking out her window. When Clo-Clo greets the girl, the camera tracks in to the Delgado home, thereafter following Teresa's actions until she meets her death. The second murder sequence begins similarly, with Clo-Clo encountering Rosita, Consuelo Contreras's maid, whom the camera, as if randomly shifting its focus, then follows back to her mistress to begin her story. In several other instances as well such chance meetings, which seem quite natural in a world marked by random events, allow for an abrupt shift in scenes or the introduction of an entirely new line of action. This technique provides a mechanism for acknowledging the jarring multiplicity of events and character concerns, while at the same time smoothing the transitions between them and thus injecting an overriding sense of human complicity in all that transpires.

Once the different murder sequences begin, we become caught up in their dreamlike realms and the abrupt shifts are quickly forgotten, for the sequences function like separate interpolated narratives, asserting their own logic against the larger plot which shifts into the background. Each of these embedded narratives adds to the larger labyrinthine pattern, however, by describing its own maze in which some Minotaur-like half-man, half-beast waits for his victim. And once again the tracking camera with its discomfitingly mobile perspective draws us into these intricacies. As we wander through this dark realm, we are not only forced to experience the anxieties of a potential victim, but also are reminded of our tendency to project the shape of mind, especially its amorphous fears, onto this landscape. From these simultaneous impulses, a tension arises which undermines any relief we might derive from the sense that this is all simply part of the natural environment seen from a different, more revealing perspective. Consequently, we find ourselves drawn into the same sort of maze as the characters, with their movements increasingly suggesting our own progress into the territory of the psyche and the realm of fantasy. When the girl Teresa makes her way through the streets of the town and across an arroyo on what would normally be a simple trip to the grocery, it soon turns into a nightmarish wandering and wondering at the eerie transformations which darkness can work on even familiar geography. Repeatedly frightened by such commonplace objects as a tumbleweed and a train, transformed by the shadows, she is finally attacked and killed by the leopard just when she seems to have reached a safe exit from that maze—the door of her own home which her mother, in chastising the child for her imagined fears, has bolted against her. The labyrinth which Consuelo enters is appropriately the cemetery, where she goes to lay flowers on her father's grave and meet her boyfriend Raoul. Accidentally locked in as darkness comes on, she meanders through a maze of statues, trees, and surrealistically twisted and angled crosses, looking for an exit or help of any sort. Like Teresa, she finds only a locked gate, a blank wall, and finally a killer just when help seems at hand. For Clo-Clo as well the familiar city streets, which she walks alone each night from the club to her home, turn into a frightening and confusing pathway. Having lost a $100 bill while coming home, she returns to the darkness, attempting to retrace her steps, to follow the thread through this labyrinth, only to meet the killer she mistakes for her boyfriend. In each situation an individual leaves the safety of her home to wander through a circuitous, ultimately imprisoning world within which there lurks sudden death. We only draw back from the darkness and the mazelike attraction of these embedded narratives to regain our sense of the larger narrative structure in the face of this ultimate connector, the one point at which, the film disturbingly suggests, life's labyrinthine stories all eventually converge— death.[12]

Each sequence thus points to another mazelike element of the narrative which is generally foreign to classical narrative and its audience's expectations. These episodes demonstrate that the most confusing yet common path which man has to traverse lies within, in the mind itself; it is the puzzle which ultimately refutes our beliefs in an intelligible cause for every action and a rationale for each fear. Once he intuits that the murders may be the work of a man rather than a leopard, Jerry Manning seeks some explanation

Kiki (Jean Brooks) enters the nightclub, her darker self under leash.

Clo-Clo (Margo) dances about the fountain, emblem of the force of fate.

Love meets death with Consuelo's (Tula Parma) cemetery tryst.

The memorial procession: human life's inexorable movement toward death.

of the killer's psychology, hoping that a rationale for these actions might help him deduce his identity or at least determine what sort of person to look for. With an irony that undercuts this explanatory intention, though, it is the killer himself, Galbraith, to whom Jerry goes for help and who explains how difficult this task will be. The murderer, he says, perhaps not even truly aware that he is speaking of himself, would "be a hard man to find . . . especially if he were clever. He'd go about his ordinary business calmly, except when the fit to kill was on him." Part of this difficulty arises from the disjunction between appearances and reality which seems so common in this world, for it is a place where, as we have seen, characters carefully cultivate their public images, and where actions may be linked to many possible causes or to no apparent ones at all. The sense of randomness and of the inexplicable, however, gives *The Leopard Man* a large measure of its unsettling and frightening atmosphere and most surely links it to the successful strategy of the earlier films.

In a further questioning of our normal assumptions, we learn that the killer is the least likely member of the community; hardly "twisted" in appearance, he is an intellectual, former college professor, curator of the local museum, and, ironically, the "expert witness" Sheriff Robles calls in as a consultant on the "cat murders." Galbraith is one more instance of the doctor or scientist who, as the Lewton films repeatedly suggest, hides his darker self behind a discourse of reason or learning. More clearly than *Cat People*'s Dr. Judd, though, Galbraith exemplifies the dangers of this disparity. Because we do so readily defer to the scientific world and its representatives, we are especially vulnerable to the hazards it purposely or unwittingly veils from common view. In their doctor and scientist characters, therefore, these films locate a telling paradox particularly suited to their fantasy formula; such figures represent both knowledge and its subversion, truth and the suppression of an unsettling truth which dwells in the human personality. Even when he confesses to the cat murders, Galbraith strikes this disturbing note of complexity, underscoring how little of these events—and of the psyche's depths—we can ever hope to understand. He tells Jerry, "You don't know what you're doing. You don't understand. Nobody understands." His declaration drives home the great danger that has been revealed here: not simply the existence of an external threat like a cat or common murderer, but a danger that is immanent and internal, lodged in the convolutions and irrational depths of every human mind. Although the murders are finally solved, the "leopard man" unmasked, we are left with a stubborn sense that a satisfying explanation for these events or for Galbraith's aberrance will never be forthcoming and that we have simply glimpsed the darker winding passages of the mind, within which motives, identities, and even a dependable sense of humanity can easily become lost.

The key to threading any labyrinth, of course, is a distance or safe perspective from which to map its pattern, discern the full figure in the carpet. For the psychic maze which we enter here, the film offers, on the one hand, a sense of detachment through the characters of Jerry and Kiki who, for much of the narrative, pretend to be untouched by the events in which they are entangled, and, on the other, an involvement resulting from our immersion in the plot's convolutions and from the mysterious nature of these tragedies. As an audience, we are never quite permitted the distance we prefer, one which might impart a sense or meaning to these deaths—and this effect is probably one reason for the critical reaction to the film. The inaccessibility of that distance, like the inaccessibility of a satisfying meaning, becomes a sign of man's "smallness," of our inability not only to perceive the larger pattern within which our lives transpire but also to discern if there is any pattern to be perceived or thread which might lead out of the labyrinth. The ball precariously balanced atop a column of water in the nightclub's courtyard almost didactically emphasizes this limitation. The narrative returns to this peculiar fountain several times, using it as both a transitional device and symbolic image, much like Ti Misery in *I Walked with a Zombie*. In another heavily ironic touch it is the mysterious Galbraith who must explain the significance of this image; as Jerry later recounts, the ball in the fountain represents humanity, people like him and Kiki who are constantly being "pushed around by things bigger than themselves. That's the way it was with us. Only we were too small to see it that way."

Ignorant of those "forces that move us," and lacking an adequate perspective on our actions, the film suggests, we continually seek, individually and collectively, some way of ordering, explaining, or safely passing through the labyrinth of life. Jerry and Kiki hope to unravel a mystery, Sheriff Robles to track down a dangerous cat and return peace to his community, Clo-Clo to find the rich man who will solve her financial problems. *The Leopard Man* pointedly comments on this human ordering impulse in two small but disturbing scenes that bracket the first murder. As Teresa hesitates to go out into the night, her brother mocks her fear, noting that "it's because of the leopard." At the same time, he uses his hands to cast the silhouette of a cat on the wall—an image effectively juxtaposed in medium shot with Teresa's frightened face. Later, at her funeral, he again amuses himself with his ability to project that fear-filled shadow of the cat on a wall, though now it serves as a silent, imaginal explanation of his sister's death; in fact, it works much like an archetypal image, a projection from the depths of our psyche, reminding us of the dark powers of our world. This action both "explains" the occurrence for the boy and demonstrates how we often try to cope with those things we fear the most, by fashioning games around them, turning them into play—even by projecting their shadowy substance onto movie screens, as the Lewton unit did. In this way we attempt to demystify our fears of the unknown and assert, however tenuously, a control over them. Of course, the very inappropriateness of this bit of play, there in the funeral parlor where Pedro's sister lies, stands out and shocks us. It is so obviously wrong given the situation, so out of place—yet at the same time an act done in innocence of its effect—that it casts an ironic light on the attempts of all the characters here to sort out, sift meaning from, and assert a control over their lives. All of their explanations begin to seem equally like forms of play in the face of the inescapable fact of death and the presence of an irrational brute force ever there in nature—even in human nature.

The real mystery which *The Leopard Man* explores, therefore, is this most persistent but unfathomable one, that of human life which moves reluctantly yet inexorably toward death, while the mind persistently but frustratedly tries to locate some pattern or meaning in this movement. The film climaxes with a fitting image of these concerns in the black-robed and hooded processionists who, as if blindly, wind their way past the scenes of the previous murders, through the maze of city streets and out into the surrounding, open desert. Their movements take us from the comfortable world of modern civilization—now revealed to be much less than secure—into a dark and barren landscape, from the familiar dayworld into night, peopled only by the multiple images of the hooded monks. In this dreamlike imagery the film's fantasy dimension rears its head to reveal the force which has, all along, subverted the narrative's traditional mystery pattern and its impulse to render every enigma intelligible. While Galbraith explains that the procession is just a quaint local custom whose purpose "is to remind us of the great tragedy that took place here"—the massacre of a peaceful band of Indians by an army of conquistadores in the seventeenth century—the film's ensuing actions clearly transform it from a simple memorial for the dead. When Galbraith is revealed to be the cat murderer, he hides among the marchers, and when Jerry and Raoul, his pursuers, locate him, they too fall in march beside him, all becoming a part of the funereal procession. Their actions thus link the distant historical event to the modern incident to suggest a continuum of such inexplicable human horrors, the winding procession becoming emblematic of an eternal human condition. With this almost allegorical image the mystery element of *The Leopard Man* is subsumed into its horror aspect, as the film literally renders R. H. W. Dillard's description of the horror genre as a "pageantry of death," whose function is to help us to cope with a world we "can never hope to understand,"[13] in which life and death, meaning and mystery are ever inextricably intertwined.

In keeping with this image, even as the mystery seems solved and the town freed from the murderer's grip, we plunge further into a world of inexplicable and alarming events. Galbraith's compulsive and detailed description of Consuelo's murder is intercut with several close-ups of Raoul's wild, staring face—his gleaming eyes recalling those of the leopard shown in close-up during the first murder sequence, as well as Galbraith's just before he is caught—as he is moved beyond all self-control by this confession. Although one of the murderer's supposedly sane pursuers, Raoul too seems beset by a "fit to kill," a rage which suddenly prompts him to shoot his helpless captive. With the distinction between pursued and pursuer thus blurred, the killer's captor himself becoming a killer, the narrative demonstrates the frightening ease with which one may slip between normalcy and aberrance, and how from the mind itself the most harrowing creations can suddenly emerge. In this unexpected twist *The Leopard Man* disturbingly questions our ability to maintain a semblance of order and rationality in the face of unpredictable human nature and a world given to flux.

In this unsettling resolution we can discern the film's clearest departure from the narrative pattern traditionally associated with the mystery tale. A fundamental component of this formula, John Cawelti contends, is the "fantasy projection of guilt away from" the audience and onto some identified or identifiable culprit within the world of the narrative.[14] No sooner is Galbraith caught, though, than part of that guilt is transferred to Raoul. This rapid shifting and even sharing of guilt suggest how *universal* that state is here, and how difficult it ultimately is to assign. Certainly Jerry and Kiki share a blame for the murders, having unleashed the leopard which, in turn, apparently triggered those murderous instincts previously dormant in Galbraith. Some portion also falls to Teresa Delgado's mother, who locks her child out of the house and fails to open the door when the leopard attacks. Furthermore, Galbraith is painted like most of the villains in the Lewton films, as essentially a pathetic figure, hardly blameless for his reign of terror, but by no means truly evil.[15] In fact, when Kiki tries to trap him into revealing his murderous intentions by visiting him in the night and presenting herself vulnerably as another possible victim, Galbraith clearly hesitates, fearful of turning off the lights in his office because some part of him recognizes what sort of fall he is prey to in that darkened world, what terrible depth of his psyche may thus be tapped. Although the sheriff throughout the film makes a practice of absolving characters of guilt, repeatedly assuring them that the killings are not their fault, what becomes obvious is how all-inclusive and unprojectable the guilt really is. In keeping with the film's narrative style, the world fashioned here seems characterized by a broken teleology, a fall from both moral and logical meaning. The threats this realm contains are not simply the random and frightening aberrations from some larger design—signified by the accidental escape of a leopard from his normal captive state—but an apparent lack of design or at least a fundamental weakness in man's capacity to project and conscientiously maintain a humane pattern in the confusing environment he inhabits.

Having revealed the disconcerting mazes in which the human psyche can easily become lost, the narrative attempts to pull back and reassert, if only tenuously, some hope or lesson to be learned from this encounter with the darker possibilities of the self. Jerry and Kiki have continually reminded each other not to "be soft" and blame themselves for what has happened. As Jerry confesses, this attitude was instilled in him by the world in which he grew up: "Where I was brought up you had to be tough. It was a tough neighborhood. I learned it didn't pay to let anybody know how you feel or really think." Faced with a realization of how unreliable that individual detachment is, and paradoxically how vulnerable it ultimately makes one, both adopt a new principle of behavior. Kiki admits that she is "tired of pretending that nothing bothers me, that all I care about is myself, myself and my two-by-four career," while Jerry allows that he is really "a softie" who wants "to do something about all of this." It is a humane if somewhat naive response to the horrors they have witnessed, but it is a reaction that acknowledges and begins to grapple with the disparity between their true selves and the deceptive images of "hardness" they cultivated for a world clearly too prone to deception and misleading appearances, and for a human nature frequently incapable of coping with its own unmeasured depths.

Between our expectations of the formulaic fictional world and the demands of the film's nonclassical structure, the narrative indeed seems strained, its suddenly harmonious end incommensurate with all that has gone before. The publicity agent–detective has played his hunch and unraveled a murder mystery; the killer has confessed and is killed in retribution. Such a neat resolution and questionable justice could not stand unquestioned, however, at least not in an era which was witnessing the apparent breakdown of order and justice on a world scale. Even as Jerry and Kiki walk off, satisfied with this conclusion and their resolve to take a more humane perspective, then, the in-depth composition reveals in the background the coroner's office where Raoul, told he must stand trial for Galbraith's murder, convulsively breaks down. The agent of a melodramatic justice (that which the Motion Picture Production Code usually dictated), the revenger, must face an inevitable if unpopular justice since, as we have seen, he too bears that murderous potential, a dark and unpredictable possibility that society, for its own preservation, has to repress. As a result, we are left with a sense that there is no real ending yet in sight, certainly no true consolation here for the victims' families, and no satisfying feeling that things have at last been "made right," just a disturbing residue from these terrible events.

In juxtaposing such residual concerns with the two central characters who are free to leave this tragic scene, satisfied in their resolve for the future, *The Leopard Man* embodies the tensions that mark its narrative and that have contributed to the differing estimations of the film. It achieves a resolution neither open nor closed, not quite modern but neither truly classical in style, and yet one whose very ambiguity probably best indicates the sort of complex perspective which characterizes the Lewton works and accounts for the attraction of even the more rudely crafted entries in the series. A film like *The Leopard Man* measures off the potential of narrative to open onto human mystery against the traditional demands of genre, a truly labyrinthine impression of reality against the linear, ordered world audiences of the period expected to see. Through this tension the film effectively reveals the leopard in the labyrinth—the dark and mysterious alter ego of man in modern society—while also pointing the way to a more involving, vesperal style of genre narrative.

5 Repetition and the Experience of Limitation: *The Seventh Victim*

> Repetition is an absence of direction, a failure of
> coherence: the return to the same in order to abolish the
> difficult time of desire, it produces in that very moment
> the resurgence of the inescapable difference, produces
> indeed the poles of "same" and "different"; its edge, its
> final horizon, is thus death, the ultimate collapse of same
> and different, pure totality of indifference.
>
> —Stephen Heath
> *Questions of Cinema*

In its first three films the Lewton unit established a consistent concern with the problematic nature of human knowledge, a concern rooted in the films' haunting imagery, narrative structures, and generic conventions. Although directed by Mark Robson instead of Jacques Tourneur, the unit's next production, *The Seventh Victim* (1943), maintained that focus through its thematic and structural exploration of the common human experience of limitation. Because it seems to sum up many of the earlier films' concerns, Joel Siegel sees it as the most characteristic work of the series, although he also describes it as a "most forthright negation," "a film in which existence is portrayed as a hellish void from which all souls yearn for the sweet release of death."[1] More than the nihilistic statement Siegel's comment might suggest, though, *The Seventh Victim* explores certain ineffable fears that always haunt the human psyche, especially a fear of meaninglessness or the irrational which can make death seem almost a welcome release from life. In short, it evokes the disparity between what we know and what we long to know in order to examine that "experience of limits" which, according to Tzvetan Todorov, is the hallmark of fantasy.[2] In the film's mechanism for describing this human experience, the vesperal impulse which characterizes the Lewton series clearly shows through. As its very title implies, *The Seventh Victim* is concerned with repetition, although not simply as a recurrence of victimization, as in *The Leopard Man*'s multiple murders or those which horror movies so often deploy to generate shock. Rather, the film explores repetition as a common denominator of human action and a fundamental element of the psyche which, viewed in its narrative application, might afford a clearer perspective on man's persistent drive for knowledge.

The basic concept of repetition automatically suggests a sequence of events which might conceivably lead back into the past or allow for extrapolation into the future. This sense of progression, as James Hillman explains, can afford an important perspective on the workings of the human psyche: "Reversion through likeness, *resemblance*, is a primary principle for the archetypal approach to all psychic events. Reversion is a bridge too, a method which connects an event to its image, a psychic process to its myth, a suffering of the soul to the imaginal mystery expressed therein."[3] By "resemblance" Hillman refers to what he sees as the most basic psychic activity, an "image-making" process wherein the spirit is "ceaselessly talking about itself in ever-recurring motifs"; from this activity come the archetypal images we need to guide our lives. Such recurrent patterns of mental "speech" afford a convenient bridge for moving back into the depths of the human experience and for gaining a perspective on how these depths affect our lives. In outlining the concept of depth psychology Freud isolated a repetition mechanism, what he termed a compulsion, in man. In fact, his *Beyond the Pleasure Principle* calls attention to a fundamental paradox implicit in it. On the one hand, he saw repetition as a common method of learning or mastery, which all mankind employs; on the other, he identified in it a subtle manifestation of an equally universal phenomenon, the death instinct.[4] His interpretation, however, essentially separated the two possibilities—for understanding and extinction—as alternative forms that the act of repetition can signify. Instead of exploring their curiously paradoxical intertwining in the human psyche, therefore, he treated them as what Hillman terms "morning traffic," a means of explaining the ego's activities, although at the cost of understanding the archetypal significance that underlies their appearance.

In recent studies of repetition as a narrative mechanism, however, this paradox has come more clearly into focus. As a narrative device, repetition obviously promises to increase knowledge or clarity, since by offering minor variations on a character, event, or motif, it generates a sense that our expectations and narrative reality correspond in a dependable way. At the same time, though, it can complicate the narrative experience, as we saw in the case of *The Leopard Man*, by subverting expectations of linearity and cause-effect relationships; this subversive potential is explicit in J. Hillis Miller's explanation of repetition as "something occurring along the line which disintegrates the continuity of the line . . . even though the series of repetitions may appear as the gradual covering over of a subversive implication."[5] Even as it seems to propel us toward some narrative understanding, then, repetition may also open up a potential aporia or ambiguity; hence, it carries a dual, even paradoxical potential to inform and subvert the act of narration. Bruce Kawin echoes this view when he describes filmic repetition as possessing both "constructive" and "destructive" properties[6] which hold out the possibility for knowledge and ambiguity. This dual potential probably shows forth most clearly in the repetition structure of a film like *Citizen Kane*. To fashion the ambiguous portrait of his title character, Orson Welles doubled and redoubled the various perspectives afforded by the dead man's acquaintances, while he also destroyed the one object which promised to lend some coherence to those multiple, often contradictory views. The film leaves us, consequently, simply with a sense of limits, of boundary—like the "No Trespassing" sign with which it concludes—that no further commentary or additional point of view might dispel. The narrative paradox which repetition indicates was in this case employed to reveal the character of Kane, who is described variously as "a communist," "a fascist," and "an American," and at the same time to remind us of the ultimate limits of interpretation. In *Citizen Kane* Welles thus succeeded not only in demonstrating the narrative potential of repetition, but also in crafting the necessary image—his film—of the psychic paradox which repetition indicates.

Of course, the technique for which the Lewton unit's films are most noted, the bus suspense mechanism, reveals a fundamental consciousness of and reliance upon the potential of narrative repetition. This technique evokes an atmosphere of menace by fashioning a sequence of possibly threatening situations which hint of some frightening, almost predictable conclusion. Primed with a vague foreboding by this structural repetition, we readily see in even the most commonplace of objects and encounters a deeper, sinister purpose, as they suddenly appear. This general pattern, moreover, also informs the larger structure of the films, as Lewton himself readily pointed out: "Our formula is simple. A love story, three scenes of suggested horror and one of actual violence. Fade-out."[7] What he clearly recognized is that there exists in man an absolute need for formulation, for certitude of the sort normally felt to be provided by repetition, so that whatever remains unformulated, beyond the pale in life or narrative, can evoke a psychic disability or anxiety. The narrative rhythms of the Lewton films consequently employ repetition to set the individual imagination to work, confronting it with a most ambiguous atmosphere and forcing it to seek some closure for what has come to seem a disconcertingly open world. On this structural level, repetition holds out a promise of alleviating anxiety by fostering a familiarity, even as it injects a most fundamental discomfort by playing upon our desires for verification and knowledge. If the promise implicit in those repetitions is never quite fulfilled, the anxiety never fully allayed in the Lewton films, it is because of the epistemological paradox they successfully tap. They disclose a subversive element at work in the human psyche, as in the repetition mechanism itself and the narratives in which we project the mind's own image.

The Seventh Victim is a film about a sequence of sacrificial killings designed to suppress knowledge of a satanic cult, the Palladists, and it draws its structure from a series of doublings or repetitions, as every character seems provided with a double or alter ego and every action paired with or qualified by its mirror image. The story focuses primarily on two sisters, Mary and Jacqueline Gibson, who are both threatened by older women at various times and who eventually become competitors for the love of the same man. When Jacqueline, the older, mysteriously disappears, she becomes the object of a series of searches, first by her sister, then by two detectives—one working for Mary, the other for Jacqueline's husband Gregory Ward—and finally by a poet and a psychiatrist who offer their help. However, even as these many people—all doubles, it seems—pursue her, Jacqueline constantly flees, afraid of rejoining the everyday world which she associates with sameness, meaninglessness, and death. It is a theme announced at the film's opening in an epigraph that recurs on the soundtrack at the film's conclusion; echoing a central theme of all the Lewton films, the statement comes from John Donne's Holy Sonnets: "I run to death and death meets me as fast, and all my pleasures are like yesterday." First appearing on a stained glass window in the school Mary attends, this verse is later recited by Jacqueline as she hangs herself at the film's end. These two different contexts suggest a Freudian view of repetition as part of both the learning process and the death instinct, and the narrative they enclose in their rhyme seems concerned with disclosing this paradox and exploring its implications for human activity.

Both the informative and subversive implications of repetition surface in the film's initial sequence, the first appearance of the Donne epigraph, as the camera tracks back from the enscribed window to reveal a bordering staircase down which file happy children, oblivious to the morbid message they pass with each change of classes. After this first group of children passes downstairs, Mary moves past the same window but in the opposite direction, up the stairs to the headmistress's office. There she learns that her sister, her only relative and apparently her alter ego, has stopped paying her tuition and disappeared. This unsettling knowledge comes as Mary's first hint of a disconcerting absence in her world—an absence of all she has come to rely upon; and while it offers her a kind of individuality, it does so by asserting how alone in the world she is. To compensate for the loss of the double who has made her life possible, however, Mrs. Lowood offers Mary a position at the school as an assistant teacher, which she is immediately warned against accepting by Miss Gilchrist, the headmistress's assistant. It would only repeat her own mistake, she explains, for like Mary she went through a traumatic departure and then a return to the school: "I left as you are leaving; but I didn't have courage. One must have courage to really live in the world. I came back." To avoid repeating her failure, then, Mary is urged to another, archetypal repetition, a movement out from the security of school into the real world. It is a kind of repetition which could lead to life or death, fulfillment or frustration, although it might also allow her to break with the limiting models of her past in the struggle for her own identity.

When viewed in this light, Mary's pursuit of her sister takes on an epistemological shape, underscored when she once more descends her school's central staircase. While she repeats the earlier action of her fellow students, there is a clear difference, which Mary senses, as she smiles and shakes her head at the sounds of her former classmates reciting their lessons, trying to gain knowledge by rote. The various lessons she overhears include repetition of the French verb for "to search," a conjugation of the Latin for "to love," and a recitation of Oliver Wendell Holmes's "The Chambered Nautilus"—each element in this sequence ironically reflecting on her new situation. Leaving this sheltered world, a world of comforting repetitions, Mary must search for both her sister and herself; as part of this exploration, she is to experience the awakening of love; and, following Holmes's admonition to "build . . . more stately mansions" and "leave thy low-vaulted past," she must finally begin to grow out of the limiting shell previously provided by the hermetic schoolhouse. From this world of safe models, she must venture out into a new realm, whose potential for the inexplicable, the unthinkable, the unmodeled has just begun to come into focus.

Outside the Dante Restaurant, the poet Jason (Erford Gage) passes his inspiration Mary (Kim Hunter).

Mary leaves her school and its "safe" existence.

Jacqueline (Jean Brooks) recounts her experience with the devil worshippers.

A complementary doubling: Dr. Judd (Tom Conway) and Jason join against the devil worshippers.

Reaching New York, a realm of unknown but immense possibility, Mary finds that mystery is almost the norm, unexplained disappearances such as Jacqueline's a fact of life. A long tracking shot of similar seekers at the Bureau of Missing Persons underscores this fact. Despite this world's larger bounds, Mary seems to have simply exchanged one "low-vaulted" enclosure for another, as the narrative develops a telling structural repetition, an encounter with a series of small rooms, to emphasize the difficulty of her quest for knowledge and the growing anxiety which results from it. At the Dante Restaurant where Jacqueline was last seen, Mary learns that her sister rented a room which, when opened, reveals only a solitary chair and a noose hanging menacingly from the ceiling. When the detective Irving August tries to locate Jacqueline, he discovers another such locked room in the rear of La Sagesse Cosmetics, a company she formerly owned, and with Mary breaks into the building to discover its secrets. Although he finds Jacqueline there, he also meets his death, as she stabs him out of fright and then flees into the night. Shortly thereafter, Dr. Louis Judd, Jacqueline's psychiatrist and lover, takes Mary to a rooming-house where he is hiding her. When he unlocks the door, however, the room proves empty, a burning cigarette indicating that Jacqueline has recently fled. Judd's unexplained fright at this turn of events and his cryptic statement that "she's left me to meet them alone" underscore the sort of mystery and foreboding that, through these frustrating repetitions, has gradually attached to such emptiness. This sequence of encounters with empty rooms marking Mary's pursuit of her sister suggests the sense of absence which plagues her consciousness, much as it does the heroines of both *Cat People* and *I Walked with a Zombie*. In this case it is actually a pointed lack of knowledge which follows from the recurrent threshold crossings, as these empty repetitions hint at a larger and more disconcerting emptiness distinguishing this world she has entered.

The recurrent problem of threshold crossing is even more firmly linked to Mary's quest for knowledge in the shower scene, later adapted as the centerpiece of Hitchcock's thriller *Psycho*. In her

own room and in that most private of rooms, the bathroom, Mary
sings as she showers, happy that she has begun to make some
progress in her investigation. Working against this atmosphere, in
the background, indistinctly outlined against the shower curtain,
a shadowy presence suddenly enters the room and identifies itself
as Mrs. Redi, Jacqueline's former partner to whom she supposedly
sold La Sagesse. Throughout this scene the shower curtain remains
drawn, forming a translucent barrier between the two characters,
while also recalling that "certain hesitation" which Todorov terms
a hallmark of the fantastic. Reluctant to broach this limit, Mary
converses with the intruder across the barrier, while the annoying
drip of water from the shower head in the foreground effectively
visualizes the tension here, providing an objective correlative for
Mrs. Redi's urging of a sort of repetition, as she tells Mary to "go
back. You don't know what you're doing or what dreadful things
you might bring about by looking for your sister." More than a
physical barrier separating these two people, the curtain objecti-
fies Mary's essential innocence; it is a barrier that must be pulled
aside if she is to locate her sister and live in this world. Her hes-
itance simply marks a growing awareness of the difficulties and
dangers that attend such a drawing aside of the veil and any encounter with that which remains outside the pattern of her prior
repetitions. It suggests as well something within Mary that implicitly resists opening onto any darker possibilities, as the poet Jason
Hoag recognizes when he challenges her to "look into your heart.
Do you really want to find your sister?" The only alternative,
though, seems to be the return, and thus, as Gilchrist warned, a
repetition of a fruitless and empty pattern of existence.

In Jacqueline we can see more starkly both a strong impulse
away from repetition or models of any sort and the dangers which
might attend such a movement. As Dr. Judd notes, Jacqueline
"was always a sensationalist, trying to seize onto something, anything to bring her happiness," and Gregory Ward admits that as a
result she seemed to inhabit "a world of her own fancy. She didn't
always tell the truth. In fact . . . she didn't know what the truth
was." The portrait that emerges from these descriptions and Mary's

investigations suggests a person possessed by the absence of meaning at the core of her life, the lack of a suitable model or example. Because of this lack, she has rushed to embrace anything new in an attempt to fill the void, to dispel that besetting ambiguity, or to give meaning and direction to her existence. In effect, she has entered into a fantasy world, constructed and furnished from the dark projections of her own psyche. As Rosemary Jackson explains, fantasies typically "express a longing for an absolute meaning, for something other than the limited 'known' world."[8] This longing finds its most disconcerting expression in Jacqueline's noose-equipped room above the Dante Restaurant. In a universe that seems quite meaningless, it places the ultimate power of negation—of death—in her own hands, letting her choose, existentially, to impose or revoke a sense of meaning, and thus to assert, in a final way, the force of her individuality. Of course, even as it intends to counter a world of apparently meaningless repetition by a singular assertion, such an act firmly locks Jacqueline within the ultimate archetypal repetition, Freud's death instinct.

Because Jacqueline, even as she demonstrates the dangers of abandoning an informing repetition, also mirrors a darkly alluring side of Mary's nature, the younger girl feels compelled to pursue her sister despite those threats. We might see in the two sisters an allusion to the workings of the human psyche, the Jungian persona fleetingly glimpsing and fascinatedly pursuing the self's shadow, as it strives for the completion that leads to individuation. Such a perspective sheds light on the distinct physical resemblance between the two sisters—a doubling which the Romeris, who own the Dante, remark upon when Mary first inquires about her sister—as well as on that unsettling feeling of estrangement which Mary notes: "I almost feel as if I've never known my sister." When Judd takes Mary to the room where her sister has been hiding, Mary handles Jacqueline's things, particularly her monogrammed hand mirror, and when she answers a knock at the door, finds her sister standing there, poised as if a mirror image of herself. Not quite doubles, though, as their hair styles and attitudes emphasize, they resemble light and dark versions of the same character, different potentials such as *Cat People* depicted in Irena and Alice, or *I Walked with a Zombie* with the half-brothers Paul Holland and Wesley Rand. Such a complex combination of doubling and difference or repetition and individuation opens onto the deep ambiguities of character with which *The Seventh Victim* is fundamentally concerned.

Such a doubling of character, seen as well in the psychiatrist Judd and the poet Hoag, suggests a complexity of motivation which usually goes unperceived. Dr. Louis Judd obviously recalls the character of the same name in *Cat People;* in fact, his curious mix of popularized Freudianism and sexual intrigues with his clients seems consistent in the two films. His smooth manner and success in publishing his psychoanalytic theories, however, only cloak a deeper sense of failure—which perhaps prompts his sexual pursuits, as if by sating one appetite, he might still another. As Judd informs Gregory's secretary when she asks for advice about her father, "I don't practice anymore. I find it easier to write about mental illness and leave the care to others." What prompts this abdication from care, however, is his failure in treating Jacqueline and, some years before, another girl now hopelessly institutionalized, as he eventually reveals to Jason. Hoag, though, seems remarkably similar. Once a promising poet, he has fallen into a ten-year silence after losing his inspiration—the same girl whom Judd had institutionalized. Now he simply works in a bookstore by day and takes his meals beneath the mural of Dante in the Romeris' restaurant, as he waits for another Beatrice. His impractical, romantic side, embodied in his vision of himself as Cyrano de Bergerac, seems a fitting complement to Judd's cold, rational perspective; in fact, the interaction of these two failures reveals just how much each represents what the other lacks, as Judd confesses his admiration for Jason's poetic skills, and the latter tries a bit of psychoanalysis on Mary in an effort to convince her to abandon her search for Jacqueline. That, unlike in *Cat People* and the other Lewton films, the rational world seems far less menacing here is probably due to this effective balancing of doubles—a balance made even more prominent when Judd and Hoag combine forces to upbraid the Palladists who are pursuing Jacqueline. If the common ground from which they counter the cultists' nihilism—a recitation of the Lord's prayer—strikes some viewers as contrived and too redolent of a conventional morality, it is nonetheless a fitting demonstration of the way in which myth and religion have always furnished a fundamental point of unity for the different impulses which drive the individual.

In the absence of such a balance, however, the fact of difference becomes both a retreat and a psychic burden for the self. Two rhyming sequences, one as Mary searches for her sister and the other as Jacqueline flees a Palladist assassin, underscore the complex character of difference as it influences these two girls' lives, marking them off from all others, even as it all the more surely affirms their sisterhood. In pursuing her sister, Mary breaks into the La Sagesse building one night, and as she threads its dark corridors, the shadow of the company trademark—which is also the Palladist insignia—is momentarily cast on her back, as if a mark of the dark and threatening world into which she has moved; and when Irving August meets his tragic end moments later, she flees to the subway system, only to encounter several of the cultists carrying off his body—an encounter which revisits the initial shock of his sudden murder. Her chance discovery of their presence and inability to get any help or even persuade anyone to believe what she has seen thrust home the horror that attaches to individuation, at least to a special knowledge or insight which bothersomely questions the appearance of normalcy to which most people eagerly cling. Later, Jacqueline's night journey through the city streets as she is pursued by one of the Palladists underscores this motif. Although the streets are crowded, she finds herself unable to get any help, just as her sister did; meanwhile, she moves, as did Mary in the film's opening scene, in the opposite direction of all those she encounters. After entering a dark alley to elude her pursuer, Jacqueline pauses outside a theater, her body covering the mask of tragedy decorating the stage door; her frightened face, framed by her severe haircut, momentarily becomes the tragic mask, her own special mark of individuation. It is an especially telling transformation, for it underscores the tragic element of both the flight from death and the process of individuation in which the sisters are equally engaged.

During this particular narrative repetition, however, a significant inversion occurs. As previously described, Jacqueline earlier killed Irving August, responding violently to his intrusion into her world; and this later scene symbolically transforms Mary's search for her sister into a murderous pursuit, hinting at the threat which Mary's emergence as an individual poses for her older sister, particularly since she has already won the heart of Jacqueline's husband. René Girard suggests that a duality such as these sisters embody typifies tragedy and that such doubling signifies a threat felt by the individual at a potential diminution of the self; Girard explains that there is "no double who does not yield a monstrous aspect upon close scrutiny,"[9] and in that explanation hints at the sort of variation on the traditional horror film which *The Seventh Victim* in particular works. Indeed, Jacqueline embodies what amounts to a monstrous, tragic vision of death and meaninglessness which must seem at all odds with Mary's pursuit of her own meaning, just as the younger girl must on some subconscious level seem like a threatening figure to her older sister, by promising to usurp her place with Gregory and asserting, naively and absolutely, the presence of something meaningful. The two sisters thus sum up the fundamental paradox of repetition in their relationship, as they suggest both a mutual comfort and reciprocal threat, the one inevitably implying the other as its mirror image.

The final destruction of this particular doubling, which occurs with Jacqueline's suicide and Gregory's avowal of his love for Mary, underscores the tragic component of the fantasy formula. This resolution brings a certain sense of relief, as Jacqueline's death clears a path for a new beginning, a new life for Mary and Gregory, although this possibility is necessarily haunted by the tragic events which precede, as well as by the hint of another repetition; even as Mary takes Jacqueline's place, she begins following the pattern which eventually led to her doom. A more traditional name for the effect achieved by this ambiguous resolution, then, might be the one we normally attribute to the tragic effect, namely *katharsis*. Girard again provides a guide with his theory that the term originally denoted "a process of victimage," and thus a sacrificial component inherent in all tragedy.[10] Of course, the film's title clearly establishes a link between the pervasive pattern of repetitions and victimization, but its implications might initially seem limited to Jacqueline's involvement with the Palladists who have marked her for death, as they have six others. In this troubling notion, though, we should also see the ghost of the larger epistemological problem with which this film in particular and fantasy in general are concerned: the human compulsion for knowledge which always runs headlong into the unsettling recognition of human limitation.

The Palladists represent one manner of coping with this fundamental paradox. They are a small group of devil worshippers who pointedly assert, despite all their culture's denials, a singular faith; they choose to believe that a force of evil and destruction affords the only organizing principle in the universe. Within this society, which Jacqueline joined in her fruitless attempts to "seize onto something" meaningful, are people like the frustrated Mrs. Redi, the one-armed socialite Natalie, and the mousy hairdresser Frances, all seeking some framework for their lives, a way of imposing meaning on what otherwise seems a dark and meaningless void. In the face of life's sameness and apparent absence of meaning, they have sought to differentiate themselves, as Irena finally does in *Cat People*, by embracing the power of absence, the unknown and threatening forces of darkness which they implicitly fear. And it is a purely arbitrary choice, as one of their number attests when he defies Judd and Hoag to gainsay their beliefs: "Who knows what is wrong or right? If I choose to believe his satanic majesty is in power, who can prove me wrong?" By willfully adopting a belief which asserts a singular insight into the workings of their world, they both differentiate themselves from the mass of people and hold out a hope for an equally singular sense of power, a freedom of sorts from utter meaninglessness, on the one hand, and, on the other, from the traditional models and unsatisfactory beliefs to which man seems enigmatically consigned.

It is with these devil worshippers, a more traditional trapping of the horror film, then, that the problems of repetition and victimization merge to reveal a compelling concern with human knowledge. By talking of the Palladist cult to her psychiatrist, Jacqueline has both set herself apart from this select group which she previously embraced and violated its secrets, in the process pointing up the inadequacy of the differentiating knowledge it claims to possess. The decision to kill Jacqueline naturally follows from this revelation, and the repetition of murders is shown to result from a need to suppress any real individuation and all sense of the inadequacy of their manner of knowing. That the Palladist history is marked by this long succession of victims, a tradition of members who had to be murdered to check their *recit*, points up both the weakness of their arbitrary system and the failure of the alternative knowledge they claim to possess.

What the Palladists actually represent is a knowledge shot through with contradiction, a small society dedicated not to maintaining a set of beliefs inviolate, but to denying the possibility of all real belief. In short, they gainsay the informing power of repetition, even as they unwittingly lapse into its subversive force. When faced with the prospect of killing Jacqueline for violating their secrecy, the Palladists must confront this inherent contradiction. Confronted by their own binding rule of nonviolence as well as the "law that whoever betrays us must die," Mrs. Redi straightway notes the "seemingly contradictory rules" of their order, while Frances protests that "I don't understand it." Highlighting their confusion is that a more pointed contradiction—between a requirement of absolute secrecy and the readily available, published history of the organization—seems to go unnoticed by the cultists. Its implication, though, that their desire for secrecy is futile, as arbitrary as their belief itself, is significant for the film's purpose. Even if the public library keeps the texts about the cult on a proscribed list, attempting to stop their general circulation and thus

submerge their narrative—just as social institutions have traditionally sought to do with any dangerous impulse or threatening
epistemology—this knowledge will surface for scrutiny, its repetition will out, as we see when Jason gains access to the Palladist
texts simply by flattering the librarian. Although the cosmetic
company to which Mrs. Redi appropriates the Palladist insignia is
called La Sagesse, or "wisdom," then, the satanist group actually
stands for its absence,[11] and Jacqueline is only the latest in a
series of scapegoats, as Girard would term them, whose deaths
mask this lack of wisdom, by disguising it as its opposite, a knowledge kept pure, inviolate, and secret by its devotees. Of course,
according to Girard, victimization always serves such a purpose;
it is a recurring effort to keep "the truth about men from becoming
known."[12]

The repetition of victimization, therefore, should point up a
larger social problem here, as is suggested by Girard's description
of the scapegoat as "a collective mechanism of projection that must
be understood in reference not to the victim . . . but to the un-
manageable and incompletely formulated problems of that collec-
tivity."[13] The proposed ritual death of Jacqueline insinuates the
absence of a true differentiating wisdom in the Palladists' closed
society, while this group, in turn, signals a key problem of the
film, since it is only a projection—or double—of the larger society
depicted, which simply seems to have substituted empty repetitions for informing ones. When Mary notes that the Palladists seem
"sort of lonely and unhappy," Frances fittingly reminds her that
"most people" are. Inhabiting a world whose ruling principle
seems one of ambiguity, wherein life seems to exist solely for a
repeated headlong rush toward death, as the opening epigraph implies, people despairingly turn to other systems to fill the gaps they
sense, to append some meaning to the human, and finally, to claim
for themselves a distinction from their fellows. It is a common
problem and the Palladists' response only another way of fleeing
the nothingness they ultimately fear, the same nothingness which
seems to haunt all the characters here and which eventually renders them essentially the same, all equally human.

The world which *The Seventh Victim* describes, therefore, is one in which repetition seems inevitable, as natural—and as human— a condition as the lack of knowledge which afflicts these characters. We might recall Mary's departure from school, begun so distinctively as she walked up the stairs, in the *opposite* direction of her classmates, and Gilchrist's warning—meant as a "redemptive" counsel, as her Christ-ly name hints—against returning to the school as a teacher. In following Jacqueline's path, or replacing her, however, Mary seems to have gradually and unconsciously begun a kind of repetition, emphasized by the job she takes at a settlement house run by Mrs. Wheeler, whose name suggests the full—and inevitable—circle Mary's movements describe. What she teaches, of course, is colored by her experiences, as we see in the song she sings for her students: "Here comes the candle to light you to bed; here comes the chopper to chop off your head."[14] This subtly brutal message, however, that the "light" of understanding goes hand-in-hand with death implies that she also sees a certain fatalism in human action, at very least the alternatives Freud described in the human propensity for repetition: the desire for knowledge and the correlative drive toward death.

The Seventh Victim initially seems to offer two possibilities for man, either an endless repetition of actions—like an eternal childhood—or a break with the past by asserting individuality. These alternatives are seen in the initial states of Mary and her sister. The former possibility promises security, a model for action, and an apparent source of meaning; the latter consigns the individual to an ambiguous realm, marked by constant reminders of human limitation. What this second direction does make clear is a fundamental if tragic truth, for it invokes a pain implicit in the fact of otherness, of being different in a world of doubles, and explicit in the scapegoat status which inevitably follows from the condition of difference. Consigned to sameness or damned to individuality, the self remains caught within a larger cycle of repetition, as we see in the film's end which repeats the beginning. Jacqueline and Mary are both bound by the recurrence of the Donne epigraph—imprisoned by rhyme, as it were. That very doubling, moreover, suggests both repetition's essential paradox and its ultimate sway over the psyche. In a life that seems to exist only for the headlong rush to its own extinction, death easily appears to be the only exit; this compulsiveness, of course, ultimately assures us that even in that fatalistic movement one finds no real exit, in this instance, that the pattern of Jacqueline's escape is indeed familiar, and that her experience could well find a subsequent double in Mary's life.

In these characters and their condition, therefore, we can see mirrored the fundamental complexity of narrative repetition, as they find themselves trapped within a continuity, even as they individually seek to deny that continuity. Of course, we normally think of classical narrative as allowing little room for such ambiguous and frustrating situations, its repetitions typically suggesting an ordered world wherein everything might conceivably be known or shown to correspond to some prior, even familiar model. Even within such pleasantly reassuring rhymes, however, there inheres a subtly subversive force, akin to the power of fantasy itself. It is this capacity that Stephen Heath notes when he describes repetition as "the return to the same in order to abolish the difficult time of desire and the resurgence in that moment of inescapable difference."[15] We need to remember that this pattern disguises more than abolishes; it is a model for meaning that, when held up to a mirror, reveals the meaningless as well through its lack of any reflection. As did *The Leopard Man*, *The Seventh Victim* turns this complexity to a way of describing the larger human story through its sisters who seek an identity, only to find that individuality denied, unsatisfactory, or already modeled. The result is a discomfiting sense of how frustrating man's conventional drive for knowledge can be and how much we all share in the victim's condition.

The Specter of
The Ghost Ship

There are many mansions and a house divided does
indeed stand, even in hatred. The necessity of schism?
To end the illusion of unity, of any delusional system that
does not give place to the distinctive multiplicity of the
archetypal powers affecting our lives.

—James Hillman
Loose Ends

In dramatizing man's yearning for explanation or certainty, *The
Seventh Victim* provided a thematic correlative for the structural
complexities of the earlier films in the Lewton series. *The Ghost
Ship* (1943), Mark Robson's second directorial effort, further develops that link by embodying in a ship's captain, whose obsession
with authority, discipline, and order leads to his destruction, the
previous film's concern with human limitation. In its structure the
film is marked by a tension which haunts its narrative, as various
points of view—or what we might term the dialogical aspect of the
tale—come into conflict with a thematic emphasis on a single authoritative perspective or monological vision of the world. While
essentially an initiation story, *The Ghost Ship* finds its darker pattern of the fantastic in this informing tension. In this respect the
film calls to mind the basic questioning project of textual deconstruction, as J. Hillis Miller describes it, for it attempts to show
that the monological is "a derived effect of the dialogical rather
than . . . the noble affirmation of which the dialogical is a distur-
bance, a secondary shadow in the originating light."[1] Just as *I
Walked with a Zombie* gradually exposed a subversive potential of
narrative by splintering a single perspective into a litany of possible narrators, *The Ghost Ship* develops this vision of a disconcerting multiplicity as a struggle between the one and the many,

the reasoned and the ambiguous, the monological and the dialogical. By so doing, it demonstrates that the ambiguous, multiple perspective is indeed a kind of shadow or ghost, haunting our dreams of order and certitude. At the same time the film defines this shadow as an insistent, even necessary specter that reminds us, as James Hillman asserts, that "multiplicity" and "ambiguity" constitute "the essence of psyche"[2] and thus a basic truth upon which the human world is constructed.

Certainly a strange offering for a Christmas season, *The Ghost Ship* reached audiences in late December 1943 and, like the four prior releases from the Lewton unit, met with generally favorable reviews. In keeping with the season Bosley Crowther, for instance, described it as "a nice little package of morbidity all wrapped around in gloom."[3] Such reviews, however, tended to suggest that the film was precisely what its title implied, yet another entry in a long tradition of horror or ghost pictures, better done, of course, but essentially concerned with crafting a menacing world from which the usual quota of audience fears might be elicited. Manny Farber's recollection of the film's emphasis on "the voluptuous reality of things, such as a dangerously swinging ship's hook, which was inconspicuously knocking men overboard like tenpins,"[4] more accurately assesses its dark shadings by emphasizing the visual allure of the world depicted here—an allure which invites both interpretation and misinterpretation. Hardly a traditional horror film, *The Ghost Ship* marshals the atmosphere and trappings of the genre to comment upon the importance of the perspective we typically take to our world and the frailty of the human community which it fashions. In short, by a kind of indirect vision the film reminds us how much depends on our own shaping eye.

The Ghost Ship's plot is fairly simple, drawing on the themes and conventions established by a number of popular literary narratives of seafaring, most notably Jack London's *The Sea Wolf* and Joseph Conrad's *The Secret Sharer*. The naturalistic influence of the former and the latter's emphasis on doubling are particularly evident.[5] As in London's tale, the central action follows the encounter between a young man on his first voyage and his new ship's disciplinarian captain. Fresh from the Merchant Marine Academy, Tom Merriam joins the *Altair* as a replacement for the previous third mate, who has died under mysterious circumstances. On board he finds a motley crew, assembled from all parts of the globe, and a captain who maintains order among the disparate group by a harsh exercise of authority; as he ominously informs Merriam, in his role as ship's master he claims "the right to do what I want with the men." Prodded by such remarks and the inexplicable deaths which occur during the *Altair*'s voyage, Tom concludes that Captain Stone, like London's Wolf Larsen, has gone insane and is murdering those of the crew who seem to threaten his authority. Because of the sailors' fear of the captain and their lack of cohesiveness, however, Tom can find no help and is even imprisoned on the ship—just as the previous third mate had been—as Stone convinces everyone that it is Merriam who is insane. When the captain eventually tries to kill the young mate, he is himself done in by a sailor who has been closely watching them. With this murderous "ghost" vanquished from the ship and Tom vindicated, a voice-over intones a concluding message that "all is well"—a sharp contrast to the fatalistic commentary with which *The Seventh Victim* closed.

Clearly, such a narrative draws its basic shape from the classic initiation tale, as it thrusts its young hero into a new and threatening situation, employs his encounter with the unknown to reveal the complexities of human nature and the world he must inhabit, and then returns him to his home port to bear the burden of a new awareness. As in *I Walked with a Zombie* and *The Leopard Man*, however, this simple story line benefits from a degree of narrative complexity which, in the fantasy tradition, emphasizes the problematic perspective we normally take to such unsettling events. Like *Zombie* in particular, the film lacks a consistent point of view, as it begins with a detached perspective to introduce Tom Merriam, periodically intrudes a voice-over commentary from the Finn, the sailor who eventually saves Tom's life, and at times, through a subjective focus, links our point of view with that of Merriam. While this shifting perspective ultimately develops the same theme of human involvement found in *Zombie*, its primary effect here is to generate a disturbing sense of indeterminacy which heightens tensions through the audience's unease at witnessing a menacing world without the comfort of either a stable point of view or a full detachment from events. Because of the film's concern with the problems of perceiving the truth and its vesperal thrust toward gaining a new perspective on the self, a narrative styling which repeatedly yanks us back from the objective to the subjective seems singularly appropriate.

Adding to the disorienting effect of this narrative indeterminacy is a generally elliptical construction in which a number of scenes initially seem little concerned with furthering the simple initiation plot. Farber suggests that this approach typifies the Lewton films and their "shorthand method."[6] Robson readily admits that *The Ghost Ship*, like many other films in the series on which he worked, "broke many of the rules of story telling," being "much freer" in construction and following "very few dramaturgical rules."[7] While keeping to a normal temporal sequence, for instance, the narrative can subvert our expectations by inserting at several points seemingly disconnected details, whose significance, in the absence of a controlling point of view, is postponed until larger narrative connections emerge. In place of an obvious causality, therefore, there develops the discomfiting sense of a casual, yet labyrinthine series of events, what we might term, using Frank Kermode's terminology, "secrets" which seem "at odds with" the narrative's sequentiality.[8]

One consequence of the confounding of narrative order or determinable meaning, as J. Hillis Miller explains, is an increase in the ironic nature of a story.[9] That this aspect of the narrative corresponds to—and speaks of—our own perspective on events is emphasized by the source of the tale's single voice-over. Although we hear his thoughts directly, the Finn is a mute, incapable of communicating to his fellow crew members; hence, the narrative voice is his *only* voice, and a limited one at that, since it is restricted—or muted—by the narrative which freely shifts from his point of view. The Finn's words, moreover, project a most sympathetic character, which undercuts his initially menacing appearance and makes us mindful of a constant potential for disparity.

A similarly privileged and ironic perspective develops through a recurrent pairing of scenes, as one takes its full value and thematic weight only in juxtaposition to the preceding or following scenes. For instance, as Merriam and Captain Stone cross the ship's deck, the camera tracks with them until they encounter two sailors who, on detecting the officers, immediately cease talking; when the officers move off, the camera lingers on the seamen as they resume conversing. The result is a seemingly chance transition of the type which dominates *The Leopard Man*. While one of the seamen complains about a sharp pain, several later scenes must explain the significance of this pain and its bearing on the captain and Merriam, who prompted the silencing of the man's complaint. We learn that Stone does not like to be troubled by complaints from his crew, seeing in such expressions a kind of malingering that calls for discipline. Later still, this sailor is revealed to be suffering from appendicitis; in lieu of a doctor on board and as a challenge to his frequent assertions of "responsibility" for the crew, Stone is required to operate to save the sailor's life. The most significant revelation of these linked scenes is one that initially eludes Tom's perspective and only gradually becomes obvious to the viewers, that is, the crew's tendency to suppress their feelings, even their most vital needs, and to lapse into silence rather than seek help, which they suspect would not be forthcoming. This code of behavior becomes particularly significant when Tom violates it by calling on members of the crew to help him against the captain. Because his perspective is quite different, focusing on the human community and not solely on the self, he fully expects them to sympathize with and speak out for him; that they seem willfully "mute" in this case leaves him puzzled and frightened. With far less complexity, such ironic pairings of scenes operate through much of the narrative. An early scene in which Stone stops Tom from killing a helpless moth, for instance, casts its ironic light only at the last when the captain tries to dispatch the equally helpless Merriam as he lies strapped to his bunk. By this pattern of elliptically paired scenes, reminiscent of the doubling patterns which inform *The Seventh Victim, The Ghost Ship* develops a structural irony that complements its indeterminate point of view and emphasizes its larger concern with the epistemological limits confronting its characters.

The opening scene employs yet another ironic ploy, a compositional and contextual one that more obviously develops a link to the limitations of perspective and understanding which inform the rest of the film. The scene creates two focal points, a blind beggar in the foreground, singing an upbeat sea chanty, and in the background, the storefront of the Seaman's Outfitting Company. As a visual counterpoint to the singer's "invitation"—"Come all ye young fellows who follow the sea, / With a yo, ho, blow the man down"—the camera tracks in for a close-up of the store window to reveal what sort of supplies a seafaring life requires; there we see row upon row of fearsome knives neatly arrayed. Besides suggesting what Tom will need to survive his upcoming voyage, this image foreshadows the climactic knife fight in which his life is threatened and then saved. The bouyant song, hinting at the romantic illusions Merriam takes to his first voyage, counterpoints those menacing instruments to evoke an ominous atmosphere and establish a persistent narrative tension between initial appearances and a deadly reality they may mask. The blind man's subsequent comment to Tom, that the *Altair* is "a bad ship," elicits a reply which makes explicit this potential for disparity and divergent perspectives. "You can't tell about ships," Tom remarks, simultaneously hinting at the naiveté which he brings to the seafaring life and expressing the deeper pattern of indeterminacy which rules the narrative.

In establishing an initial sense of foreboding, *The Ghost Ship* does more than simply follow a typical horror film formula. Although its complexities and demands are unsuspected, the world evoked here is not depicted as malevolent, filled with monsters or the products of an unforgiving nature. The following scene, for example, as Tom boards the *Altair* and encounters the silent Finn, who is slowly and carefully sharpening his long, menacing knife, signals an ominous environment, especially in its narrative rhyme with the earlier image of the knife-stocked store window, and it may thus imply a continuing motif of menace; at the same time, though, it points to a pattern of misdirection at work in the film— as in the human realm—as many of our immediate assumptions are undercut or called into question later. It is the Finn, after all, who eventually sees in Tom a model of his own forced isolation and wields his knife to protect Merriam from the captain. The knife thus functions as either threat or defense, depending on the man who gives it a value; like so many appearances here, it simply assumes the character which man's perspective gives it. Despite the fog and darkness that dominate every scene and seem to call for anxiety, the environment is hardly a threateningly naturalistic one of "nature red in tooth and claw," such as is found in the film's literary progenitors. The night and surrounding sea actually hold relatively little danger. They simply contribute an archetypal imagery and source of psychic terror which recall the use of water in *Cat People* and *I Walked with a Zombie*, while they also echo Lewton's plans for another thriller, tentatively titled *Die Gently Stranger*, which was never filmed; as in *The Ghost Ship*, he intended to use "the average person's fear of the awe-inspiring ocean and of being lost in a fog as a motivating force . . . and the result, I hope, will be psychological horror at its best."[10]

In place of the environment, it is the individual, specifically Stone, who seems to be the true danger in this world. Behind the captain's menacing aspect is his bitter authoritarian philosophy, which asserts that the mass of men "are worthless cattle and a few men are given authority to drive them." He singlemindedly clings to this "great lesson of authority," as he terms it, and the monological perspective it affords, even as he claims to have "the welfare of the men" and the safety of his ship in mind. What terrors this world holds, consequently, originate not so much in the sea as in man himself, particularly as he persists in his own vision of things, despite the dialogical character of the realm he inhabits. While *The Ghost Ship* establishes an environment wherein appearances can be deceiving, man gradually shows himself to be the most deceptive and potentially most dangerous denizen to be encountered there. Not content with the principle of indeterminacy which governs his world—just as Stone is not content with life ashore, where he ranks as "just another captain" rather than "*the* captain"—the film reminds us, man often attempts to remake that realm in his own likeness or reorganize it around his own warped perspective, even if the task requires the destruction of those who oppose his scheme.

If the menace here is essentially of human origin, it is also something that can be dealt with by right-thinking men. Robson claims some credit for this potential for remediation, describing his view of the human condition in this way: "I'm optimistic as a person and I've tried to show this. I think that the struggle to improve the world is important and I believe that if you try hard enough you can make some dent in the wall that imprisons us."[11] Starting with *The Ghost Ship*, this positive element plays an increasing role in the Lewton series, and it might arguably be seen as one of Robson's personal signatures. Of course, we should note that a possibility for affirmation resides in the very conception of horror which informs the series. What all of the films underscore is that the real danger to the human situation is not, despite initial appearances to the contrary, an external menace, such as ghouls or monsters, but problems lodged deep within the individual which he must confront and understand. Such menaces as these, however, can be dealt with, for they call the individual to awareness, to travel what Hillman terms the *via regia* or vesperal path to the unconscious where he might gain a new perspective on the self.[12] Of course, in some cases those frightening elements seem so deeply ingrained in human nature or so formidable that they might never be rooted out. Exacerbating the problem is man's tendency to retreat ever further within the self, to the ground of his own ghosts, as does Captain Stone, who comes to deny the humanity of those around him and lose practically all concern with the world of man; as he admits, he has neither friends nor outside concerns, in fact, "no interests, just authority . . . authority." Just as monocular vision deprives reality of its depth, so does a monological perspective empty the world of its substance and reduce it to abstraction—a realm of reason, authority, discipline. Yet for those who embrace the promise of abstraction, no order or clarity results; rather, the dark realms of the psyche become a solitary refuge against the threat which, from their perspective, all others—indeed, the world itself—seem to pose.

In practice, we find this principle demonstrated when Tom boards the *Altair* and finds a crew conditioned to such a limited perspective and characterized by a callous, insolationist attitude. Instead of welcome, he meets with disinterest, suspicion, and even fear. Finding his new cabin in disarray—lingering evidence of the previous third mate's mysterious death—disturbs him less than the steward's attitude toward that enigmatic disappearance; he simply allows that, like most people, the mate "didn't want to die, but he was always telling funny stories." This non sequitur, substituting for an explanation, only emphasizes the mystery surrounding his death, while it also demonstrates the steward's minimal concern for his shipmates. This attitude characterizes the entire crew, who are all strangers, drawn together from many nations and lacking any ties to each other or common interests, save for the efficient operation of the ship. Captain Stone's roll call after the ship weighs anchor emphasizes this situation, as a Greek sailor is mistaken for a Scot, several of the men laugh at the strange names of their new shipmates, and all eye the Finn suspiciously upon learning that he is a mute and thus pointedly different from them. From the outset of the voyage, therefore, we know that these men are basically loners, isolated by their different cultures and experiences and prone to view any difference as potentially threatening.

At the same time, they also seem willing to accept the sameness which results from their mutual alienation, that is, they seem content to stay to themselves, since that attitude places few demands on them and leaves them detached from events, which seem to transpire in an abstract realm, removed from their personal concerns. Stone calls attention to this trait when he describes his crew

The threatening authority figure: Captain Stone (Richard Dix) of the *Altair*.

The pawn and the power: Tom Merriam (Russell Wade) and Captain Stone.

The Finn (Skelton Knaggs) sharpens his knife while the crew relaxes.

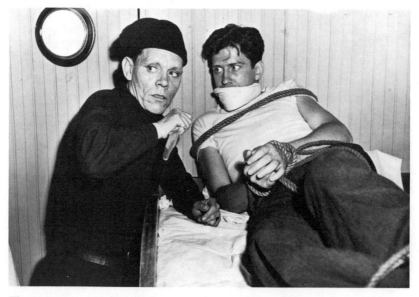

The ironic reversal: the menacing Finn rescues Tom.

as being "like sheep." It is a simile which becomes a recurring motif, reminding us of their withdrawal from events. For example, we soon learn that the *Altair* regularly carries sheep and wool as its cargo, and that the ship virtually reeks with the smell of sheep. Upon reaching port in San Sebastian, Tom searches for help against Stone—help which has not been forthcoming from his shipmates; however, his hopes for success ashore are undercut, as he is repeatedly framed in long shots with groups of sheep being herded through the city streets. Ultimately, it is the casual, even stolid manner in which the crew accept the series of mysterious deaths in their midst that underscores this group characterization. Besides reinforcing their fundamental estrangement from each other, their animallike placidity also demonstrates how much they are like sheep being led to a slaughter.

Through this group portrait, *The Ghost Ship* reveals a common human tendency to abdicate the responsibilities we bear to others as well as to ourselves. In fact, it shows this renunciation to be one of the most frightening of man's experiences. To avoid confronting the full complexity of his situation, however, man often asserts arbitrary limits for his concern, as is the case with the *Altair*'s crew. The first mate, for instance, aptly named Mr. Bowns, feels that his position demands that he strictly observe certain "bounds" of authority and interest, circumscribed by those of the captain; so when Merriam tries to convince him that Stone murdered Louie, a sailor who protested his treatment of the crew, Bowns refuses to listen, warning Tom against anything that might be construed as mutiny. Sparks the radio operator, Tom's best friend, similarly excuses himself, indicating that he believes in "keeping my nose clean, really clean." Although he recognizes that Tom's charges may have some merit, he weighs that possibility against his personal interests and decides, as he tells Merriam, "I like my job and I want to keep it." A more telling clue to Sparks's own sense of "bounds" occurs when Tom approaches him with his suspicions and finds him dancing about the radio shack with his headphones on, waltzing to the music only he can hear. This single image tells us much about Sparks's character: he apparently finds his comfort in a sort of internal music he alone can tune in—again a kind of abstraction—and he prefers to substitute such pleasurable isolation for the more demanding world of human interaction. While the other officers of the *Altair* are practically anonymous, appearing in only a few scenes, they too demonstrate a tendency to abdicate from human responsibility. Their announced concern is solely with the workings of the ship, with keeping the engines running, and when the captain appears, they usually scurry off to their privileged retreat, the engine room, whose remove from this world is only half-comically indicated by its name, "The Black Hole of Calcutta." When confronted by evidence of the captain's murderous activities, they try to dismiss their responsibility and complicity, informing Bowns that "you deck officers have a problem"; and they are little moved by his rejoinder that the problem concerns "you fellows as well. . . . We've got to do something about this. After me you're next in rank and you've got to help." Of course, the limitations these officers put on their perspective, enabling them to see little beyond their "Black Hole," are determined by the captain's model, and their restricted vision represents only the alternate, nonmalevolent, yet almost equally dangerous side of his destructive point of view.

In only Tom and the Finn, both associated with a larger perspective on events and an insight into the "secrets" of this world, do we find this gravitational pull toward isolation and abstraction effectively resisted. Outcast because of his inability to communicate with his companions and consequently distrusted by them, the Finn reveals in his choric voice-over the anguish of an enforced and unnatural isolation; on first seeing Merriam, for example, he laments that "this is another man I can never know, because I cannot talk with him. I am cut off from other men in my silence. I can hear things they never hear, know things they never know." At the same time, however, perhaps because he is an outcast, he feels the bonds of humanity even more keenly. When Tom is similarly unable to communicate with his shipmates, to convince them of the captain's murderous designs, the Finn's voice-over shows his inexpressible sympathy for the mate and his own suspicions of the captain: "I know this man's trouble. I've seen the captain's hatred. I know and I will watch." Such comments mark a gradual transformation in our perception of his character, from his initial association with the strange and threatening atmosphere of the *Altair* to the single representative of our hope for some human balancing of the scales.

Despite his complex perspective, as both an outsider and, due to the captain's initial fondness for him, a privileged participant in events, Tom Merriam seems an equally unlikely candidate to bear the film's moral weight. He is an orphan, a stranger in this world about to join his first ship and learn about the problems of the seafaring life. In effect, he seems the archetypal innocent, eager to learn and clearly with much to learn—about human nature as well as about the sea. Like the protagonists in the other Lewton films, he is a supremely ordinary and hardly heroic fellow: not overly handsome, strong, or even especially intelligent. In fact, he seems quite gullible at first, quick to accept the captain's every explanation for his actions—and for his failure to act. If he appears a hardly suitable hero, though, Tom's prosaic character is important for the narrative's ultimate thrust. His simple nature, after all, makes his predicament seem all the more human and natural, while his innocence and weakness call for assistance and thus evoke a moral imperative. In sum, his character underscores our common need for others, not simply that we might survive, but also to help fashion a truly humane environment in which to live.

At the same time, Tom is endowed with some important strengths of character, particularly an other-directedness which, as Hillman notes, is implicit in the perspective for which man's psyche commonly strives: "the nature of psychic reality [is] not I, but we; not one, but many."[13] Not content to remain a stranger in a world of strangers, Tom tries to make friends among the crew, even if it means overcoming personal obstacles, like Mary in *The Seventh Victim*. Besides striking an acquaintance with Sparks, Merriam befriends the lone black member of the crew, and when that man is accosted by a gang of sailors on shore, Tom unhesitatingly comes to his aid—only to be beaten for his efforts. This ability and willingness to reach beyond the self despite the consequences—and thus the desire to live in a human rather than an abstract realm—prepare us for his greater concern with what goes on around him on board the *Altair*. In fact, this concern may best explain why Tom is able to piece together the incidents surrounding the "accidental" death of Louie, who is found crushed to death in the ship's chain locker shortly after complaining about the captain's treatment of the men. Tom connects this incident to Stone's remarks on the necessity for discipline and his comment that, with Louie out of the way, there will be "no more insolent remarks, no more danger to the authority of the ship." What most distinguishes Tom from the rest of the crew, however, is that he refuses to ignore or passively accept this evidence. Through the more humane perspective he brings to this world, Merriam can see that what happens to his mates inevitably, even if indirectly, affects him as well. By his example, then, the film gives substance to a most fundamental moral imperative, which Tom formulates simply and straightforwardly for Sparks: "If something's wrong, I've got to do something about it."

In contrast to this human concern and the larger perspective it suggests, Captain Stone is driven by a much more primitive impulse, a Nietzschean will to power, which finds its correspondence in his single, self-centered point of view. Despite his assertions, he is not so much concerned with the condition of his crew, as he is with extending his personality and authority over all, with subordinating the concrete world of men to abstract principles. He has hired Merriam sight unseen solely because, on paper, he seemed Stone's double; as he tells Tom, "Your history could have been my own at your age—orphaned, serious, ambitious." In Tom, he claims, he thought he had found "a man who'd think as I think," someone to whom he could pass on his passion for abstractions like "the great lesson" of authority. In the character of Stone, therefore, we see both the disturbing impulse for doubling developed to such great length in *The Seventh Victim* and a dangerously assertive will, insistent on extending its thought patterns and its perspective on the world to all around.

In keeping with the narrative's pattern of misdirection and ironic revelation, however, the full implications of the captain's attitude are not immediately perceived. To the contrary, the film initially strikes a note of sympathy for Stone, as Tom sees him as a father figure after whom he might model himself. Consequently, when Sparks derides the captain's fascination with authority, Tom immediately defends him, remarking that "he's the first older man who's ever treated me like a friend." And despite Stone's often twisted logic and explanations, Merriam makes every effort to understand his philosophy, particularly since his own goal is to occupy a similar position someday and follow what initially seems like a good example. Behind this stern father figure, however, is a violent and dangerous nature which firmly believes that "authority cannot be questioned or defied." When Tom first enters the captain's cabin, we note in the background a plaque which reads, "Who Does Not Heed The Rudder Shall Meet The Rock." Less a motto for Stone's life than a warning to others, that maxim cautions everyone to accept the captain's every command or suffer the consequences—Meet The Stone, as it were. The viciously authoritarian rule of this "father" ultimately becomes the chief terror in the lives of the *Altair*'s sailors, his concern with the abstract principles of power and discipline providing the real "ghosts" which haunt the ship.

If Stone lacks any perspective on himself and his effect on the crew, it is because of his strong ego, which readily dispels the dark shadows his actions cast. To his mind, any fault rests not with him but with those who question his actions; and this thinking is manifested by his compulsion to rationalize or explain his every deed—a tendency which, as we have seen, recurs in the Lewton films and typically signals a dangerous refusal to see the depth and complexity that characterize both man and his world. In keeping with this pattern, Stone's explanations ultimately have an effect almost opposite to what he intends, only making his "reasoned" actions seem more unreasonable and disturbing in light of their consequences. As captain of the ship, he tells Merriam, "I have the right to do what I want with the men. Because their safety does depend on me, I stand ready at any hour of the day or night to give my life for their safety and the safety of this vessel. Because I do, I have certain rights of risk over them." This explanation, which covers so many faults, rings hollow almost immediately, however, when after his disquisition on authority Stone must operate on the sailor who is suffering from appendicitis. As instructions for the operation are relayed over the ship's radio, Stone freezes and cannot function; so with the sailor's life at stake, Tom must step in and bring the operation to a successful conclusion. Although Stone later tries to explain away his lapse, noting that he is "not afraid of anything but failure" and that, in any case, a captain also has the right to refuse to act, Sparks knowingly dismisses the excuses, reminding Tom that "he's a smooth man with the words, the captain." Detached from humanity, reason simply draws out from itself its own justifications, as Stone repeatedly relies on his ability to manipulate words as a way of maintaining his ego and validating its limited perspective.

Stone functions, therefore, not simply to voice a challenge to social order after the fashion of so many naturalistic narratives, but to demonstrate the flimsiness of a rational faculty which man often depends too heavily upon to organize and demystify his world. With this rather fragile support called into question, as we see, the self can easily become a thing of horror, especially if it refuses to acknowledge its inherent weakness. Haunting Stone's psyche is the memory of his former commander, Captain Blake of the ship *Ajax*, who lost his reason and with it his ship—apparently the extension of his ego, just as the *Altair* has become for Stone. As a young man like Merriam, he recalls, he helplessly watched his captain "lose his mind little by little," until he wrecked the *Ajax* and went down with it. Now Stone fears a repetition of this pattern, that he might duplicate Blake's fall. As he confesses to his fiancée Ellen, "I've done things I couldn't remember doing," and, in spite of his mania for absolute discipline, he increasingly feels that "I don't know myself . . . I don't control my thoughts, my actions." In the face of this deterioration and mindful of its consequences for his former captain, however, Stone seeks no help and depends no less on his reason; he simply retreats further into ego-consciousness, behind the empty abstractions of discipline and unquestionable authority, what one of the sailors describes as "his hobbyhorse." He even rejects Ellen who, for fifteen years, has "tried to give him love and failed," and who consequently has had to watch him—just as he witnessed Captain Blake—slowly turn into a "lonely, austere, bitter" man. In Jungian terms Stone represents a self incapable of individuation, as his persona rejects the anima or feminine aspect of his life and constantly seeks to deny, although with ever-decreasing success, his shadow component. Consequently, every person and every action have come to seem threatening; he confesses to Ellen, for instance, that "people seem to be turning against me, the boy, some of the crew; I feel their dislike, their distrust." For this reason Stone interprets Louie's legitimate complaint as a challenge to his authority and does away with him, and when Tom learns of it, Stone tries to eliminate him as well. As Stone teeters on the edge of insanity, rationalizing such actions comes to pose less and less a problem for him, particularly since he sees his crew not as rational men like himself but as animals—"cattle" or "sheep"—who are, as he informs Tom, "too lazy, too cowardly, too disinterested" to care what happens to anyone else.

His monological voice and monocular perspective thus form the substance of the film's challenge to the nature of society, here represented by the small community aboard the *Altair*. *The Ghost Ship*, however, not only evokes such a formidable specter, one always latent in human nature, but seeks to exorcize it as well by demonstrating the viability of the alternative attitude espoused by Merriam. He tells Stone that he cannot prove people are such pitiable creatures, "not even with a gun. I know people aren't that way. They're good, kind; they help each other. It's only hard to get them to understand." And after repeated appeals and denials, Tom does convince a few "to understand" and even offer their help: first Sparks, whom Stone immediately kills and dismisses as having been "lost overboard in heavy seas," and then Mr. Bowns, who tries to talk the other officers into acting against the captain. In these tentative successes the film suggests a potential for right action which remains to be tapped and a sense of human complicity to be affirmed.

Of course, what may be the film's heaviest note of irony derives from the Finn's having to carry the burden of this social affirmation. As we have seen, he seems alienated from his shipmates and looks to be the most enigmatic and menacing figure of this group. In another instance which plays upon the motif of a failed communication, we also learn that the Finn is illiterate; as a result, he cannot read a note which Sparks leaves, detailing the captain's murderous plans for Merriam. Still, because he feels some sympathy for one who has also become a pariah, he watches over Tom and, in an effective reworking of the various elements of the film's opening, intervenes to save the young mate. In place of the blind beggar singing his chanty, the crew, gathered on deck, sing an upbeat song of how the sailor's life "is the life for me." Not only does their light-hearted song ironically contrast with the main action, as the knives that formed the backdrop of the opening scene become the weapons in a life-and-death fight between Stone and the Finn, but it also suggests how "blind" these sailors are to what is going on below decks. As the bound Merriam watches helplessly, the Finn stands alone as a final and small human buffer between the captain and his victim. What this scene dramatically thrusts home is how, in our weakness or simple unknowing, we must depend on a sense of fellow feeling, since only our capacity for a more complex perspective, particularly the ability to see ourselves in others and react to their situation, enables us to overcome the horrors we may encounter—or perhaps unwittingly engender. While the captain's actions and the crew's abdication from responsibility have made that capacity seem questionable here, the mute's intervention is reassuring; it affirms, just as his voice-over at the conclusion notes, that for the time being at least "man's essential goodness is secure."

In a way that none of the earlier films in the RKO series does, therefore, The Ghost Ship leaves us with a sense of promise fulfilled and some hope for the future. As in The Seventh Victim, with which it clearly has much in common, a full circle has been described, but to a more positive effect. As the *Altair* again docks at its home port, Merriam is accosted once more by the blind beggar, who affirms that he has become "a sailor all right." The presence of Ellen's younger sister, there to meet Tom, promises not a repetition of Stone's pattern but a break with it, as she offers to help ensure that he does not "become another Captain Stone." In marked contrast to his captain who chose isolation and authority, then, Tom goes off with the girl, electing, as Ellen has suggested, "to embrace warmth and life" rather than cold abstraction. It is clearly an affirmative ending, indicating an initiation accomplished and an individuation hard won. Although Tom and the girl walk into the night, the dark background is less foreboding than emblematic of the vesperal path which he has so far followed and must continue to follow if he wishes to live in this world.

Like the other films in the series, *The Ghost Ship* clearly belies its studio-assigned title. Offering neither ghosts nor monsters, it reveals only the dark, murderous spirits which man conjures up from within himself and projects into his world by means of the faulty or limited perspective he often takes to it and to his fellow men. Of course, horror, as the Lewton team saw it, was a fundamental component of our normalcy, a potential in even the most ordinary elements of our lives. It springs from within man, often even as he tries, like Captain Stone, to avert its force at all costs, for instance, by setting up reason and abstraction as bulwarks against chaos. What this human measure of horror forces us to see, though, is just how tenuous that order and how commonplace those threats to it ultimately are. In man's capacity for a larger, dialogical perspective, this film implies, there lies the possibility for recognizing these human failings, effectively responding to them, and thereby maintaining the fragile, often enigmatic world we inhabit.

7 Fantasy as Reality, Reality as Fantasy: *Curse of the Cat People*

> The child *per se* makes us uneasy, ambivalent; we are
> anxious about the human propensities concentrated by
> the child symbol. It evokes too much of what has been
> left out or is unknown, becoming easily associated with
> the primitive, mad and mystical.
>
> —James Hillman
> "Abandoning the Child" in *Loose Ends*

For the first production of 1944, the Lewton unit offered a film that underscored, more than any of the earlier works, the sharp disparity between their movies' lurid, studio-assigned titles and their challenging fantasy themes. *Curse of the Cat People* obviously shares important links with the first and most successful film of the series, *Cat People,* to which it was ostensibly a sequel. However, in place of the earlier film's horror trappings and elaborately choreographed shock effects, the later work concerns itself in an unsensational manner with the experiences and emotions of childhood, and especially the proclivity for fantasizing which typically plays a large role in a child's developing understanding of his world and himself. In fact, this film appears to have at least as much in common with its immediate predecessor in the RKO series, *The Ghost Ship,* as it does with *Cat People.* Like the preceding film, it elaborates on the motifs of initiation, parent-offspring relations, and disparate perspectives, all of which it joins to its namesake's disquieting interrogation of all normal seeming. By grounding these concerns specifically in the figure of the child, moreover, *Curse of the Cat People* effects an important development of these earlier elements, which casts the normal human activity of fantasizing into a most revealing light.

The generally good reviews which greeted *Curse of the Cat People*, Robert Wise's first directorial effort for the group, praised it precisely for this more familiar and human focus. James Agee, for instance, lauded the "rather gentle, pleasing, resourceful kind of talent" which the picture displayed in its careful evocation of "the poetry and danger of childhood."[1] And a few years later, David Riesman in his book *The Lonely Crowd* was to single out the film for its accurate and touching depiction of childhood and the anxieties which accompany this stage of life.[2] Of course, children figured prominently in other films produced by the Lewton unit, most notably *The Leopard Man* and *The Seventh Victim*, but never before did they so fully occupy the narrative foregound or provide a film with its central symbol. With *Curse*, however, Lewton and his colleagues began to explore the larger possibilities of their usual subject matter, especially the potential for a subtle kind of fantasy vision which might be brought into focus through the image of childhood. Despite a typically disarming presence, the child can furnish an image fully capable of challenging the adult world and its customary perspective; in fact, as James Hillman notes, it seems to be an image which evokes an ambiguity and even a secret anxiety in the adult realm, for the figure of the child reflects many of the fears and insecurities man has managed to dispel or block out with the concrete concerns of his daily existence. What the Lewton unit sought to do in this film was to grant us that disturbing reflective vision. Through the complex image of the child and his fondness for fantasizing—a fondness which can become lost in the course of growing up—*Curse of the Cat People* locates a valuable touchstone for the larger human vesperal experience, one which marks the path by which we come to "experience the fantasy in all realities and the basic reality of fantasy."[3]

As we have already suggested, the Lewton films all treat a common human problem, our desire to understand and explain a world that is consistently mystifying or frightening. As both *The Seventh Victim* and *The Ghost Ship* especially demonstrate, this epistemological dimension finds a ready metaphor in the difficult process of growth and maturation. It is an analogy, of course, which has been frequently employed in the fantasy tradition, for children have been repeatedly exploited to evoke our normal fears or stir alarm. A child, after all, almost automatically projects a sense of helplessness and innocence which can be used to manipulate an audience's natural sympathies or touch its protective instincts. As Henry James frequently demonstrated, one might easily provoke the fantastic imagination into a sense of horror or uneasiness by playing upon a perception of innocence, what he termed "the exposure . . . the helpless plasticity of childhood that isn't dear or sacred to somebody!"[4] The tension between an external evil force and such a threatened innocence lies at the heart of many traditional horror films. Whether it is the case of the Frankenstein monster accidentally murdering a little girl in the 1931 film or that of a murderous maniac menacing unsuspecting teenagers in the recent *Halloween,* the horror genre has repeatedly demonstrated the potential for generating anxiety or alarm simply by the absence of an effective adult protection for the young and unaware, especially as they set about the common task of becoming initiated into what often seems a most frightening world.

The Lewton films certainty give every appearance of abounding in such threats—cats, zombies, and crazed killers—although they eventually suggest that man is often his own worst enemy, his own monster. One way in which he poses a threat to the self is in his unyielding distinctions between fact and fancy, reality and the realm of the fantastic, as man clings to his faith in the appearance of normalcy, especially in the secure seeming of his daily surroundings. Children obviously offer an especially effective image of this naiveté, and the Lewton team clearly appreciated this metaphoric potential. Through the child, a typically human attitude could thus be evoked. The children populating these films consequently represent something more than potential victims; they hint at an adult world fragile in order and limited in self-knowledge. Furthermore, this metaphoric use of the child raises another disconcerting specter, one to haunt the sense of self-satisfaction and well-being which typically marks the adult characters in these films. This complex use of the child elicits an unexpectedly challenging tone in many of these supposedly simple genre programmers, as the child plays not only on our usual fears for the safety of some innocent but also upon our own deep-seated, often denied feelings of insecurity and doubts of the adult ability to cope with the unknown.

The Seventh Victim attempted the most complex rendering of this pattern by situating Mary Gibson in both child and adult roles during the course of the narrative. Having been turned out from her child's world because of adult neglect—her older sister's failure to pay her tuition—Mary suddenly and disturbingly finds herself thrust into an adult environment, the complexities of which her schooling has ill prepared her for. There she goes through a difficult initiation, ending in her supplanting her sister as the film's love interest. In later films like *The Body Snatcher* (1945) and *Bedlam* (1946), children serve in a more conventional but equally effective manner, their victimization prompting an adult awakening to the callousness and irresponsibility of the world. *The Body Snatcher,* for instance, tells of young Georgina Marsh who has been crippled in a carriage accident caused by her father. Although the famous surgeon Dr. MacFarlane promises to operate and cure her paralysis, he must first obtain a cadaver on which to practice the operation, and this need prompts another young girl's murder. Thus the victimization continues, despite the best of intentions from the adult world. *Bedlam* reveals equally discomfiting circumstances in its exploration of the problems of the insane. One of its more telling sequences focuses on a young inmate of the asylum who has been painted gold to represent Reason in a play staged by the institution's headmaster. With the boy's subsequent death from this treatment, his society's pretensions to an "enlightened" humanism are eloquently indicted. By placing children or innocents in such precarious positions, these films warn of our need for a greater sense of human responsibility, especially to those who must trust in an adult watchfulness, and they challenge us to a new perspective on our own part in the terrorizing of our world.

At the same time these narratives reveal an element of their complexity and anticipate a recent vogue in horror movies by also including some children endowed with disconcerting or even frightening characteristics. The kids who taunt Amy and exclude her from their games in *Curse of the Cat People* and the juvenile delinquents of the nonfantasy film *Youth Runs Wild* are obvious examples. The latter especially, though tame by current standards, struck a contemporary reviewer as "extreme rather than average cases of war-neglected youngsters" and their troubles.[5] In *Leopard Man,* too, we might recall the brief but unsettling portrayal of Pedro Delgado, whose sister is the leopard's first victim. Before her murder, he taunts her with shadows of the cat which she fears, and during her funeral he amuses himself by casting images of the killer cat on a wall. By juxtaposing such disconcerting, even threatening child characters with innocent victims, however, these films more accurately take the measure of our world. As a survey of the Lewton films demonstrates, their main focus was never simply the children, but the relationships between characters, particularly the lack of a proper relationship which often occurs between parents and their offspring. The children serve to point up this failing, as well as one of its major causes, namely the childish, unreflective qualities which adults themselves frequently manifest. For like the children, the adults in these films seem markedly unaware of the complexities of their world and often naively fumble about in their efforts to puzzle out the situations in which they seem so inexplicably trapped.

In films like *I Walked with a Zombie* and *The Ghost Ship,* this parent-offspring motif operates in an obviously metaphoric manner to sketch the relationships of the adult characters. In the former, the widowed Mrs. Rand consistently refers to her two grown sons as "good boys" and describes the island natives over whom she watches with a maternal affection as her "children." While she helps the natives by providing medical advice couched in the childish voodoo terminology they understand, she is far less successful in communicating to and helping her own family, as her sons fight over the elder one's wife and two deaths ensue. This parent-child relationship thus brings into sharper focus a sense of confusion and helplessness which afflicts both generations. In the latter film, a similar relationship develops between Captain Stone and the young Tom Merriam, who sees in the captain the father he never knew. Falling afoul of Stone's paranoid personality, however, Tom is almost killed and only the death of this murderous "father" saves him. In this case the parent-offspring relationship assumes an added dimension, almost a mythic character, by suggesting an original fall from this human relation, a fall leading almost inexorably to the death of the stifling, identity-denying parent. In this mythic pattern the film speaks of an inborn desire for a primal human rapport with its promise of protection and happiness, as well as of an inevitable sundering of that relationship, a fall from innocence—and perhaps from a primal knowledge—that typically accompanies our maturation.

The perspective afforded by this pattern, and especially by the image of the child, is a particularly appropriate one to take to *Curse of the Cat People,* for it interweaves all these various formulations of the motif. The film parallels the tensions between six-year-old Amy Reed and her taunting playmates; between Amy and her bumbling, misunderstanding father Oliver; and between the old actress Julia Farren and her middle-aged daughter Barbara. In each case a brooding sense of anxiety or unease at some internal problem, particularly a person's inability to cope with his own needs or the demands of his world, is evoked. Through these parallels, we see how similar children and adults really are, and how equally fragile are the worlds constructed by their psyches. Viewed against the pattern of their offspring, parents like Oliver and Julia indeed seem quite childish, as petulant, irrational, and given to play as any youngsters.

By noting the generally childish nature of many of these adults, we can also better understand the subtle relations between this film and its more famous progenitor, *Cat People.* Both films explore the fantasy impulse which their characters draw upon in order to make some sense of the mysterious or threatening aspects of their world, and both depict a skeptical, supposedly more knowing figure—Oliver Reed in both cases—who scoffs at that fantasizing activity. The problems of Oliver and Amy thus find their origin in the earlier story of the sexual difficulties between Oliver and his first wife Irena. While she fears being possessed by demons who might turn her into a killer cat, he can only laugh at her deep-rooted folk beliefs and, with an air of adult superiority, dismiss their power, as if he were simply dealing with the baseless fears of a child. Appropriately, then, their relationship more resembles that of father and daughter than of husband and wife, their marriage going unconsummated because of Irena's fears. In *Curse* this asexual relationship obviously translates into the father-daughter situation, as Oliver's attitude remains basically unchanged. In his daughter's fantasizing, he senses "something moody, sickly," as if Amy were Irena's child, and he tells Miss Callahan, her teacher, that from past experience he knows "what can happen when people begin to lie to themselves, imagine things." Amy's subsequent comments about an imaginary friend suggest that she, like Irena before, dwells in a fantasy world, and he fears similar unfortunate, perhaps even tragic consequences. This tension between the imagined and the real, the unknown and the known, informs both films; they similarly depict seemingly childish anxieties confronted by a stubborn and equally childish assurance that there is no cause for anxiety, that the world is indeed a simple and secure place over which the individual has full control, provided he does not fall prey to his imaginings—to fantasy. To ensure this control, reason persistently tries to proscribe the imagination and its fantasizing impulse, thus holding fast to its presumptive role as the psyche's ruler. And once again this psychic pattern translates the mythic formula of the father's necessary displacement, which we saw acted out most clearly in *The Ghost Ship*.

What this film, like its predecessors in the series, underscores is that such certitude, evidenced in Oliver's oversolicitousness and self-assuredness, is itself a most potent threat. Amy's parents are so fearful of her excursions into fantasy that they become overly protective, stifling their child's individuality and denying her needs, including that of fantasizing. As Bruno Bettelheim points out, a child learns to cope with his complex world "not through rational comprehension of the nature and content of his unconscious, but by becoming familiar with it through spinning out daydreams—ruminating, rearranging, and fantasizing about suitable story elements in response to unconscious pressures."[6] If that fantasy experience sometimes seems chaotic, it appears so largely because it is glimpsed "from an adult point of view," or what Hillman would term the "dayworld perspective." And because of this discrepancy in perspectives, both parents and child in a case like this can suffer from a similar problem: not an external threat, not something which, in Amy's case, any vigilance might ward off, but a complex psychological problem, an anxiety in the face of anything unknown, including the forces lodged in the self. Her imaginings, like those of her parents, stand ready to assume dark and frightening or brightly comforting shapes, depending on the pressures and reassurances she receives.

In helping to shape this relationship, Lewton probably drew heavily on his own experience, since he was the product of a broken home and never knew his father. To fill the void which resulted, he developed what Joel Siegel terms a "wildly imaginative" streak, leading him to invent highly improbable tales with which he would "amuse and annoy" his elders.[7] Although not fatherless, Amy echoes this pattern in her estrangement from those around her and her attempts to compensate for that alienation by fantasizing a more hospitable world, complete with imaginary friends. While her mother Alice and Miss Callahan see this "active imagination" as one of the child's attributes, a distinctive feature of her personality, Oliver fears its effects and remarks that "Amy has too many fantasies and too few friends, and it worries me." Consequently, he tries to mold her in his image of normalcy at all costs. In the Farren house a similar gulf separates parent and child, making Julia and the fatherless Barbara virtually strangers. Julia, because of an illness which has affected her mind, believes that her "real daughter" died at the age of six—Amy's present age—and that Barbara is "an impostor . . . a liar and a cheat," nothing more than "the woman who takes care of me." Barbara, in turn, has become resentful and withdrawn, suspicious of outsiders like Amy who threaten to further alienate her mother's feelings. Like the Reeds, then, the Farrens are a sundered family; however, this fall from an original unity eventually propels both children and adults to a more mature vision of their complex, often irrational world, and of the power of fantasy to help them cope with that environment.

The resulting impression that there are two parallel worlds— the simple environment inhabited by adults like Oliver, where everything is just as it seems, and a far more extensive and frightening fantasy world wherein children like Amy often dwell—is a primary source of the film's consistently ironic tone and a clear link to *The Ghost Ship*. In fact, much of *Curse*'s complexity emerges from the irony that the adults themselves unwittingly encourage the play of imagination which they ultimately find so disturbing in their children. The grown-ups have naturally passed on the myths and fantasies of their own childhood, in some cases even creating new ones for their offspring, but without considering the full impact or import of those tales. The film opens on this note with Amy's class on a field trip; as the children walk along a tree-shaded lane in Tarrytown, Miss Callahan instructs them to "take a good look. . . . It may seem to be just a little valley with a little stream running through it, but there are songs and stories and lovely legends about this one blessed spot." The notion that there is more here than meets the eye gets repeated mention, starting the motif of an intertwining between fantasy and reality. Naturally, this idea creates some confusion for a child who is also being initiated into a normative, dayworld perspective. Informed that a misshapen tree in her yard is actually a "magic mailbox," Amy thus proceeds to mail the invitations to her birthday party in it. Upon discovering the mistake, Oliver compounds her perplexity with his explanation, "That wasn't real; that was just a story." What he fails to understand, though, is the unpredictable residue such stories can leave when filtered through a receptive imagination. The familiar tale of "The Headless Horseman," which Amy first hears from her teacher and which Julia later dramatizes for

Oliver (Kent Smith) relates his fears to Amy's teacher (Eve March).

Amy (Ann Carter) observes her father "at play."

The image of threatened innocence: Amy bound by shadows and fantasy.

her, provides another example of this incalculable effect, for what was intended as a quaint and entertaining legend, having no real bearing on her life, returns to haunt the child at various times, repeatedly intruding its frightening reality into her fragile, formative world. Alice, Oliver, and Edward the servant can wink at the fantasies which they relate to Amy, for theirs is a secure and strictly defined reality, a realm ruled by reason and light. Oliver, a ship designer, and Alice, his former assistant,[8] are accustomed to working with facts, figures, weights, and dimensions—things one can see and measure. Those which fail to conform they naturally distrust or totally dismiss—as Oliver does Amy's reports of a mysterious friend—as "lies."

For children like Amy who have yet to undergo the delimiting process of acculturation, those real and imagined realms do coincide. As Freud notes in *Beyond the Pleasure Principle*, the fantasizing impulse is one of a child's basic methods of ordering his environment and constructing a meaningful world for himself.[9] It is not, of course, the rational approach which parents like Oliver might prefer, but, as Bettelheim points out, "to offer a child rational thought as his major instrument for sorting out his feelings and understanding the world will only confuse and restrict him," since it does not provide the appropriate models he needs for coping with and transcending his present state of development.[10] It is in fantasizing that he finds the mythic signposts which will aid "in reaching the next stage on his progress toward mature integration."[11] The fantasy process is subject to certain "ground rules" which children must learn as they grow up; and while Amy is in the process of learning those rules, she finds them frustratingly fluid, quickly changed to suit their adult arbiters. After Oliver warns her about fantasizing, for instance, Amy balks at wishing on the candles of her birthday cake. "Wishes don't come true," she knowingly asserts, only to be met with her father's confusing equivocation, "Certain wishes do." His repeated warnings about lying only compound Amy's perplexity, especially since they seem so at odds with what she observes. While Amy watches, Oliver shouts at Alice that he is "not shouting," and she, after a heated exchange with him, attempts to comfort Amy by explaining that they were "not really fighting . . . just having a little discussion." The world which Amy observes and tries to react to is indeed puzzling and inconsistent, as far as she can tell; and it appears that way because adults too live by certain unrecognized or unquestioned fictions. In Julia Farren's case the fantasy of her daughter's death is simply more obvious, the truth which belies it—Barbara's presence—so evident that we may think the old woman crazy. In most cases, however, those determinations are much more problematic. As *Bedlam* pointedly demonstrates in its juxtaposition of the sane and insane, such judgments often depend largely on the whims or irrational canons of acceptance of those in power.

This unwitting employment of fictions by the adults here points up a basic similarity between grown-ups and children which the Lewton films consistently explore. *Bedlam*'s childlike adults, incarcerated by people who have no more claim to sanity and are just as frightened by their world as the asylum's inmates, are simply a later development of this motif. In *Curse* this parallel is underscored by the play in which both children and adults engage. For the children, games provide a means of organizing their energies and activities into a meaningful form; and the film fittingly introduces Amy and her classmates playing various games under the instruction of Miss Callahan. Among many activities, they are shown playing ball, family, "pass the shoe," jacks, and tag. Of course, the very number of these games should catch our attention, especially since they point up an equally prodigious amount of playing among the adults. This side of Oliver's character receives particular emphasis, as we see him engrossed in a tiddlywinks game set out for his daughter's party, building model ships, and playing cards with Alice and another couple. In this last instance Oliver is so preoccupied with Amy's troubles that he cannot concentrate on the game and lapses into a trancelike state, just as Amy does in an earlier "play" scene. Edward's toying with Oliver's models and Julia Farren's acting and storytelling are only a few of the other forms this play activity takes. Together these activities reveal a fundamental if often unrecognized similarity between the children and grown-ups, while they also foster a feeling of just how much the fantasizing impulse lingers, almost unnoticed, in all human activities.

Having drawn this likeness between the different age groups, the film can more ironically emphasize the lack of understanding which afflicts these characters and suggest how this deficiency starts many of their fears. We expect children like Amy, faced with a complex and confusing world, to have difficulty in distinguishing, as her parents insist she must, between the imagined and the real, especially when the two seem so clearly cut from the same fabric. The affecting combination of sincerity and confusion she projects, however, throws into relief the similar inability of her parents to understand themselves, much less respond adequately to her needs for friendship and reassurance. Oliver's failings are especially marked, for he is certain that he knows what constitutes proper behavior for his child, yet his certitude rings hollow in light of his own lack of reflection. He claims, for instance, that he wants to rid himself of the troubling memories of his former wife Irena, yet he displays her favorite painting with its sinister cat motif, even though, as Alice points out, it ill fits the decor of their new home. When Alice asks him to destroy the many photographs he keeps of Irena, Oliver secretly holds one back, which Amy later discovers, announcing that it looks just like the "special friend" whom only she can see. In effect, it is Oliver who conjures up Irena's specter, who maintains the ghosts which haunt him and his family. A similar lack of perspective characterizes the relationship of Julia and Barbara Farren. In the mother it takes the form of a senility which denies her daughter's identity and the happiness of them both, while her inability to understand or accept her mother's condition leaves Barbara bitter and withdrawn, suspicious of everyone with whom she comes in contact.

Such circumscribed views inevitably lead to a kind of isolation, a state underscored by an emphasis on the boundaries of the world these people inhabit. The film's opening stresses a sense of physical limitation, as Miss Callahan cautions her students not to wander off, and Amy's parents echo this admonition in their worrying over her whereabouts and sending Edward after her when she strays from their sight. The fenced-in front and rear yards of the Reed home, like those of the neighboring houses, restate the protective attitude the parents here all seem to maintain. Confined in this way, Amy naturally tries to broaden her world by turning within and fantasizing, transforming her yard into an imaginary realm complete with the special friend she is unable to find elsewhere. The gloomy Farren house, surrounded by its high iron fence—later used in the *Bedlam* set to emphasize the imprisonment of the asylum's inmates—and overgrown with weeds and bushes, similarly suggests the reclusive life-style its occupants have adopted; no one, as Alice remarks, has seen the mother or daughter. The doors that mysteriously lock themselves, the shuttered windows, and the stuffed cat and birds decorating the parlor only emphasize the hermetic and lifeless world Julia and Barbara have fashioned by their inability to understand and deal with each other.

These images of enclosure combine with other visual compositions to suggest a sense of entrapment, which forges yet another link to *Cat People* and its recurrent cage imagery, and also points up the confinement these people endure and impose upon themselves. Bar or weblike shadows again abound, marking the virtual imprisonment of the characters upon whom they are cast. Oliver, for example, from the start seems bound by some unseen force, as he is initially shown in a pattern of criss-crossing shadows while he attempts to explain Amy's odd behavior to Miss Callahan. The composition ironically hints that he may be as circumscribed by his imaginings as he fears Amy is by hers. A later shot, depicting her in a similar composition, underscores this likeness and confirms our suspicions. After hearing Julia's story of the Headless Horseman, Amy appears in bed, the same bar shadows playing upon her as she wakes up screaming, still possessed by the horror tale told to amuse her. Similar images recur when we see Barbara, framed within the shadow cast by a door or through the rails of a staircase—compositions which insistently note how psychologically trapped she is by her fears and insecurities.

Complementing these moody images are several compositions that emphasize the characters' unawareness of their circumscribed situations. Repeatedly frame-within-a-frame compositions suggest the Reed family's imprisonment within their dream of normalcy. Gathered around the Christmas tree, the family seems happy in the renewed hopes that this season normally brings; we view this tableau, however, in an extreme long shot through a small window whose frame imposes a sense of entrapment upon this image of good cheer. When carolers come to the house, this composition recurs, as Oliver, Alice, Amy, and Edward again form a tableau standing in the dutch door, listening to the singers. Once more a long shot frames them within the tightly confined space and casts an ironic light on their manifest happiness. It is an irony, moreover, immediately reinforced by the appearance of Irena, serenading Amy from the rear of the house with a French version of one of the carolers' songs and thus testifying to the existence of another, alternate reality which casts its shadow on this world. The subsequent view of Amy in another enclosed composition also comments upon the normal appearance which these people all seem to project, while it reemphasizes their very limited perspectives.

Like the wartime society depicted in *Youth Runs Wild*, then, it is explicitly a circumscribed world which these characters inhabit, and for this reason an environment quite as threatening as that found in those films which hint of a more pointedly physical menace. The threat here, however, is not so much the world itself but a certain lack which that environment points up within the human community—and the self; for these people are unable to understand or find understanding, and in the sense of isolation which results, they project a fear onto their world, coloring all they encounter with their darkest imaginings. Not only is this the case for Amy whose imagination, prodded by a simple story, can quite transform her world, but also for Oliver, Alice, Julia, and Barbara as well. The problem is simply made most obvious by Amy's creation of an imaginary playmate, for what she conjures up is both friend and parent figure—appropriately, Oliver's first wife—a single entity by which she attempts to bring the worlds of innocence and experience, the adult and the child, into some harmony. And it is, as Bettelheim reminds, a common response to such anxieties, for a child, "as long as he is not sure his immediate environment will protect him, needs to believe that superior powers, such as a guardian angel, watch over him, and that the world and his place within it are of paramount importance."[12] Unable to find a real playmate, then, Amy wanders past the Farren house, where she hears a mysterious, disembodied voice—Julia's—beckoning her to "come into the garden; it's nice and cool here. Come into the garden." Within that Edenic locale she finds a special wishing ring, a gift as if from the heavens, which permits her to evoke that longed-for friend. This scene clearly carries strong mythic resonances, broadly suggesting a common human desire for some sort of primal return, a reentry into a lost garden of innocence and a reunion there with an original parent from which one has been estranged. Of course, this pattern of separation and a desired reconciliation shows up in several of the Lewton films, and it reminds us of their recurrent concern with a psychic need for completion, personified in a lost or absent parent figure. Such desires, though, are especially appropriate for a child engaged in the difficult process of initiation. This particular scene, therefore, points up the child's normal wish for a perfect world, a perfect parent, and a perfect friend, as Amy increasingly finds herself thrust into a less-than-perfect world by the inevitable pattern of growth and acculturation.

In response to this feeling of expulsion and disappointment, a child typically tries to reject an undesirable reality; thus Amy attempts to abandon her parents' world in favor of Irena and her fantasy domain. The child has always met her friend in the yard, so when Irena vanishes Amy pursues her disappearing image through the yard, beyond its fenced boundary, and into darkness, almost literally enacting Hillman's notion of the psyche's vesperal movement. Outside of her circumscribed, protected world, however, she becomes disoriented and wanders in an eerie darkness; it is the sinister side of her fantasies, previously kept to the periphery of her experience, relegated to the night and dreams. Beyond those familiar boundaries lies a dense forest, transformed by the night, a snowstorm, and the child's vivid imagination into a terrifying landscape where darker fantasies hold free reign.[13] As she wanders among the trees and snowbanks, Amy finds every shape and sound threatening; the dogs used by the police to track her and an old rattling car, which passes on a wooden bridge, become frightening visitations of the Headless Horseman story that has periodically haunted her dreams. Its recurrence in this instance seems especially appropriate, since the Horseman's headlessness suggests an abandonment of the limiting rationality which marks her parents' perspective. This imagined threat, however, foreshadows the real physical danger that Amy faces: becoming lost in the snow and freezing to death, or, after stumbling upon the Farren house, being killed by Barbara who blames the child for stealing her mother's love. In contrast, the loss of the rational perspective hardly seems the menace that Oliver conceives it to be, although these potential dangers suggest that reason—a "head" or fatherly guidance—properly employed might indeed be useful in warding off the menaces which mark this world.

Inevitably, children must grow up and in a world that is complex and often frightening, even if only because it is so unknown. Simply denying the full breadth of human experience, including the world of fantasy, as Amy's parents try to do, can be as debilitating as the denial of love which has left Barbara a suspicious recluse. As the Lewton films typically demonstrate, an experience of the fantastic, the mysterious, even the frightening, can provide a person with the perspective on both his world and himself that he needs to function properly. In fact, this new perspective often becomes a measure of whatever maturity the films' young protagonists attain, as *The Ghost Ship* well demonstrates. In *Curse*'s climactic confrontation between Amy and a vengeful Barbara, we see how this abiding sense of menace can be met and dealt with by a degree of understanding. With the child in flight from the imagined horrors of the woods and Barbara incensed at her mother's affection for Amy, we view two children threatened most by their own anxieties. Ironically, though, her fantasizing helps Amy to resolve this situation and dispel those fears, and in precisely the manner that Bettelheim would predict. He remarks upon the child's capacity, when confronted with debilitating anxieties, to "project" bad or good impulses onto others and to "split" a parent figure or even himself "into two people" and then join them into one again when that anxious situation is resolved.[14] Thus, when Barbara threatens her, Amy invokes Irena, whose image we see superimposed over Barbara in a bit of trick photography uncommon to the Lewton films. Through her fantasizing, Amy effectively transforms Barbara into her "friend," the woman's bitterness vanishing as the child approaches and embraces her. In close-up we watch Barbara's hands, ready to strangle the child, slowly loosen their grasp and become instead a comforting embrace. With the advent of this new relationship, the threatening atmosphere vanishes—just as the storm suddenly disappears—and is replaced by a reassuring mood, as Amy's parents come to take her home. There Oliver tells her that he can now "see" her mysterious friend, too, thereby offering her the needed acknowledgment of her fantasy world. In this accommodation through the fantastic, then, child and parent come together in an understanding of each other and *both* attain a new level of maturity.

Traditionally, fantasy tales like *Curse of the Cat People*, according to Tzvetan Todorov, abide by one most important condition: the persistence of an atmosphere of uncertainty or ambiguity throughout the narrative. The audience is thus obliged "to consider the world of the characters as a world of living persons and to hesitate between a natural and a supernatural explanation" of the events in which they are involved; it is during this "certain hesitation" that the fantastic holds its powerful sway in their imaginations.[15] In the conjunction of childhood innocence with adult experience the Lewton team found an effective formula for sustaining such a tension. What the children in *Curse of the Cat People* readily see and the adults only belatedly is the complex and disturbing nature of a world where neither fact nor fancy clearly or totally rules, where no single explanation can satisfactorily account for the problems they encounter. It is a complexity which carries over to our own perspective as well, for we are left to wonder if children like Amy do perceive more than their parents, who are so inured to a certain normal vision of the world. Perhaps the imaginative realm is simply an amusing, sometimes confusing structure of myths which must eventually be abandoned for the child to function effectively in his culture. Following the fantasy tradition, the film validates neither view and leaves us in the grasp of the vesperal. As the film ends, Amy again sees Irena, but turns away from her friend—possibly because, as Irena offers, the child no longer "needs" her—while Oliver, although not looking in the right direction, claims that he now sees her. A lingering ambiguity results, as we are left to wonder what unknown elements may yet disrupt this world, what fears still hide beneath its normal seeming, waiting their turn to be acknowledged.

The Lewton works all evoke a world that is similarly disconcerting, although the fears which are revealed, the films imply, largely originate in the isolation and lack of understanding to which children and adults alike are prone. In *Curse of the Cat People* all the characters suffer after a fashion, and ironically often because of those nearest to them or their own fears and insecurities. Through such common and human problems the film dramatizes the difficulties involved in the complex and lengthy process of maturation. The child's situation effectively parallels the similar, if usually unrecognized psychic troubles which plague most adults, but especially those unwilling or unable to take their lives in hand and involve themselves in a world of human interaction and responsibility. As Hillman would predict, from the fantasy experiences of characters like Amy, Barbara, and Oliver, and from their subsequent recognition of "the substantial nature of fantasy and the fantasy aspect of all natural substances,"[16] a kind of growth follows, an internal development from which a measure of maturity and understanding can ensue.

The Mythic Path to the *Isle of the Dead*

> We return to Greece in order to rediscover the archetypes
> of our mind and of our culture. Fantasy returns there to
> become archetypal. By stepping back into the mythic,
> into what is nonfactual and nonhistorical, the psyche can
> reimagine its factual, historical predicaments from
> another vantage point. Greece becomes the multiple
> magnifiying mirror in which the psyche can recognize its
> persons and processes in configurations which are larger
> than life but which bear on the life of our secondary
> personalities.
>
> —James Hillman
> *Re-Visioning Psychology*

A primary effect of both dream and fantasy, James Hillman
convincingly argues, is that they introduce the psyche to a
sense of death—not death in a strictly literal or "gross
sense," as he terms it, but as a *telos* or notion of an ultimate purpose for the self. From our normal or dayworld perspective, of
course, death seems like the ultimate threat to the self, a negation
and destruction of all that the ego represents; but in terms of the
psyche's necessary vesperal journey it holds out a promise as well.
A descent into the realm of Hades through dream or fantasy "turns
the world upside down,"[1] forcing us into a new and deeper perspective on psychic reality. "Hades was of course the God of
depths," Hillman reminds, and our fantasy excursions into his
realm imply a psychic movement into the depths of the spirit, a
penetration to truths normally hidden from the ego's view—hence
Hades's association not only with death but throughout mythology
with concepts of wealth (Pluto) and even nourishment (Trophon-
ios). It is for this reason, Hillman notes, that "fantasies of rebirth
occur together with death fantasies"[2]; the latter, it seems, can fur-

nish the conditions for achieving the former. With this perspective we might see the usual concern of horror films with, for instance, the menace of death and a threatening supernatural imagery not simply as opportunities for gratuitous shocks and surprises, marshaled to discomfiting effect; they also represent the potential for a kind of basic psychic nourishment, in the shape of an imaginal experience of archetypal truths.

Lewton and Mark Robson's next collaboration, *Isle of the Dead* (1945), pointedly takes the mythic, rather than purely horrific, perspective to this natural and inevitable human experience. As its title and dominant imagery—a cemetery, crypt, battlefield, and backdrop based on the famous Arnold Böcklin painting *Isle of the Dead*[3]—indicate, the film suggests a meditation on death and our anxieties about it. In fact, Lewton described it as the story of a group of people who "through their sufferings come to an acceptance of death as being good—the fitting end—Shakespeare's 'little sleep.'"[4] In keeping with the other films' focus on the internal and the intangible rather than on what lies menacingly "out there," it finds in the pervasive imagery of death and morbidity a revealing mirror of the psyche, which points up the inadequate mental picture man typically has of his world and himself. Just as *Curse of the Cat People* uses the child to cast a questioning shadow on the adult, so *Isle of the Dead* draws upon the infancy of Western culture through its Greek setting and mythic attitudes to challenge our modern perspective and thereby put us back in touch with another way of seeing and understanding our place in the world.

Myths, as Claude Lévi-Strauss points out, serve both creative and destructive functions. On the one hand, they afford "a logical model capable of overcoming a contradiction" in our culture or consciousness, while, on the other, they function as "instruments for the obliteration of time,"[5] by blasting away our concern with the present and a personal history and asserting instead another, ahistorical mode of thinking. While the mythic helps us cope with cultural problems, then, it does so at a price of ego reduction, as it helps regenerate a sense of the larger and continuing human community of which the individual is a part by first requiring that he turn aside from his singular, historical identity.[6] As Joseph Campbell explains, the basic elements of such mythic thinking "are not manufactured; they cannot be ordered, invented, or permanently suppressed. They are spontaneous productions of the psyche, and each bears within it, undamaged, the germ power of its source."[7] Consequently, mythic thought does not deny the presence of mystery or ambiguity, as reason often seems to do; rather, it draws man into the mysterious and ahistorical fundament of human culture, there to admit his limitations and follow an archetypal path that leads back within the psyche to the realm of these discomfiting but fundamental mysteries. We can thereby gain the means of coping with the present and the threatening presences that seem to inhabit it. Through a mythic thinking we can fashion a meaningful structure within which we might orient the void which seems to lie at the center of the self, upwelling from time to time to remind us of how tentative our place in this world is.

The Lewton films typically depict two quite different methods of perceiving and conceiving of the world, both of which seem to contrast with what we have termed mythic thought. In Irena Dubrovna of *Cat People*, for instance, we see a person who, even while immersed in modern culture, is beset by the superstitions of her native Serbia; as a result, she isolates herself and creates of her world a fearful animistic universe with no place in it for love. A counterbalance to this vision of a mind paralyzed by superstition occurs in the sequel, *Curse of the Cat People*, wherein Oliver Reed suffers from an equally debilitating rational perspective. While he tries to reason his daughter out of her recurrent fantasies—which, we understand, she resorts to in order to fill the human gaps in her world—his logical arguments against her fantasy life nearly lead to disaster. In the characters of Irena and Oliver we see the two poles around which most of the Lewton films revolve, the superstitious and the rational, two methods of thinking about and structuring the human realm, although neither truly commensurate with human experience. While superstition seems to offer a knowledge of and control over the mysterious, it does so by eliminating the rational in favor of a more primitive but equally privileged epistemology which simply denies the validity of all appearances. Similarly, reason seeks to vanquish all trace of the unknown, the enigmatic, and hence the frightening, first by denying any mystery that threatens appearances, and then by enclosing the world and the self within a secure, humanly imposed order. In fact, Western culture has historically sought to dispel the mythic as well with reason, by evaporating it into the solutions of science, psychology, or anthropology. What the Lewton films do, therefore, is dispute this commonplace belief in an epistemological evolution from myth to reason. Instead, they discern in the mythic an archetypal ground of truth of which man has lost sight and in place of which he has substituted the inadequate explanations afforded by both superstition and reason.

Isle of the Dead brings together these rational and superstitious impulses to demonstrate their similar failings by contrasting both with the perspective afforded by mythic thought. Its resemblance to earlier films in the series, particularly *Cat People*, shows up in the opening epigraph, which announces the picture's primary concern with the place of myth in the modern human consciousness; it notes that "under conquest and oppression the people of Greece allowed their legends to disintegrate into superstition; the goddess Aphrodite giving way to the Vorvolaka. This nightmare figure was very much alive in the minds of the peasants when Greece fought the victorious war of 1912."[8] With this signpost in mind, we view the ensuing narrative in the light of Western man's cultural heritage, and especially of a major epistemological shift in that heritage. In the course of Western history, the film suggests, our mythic way of thinking about the world and our place in it has decayed and been transformed into the extremes of a fearful superstition and a proud rationalism which places man, with all of his violent capacities, at the center of this environment—from which point he futilely asserts his ability to explain and control all around him.

Even as the film announces that decay, however, we recognize a mythic pattern still at work, as the opening shot, a close-up of the victorious General Pherides washing his hands, reveals. While cleaning, he listens to a subordinate, Colonel Tolopedes, explain his regiment's failure in the recent battle. Pherides ignores his excuses, however, and offers the Colonel a pistol with which he may kill himself to "honorably" resolve the matter. This cold, harsh response hints at Pherides's thoroughly reasoned pragmatism, a concern only for results; it is, he readily admits, "my way, the only way I know." Overlaid on this cause-effect consciousness, however, is an easily recognizable mythic pattern, as the General's sanitary impulse suggests a sort of ritual cleansing. Pherides, in refusing to hear the Colonel's pleadings, resembles a modern Pilate, denying any personal responsibility for the punishment of someone he calls "friend." Moreover, his judgment signals another mythic impulse here, since it represents a scapegoat mechanism. Consequently, we immediately glimpse two systems of thought at work, the modern and the mythic, and are reminded of how much the latter persists in coloring our perceptions of the most common human actions, even while its opposite may be violently affirmed.[9]

In this violent world individual and general destruction are decreed by man himself and for a cause that is never made clear. René Girard theorizes that a tendency to violence dwells in the human spirit and that the primary function of myth and ritual is to exorcise such impulses before they rend man's world apart. In effect, the human community can be seen as "engendered by" its myths, since they represent a shared response to an impending threat and foster a "cultural unanimity" through its expulsion.[10] The rampant violence that marks *Isle of the Dead* points up the deterioration of this mythic consciousness and, as a result, the interiorization of the dangerous forces formerly projected into an animate universe. The plague that breaks out after the battle and becomes the film's central focus, then, can be viewed as a self-induced affliction, the result of violent human impulses going unchecked by mythic representation. In examining the plague's recurrence as a literary motif, Girard found it to have precisely this sort of archetypal character, serving as "a disguise for an even more terrible threat that no science has ever been able to conquer."[11] It is, he says, "a generic label for a variety of ills that affect the community as a whole and threaten or seem to threaten the very existence of social life. It may be inferred from various signs that interhuman tensions and disturbances often play the crucial role." From this perspective the plague can be interpreted here as a telling transformation of the monsters of horror film tradition. In *Isle of the Dead* those monsters go disguised, wearing the masks of men, and fragile indeed, the film suggests, is the cultural cohesion which keeps those masks in place.

Violence breeds violence, Girard explains, so naturally a lethal atmosphere rises from the Greek victory which opens the narrative, and it threatens to spread its menace to the larger community, still untouched by the war. As the General reminds, "The horseman on the pale horse is pestilence. He follows the wars" and threatens to render such human "accomplishments" meaningless. "If it isn't stopped, our victories on the field will mean nothing," he worries. This vain concern man has with giving meaning to all his actions, especially the most senselessly violent, is a common target of the Lewton films, and it is quickly scored here. As Pherides and Oliver Davis,[12] correspondent for the *Boston Star*, tour the battlefield, the corpse-littered, grotesque landscape quickly dispels the notion that some meaning might lie behind this violence which they accept so casually. Even that sanitary impulse glimpsed in the film's opening scene is here pushed to an extreme and transformed, as Dr. Drossos, his death carts piled high with corpses, hurries about cleaning up the battlefield to prevent the plague's spread. The new "enemy" that Pherides and Drossos must now combat symbolizes the human violence unleashed in the war; but unlike the enemies of the battlefield—or the usual monsters of the horror genre—it is an invisible threat that points up the specifically human "tensions and disturbances" prevalent in this world. Unable—or unwilling—to recognize this fundamental connection, General Pherides, like Captain Stone of *The Ghost Ship*, simply assumes he can control the plague like he does his army and, through his army, his enemies. By the proper application of force—physical and mental—he believes he can enclose his world in his own ordained meaning and keep those upwelling violent forces in check.

Wherever he goes, however, so too goes the plague, constantly challenging a consciousness which has put aside myth and its acceptance of society's fragility. Together with Davis, the General travels to a nearby island to visit his wife's grave, only to have the plague follow him, as if he were indeed its cause. Appropriately, this island cemetery is a place at once redolent of myth, yet a reminder of its decay. When Pherides and Davis arrive, for example, they are met by an imposing statue of Cerberus, watchdog of the ancient gods and guardian of the gates of Hades. It seems an appropriate sentry for the island, signaling their entry into a psychic netherworld. Davis also sees in it a likeness to his companion, whom he has earlier derisively described as "the watchdog" of Greece. "There's another watchdog for you," he now remarks to Pherides, who disavows the similarity, reminding Oliver that Cerberus "only guards the dead; I have to worry about the living." Despite this denial of a link between the mythic realm and the modern world, the statue becomes a haunting presence in the narrative. Used as a key transitional device, much like Ti Misery in *I Walked with a Zombie* and the fountain in *The Leopard Man*, the grim sculpture reminds us of Pherides and his menacing aspect, while it also casts a more threatening light on his supposedly beneficent watchfulness and protective militarism.

At the same time the island's history testifies to a loss of mythic consciousness. The General cannot find his wife's body in its crypt because the island's inhabitants have long since plundered its tombs and burned the disinterred bodies. This impiety resulted from the intrusion of the modern world with its new system of values and a rational perspective on life and death. Upon beginning his research in the area, the Swiss archeologist Albrecht offered the islanders money for any artifacts they might turn up, and they obligingly put aside any lingering reverence for the ancient gods, as well as the cultural taboos against violation of the dead, to pillage the ancient sites. This step, in turn, precipitated a greater falling off, which their plundering of all the island's tombs in search of other booty represents. Too late Albrecht realized that "unwittingly I had turned good, simple people into graverobbers," who then abandoned their island home when no more easy riches were to be found. Only his housekeeper Madame Kyra remains from that broken community, and she lives within her own fallen world of superstition. Without the bond of myth, apparently, only the two equally incommensurate perspectives of science and superstition survive in this fragmented world. It is on such a stage that we then witness the effects of a mythic decay on the people who have sought sanctuary from the man-made plague, the war: the British consul St. Aubyn and his wife, their servant Thea, the tinware merchant Robbins, as well as Albrecht, Kyra, the General, Davis, and later Dr. Drossos. Through them, we see how man, deprived of his myths, attempts to cope with visitations like the plague—not by recognizing its human source and letting that original "mistake" run its course, not by simply acknowledging his impotence in the face of an enigmatic and powerful nature, but by stubbornly defying that inexorable force, termed Fate by the ancients, and asserting his own controlling power of reason. In the breakdown of human society that results, *Isle of the Dead* demonstrates our feeble capacity for controlling the world we inhabit, as well as the fragility of the human community in the face of its own internally generated corrosive forces.

Like *The Ghost Ship*'s Captain Stone, the General is obsessed with the need for control, and it is the one characteristic which most sets him apart from the island's civilian inhabitants. Before the war, we learn, Pherides collected taxes from the peasants with the aid of field artillery, firing on his own people because "the laws" dictated it, and in his eyes anyone "who is against the laws of Greece is not a Greek." The argument advanced by the peasant girl Thea, that "laws can be wrong and laws can be cruel, and the people who live only by the law are both wrong and cruel," seems irrelevant to him. Denying his own peasant background, Pherides sees himself as representative of a new order, a Greece which has left behind the ancients and their divine pantheon: "These are new days for Greece. We don't believe the old, foolish tales anymore," he explains. Like Oliver Reed of *Cat People* and its sequel in this regard, he terms the old legends "nonsense," and in their place he pays homage to "what I can feel, and see, and know about." It is this rational perspective which he rigidly imposes on his world with no regard for its human consequences, certainly without recognizing the horrors and carnage it can effect.

With the advent of the plague, this conceptual framework with which Pherides overlays his world is cast in stark relief. He simply assumes control, declares himself the "watchdog" for the small, heterogeneous society, and decrees that "no one may leave the island." In effect, he declares war on the plague, treating it as he would any enemy. Through Dr. Drossos, he proclaims, "We will fight the plague," and he reminds those under his command that they "had better believe in the doctor. He's the only one who can save us." This proclamation of the myth of modern medicine—and indeed, of a modern faith in man and his scientific powers—signals a desire to substitute human capacities for explaining and controlling the environment for the primordial power of myth. Like another Greek leader whose realm was besieged by plague, King Oedipus, Pherides looks only to his own rational and ordering power for a means of overcoming that cultural affliction, and it is the ultimate weakness of these resources which the film, like the ancient myth, then demonstrates.

What *Isle of the Dead* suggests in this regard is not that reason is inherently evil or dangerous, but that, given absolute and unquestioned power, it can become a threatening, even self-destructive force, especially as it denies man access to the deep-rooted psychic constructs he always needs. To this end the film emphasizes an intimate connection between the General and Drossos, first by a form dissolve linking the two characters, and second through a similarity of actions. Following the announcement of the plague's advent, the image of Pherides dissolves into that of Drossos, clinically describing the disease's symptoms. Along with this visual assertion of identity, the General explains the nature of his relationship to the doctor—that if Drossos represents the authority

Oliver (Marc Cramer) consoles the General (Boris Karloff) who is losing his battle with the plague.

Maddened by the plague, the General menaces the innocent Thea (Ellen Drew).

Wielding Neptune's trident, Mrs. St. Aubyn (Katherine Emery) affirms the mythic forces.

of modern science, he is the force which assures its sway; as he tells the people, "The doctor will tell you what to do and I will see that you do it." The doctor's measures, however, amount to little more than distraction and sanitation, neither of which affects the plague's progress. He explains that "the disease is transmitted by fleas. Their bodies have an eighty percent moisture content. The hot wind from the South literally burns them away. If the sirocco blows, all danger will be over in 24 hours." To remind the people of their need for a favorable breeze, he then raises a pennant, which, ironically, also serves to symbolize their ultimate powerlessness in the face of these natural forces, their dependence on something outside of their control. Drossos eventually admits that his pennant functions primarily as a distraction: "Better to watch the wind and hope that it changes than to watch each other and have no hope at all," he allows. His other measure, the sanitary precaution of washing after every contact with another person, is no more beneficial. In fact, the medium shot which shows him washing his hands only points up the essential futility of these actions, while it once more underscores his similarity to the General by recalling the film's opening shot. After he warns against any personal contact and suggests that everyone should wash afterward, both Kyra and Albrecht protest, the former reminding him that "you cannot wash away evil," and the latter holding that the plague is the work of the gods and thus immune to such human precautions: "The doctor can use his science; I'll pray to Hermes," he asserts. These sanitary measures are, in any case, immediately undercut as the General, after washing, reaches out to shake hands with Albrecht, who calls his attention to this violation of his own rules. It is Drossos's subsequent death by the plague, however, preceded by his admission that the ancient gods "are more powerful than my science," which most clearly completes this questioning of the rational perspective lodged in the doctor and his commander.

The injunction against contact with others also underscores the breakdown of the human community which inevitably accompanies the visitation of the plague, since that precaution dictates an isolation from anyone who might be a carrier of the disease. It is an approach that forces each person to view the others with suspicion—an attitude especially marked in the case of Madame Kyra, who suspects the girl Thea of being a vorvolaka and thus the cause of their affliction. As the opening epigraph states, Kyra's superstitions signal a first step in the decay of mythic thought and suggest as well the flaw in the modern, rational view espoused by the General and Drossos. As Girard and others suggest, a mythic consciousness enjoins community by embodying a threat in an external figure, against which communal unanimity can be mustered. Both Kyra's superstitious mind, seeing in Thea "an evil for which the gods punish us mortals," and reason's "sanitary" approach create separation and fragment the community; only the stated reasons for isolation differ. Given this context, we can perhaps better understand why Pherides, once weakened by the plague and Kyra's harpings, so easily slips into her superstitious way of thinking and also threatens Thea. As Oliver warns him, there is a subtler danger afoot here, lodged not in the plague but within man, especially the way in which he conceives of his world: "There is something here more dangerous than septicemic plague—more dangerous as far as Thea is concerned—and that's your own crazy thoughts about her." More precisely, it is the desire for control, for a closure of ambiguity—which we have previously associated with a monological perspective on the world and the self—that is firmly lodged in man's mind and that takes shape in rational and superstitious attitudes alike.

Ironically, it is precisely because she looks so healthy and beautiful, so "full of life" as Mrs. St. Aubyn remarks, that Thea is thought to be a vorvolaka, carrying into their midst "a contagion of the soul." When death and decay seem the order of the day, life itself apparently can become suspect, largely because its almost miraculous flourishing in this context seems to defy reason. The persistence of the inexplicable reemphasizes the weakness in those rational and superstitious attitudes, as we see when Pherides inquires how he is different in his reaction to the plague; Oliver explains that the others "sort of take it, accept it, but you're fighting it. It seems to me you're fighting something bigger than the plague, wrestling with something you can't see. Kyra too." That "something bigger," of course, is his almost consuming desire to explain away troubling uncertainties, to dispel any unsettling complexity from the human realm. As a result, however, both Pherides and Kyra risk becoming themselves a source of violence by dredging up from within such an obsessive and dangerous force. For this reason Mrs. St. Aubyn, almost paraphrasing Girard, cautions the General that "evil breeds evil and in the end it will be you yourself who will suffer."

Of course, it is always the victim who suffers first, in this case Thea who is constantly watched and accused. Kyra stays awake at night, hoping to catch her in some "evil," and, after Drossos and his medicine fail, Pherides too watches and attempts to isolate Thea from the others, especially Oliver who is in love with her. Once planted, this seed of suspicion takes such deep root that it even undermines Thea's view of herself, bringing her to wonder if she has caused Mrs. St. Aubyn's poor health. Despite her mistress's reassurance that she is "good . . . kind and generous. How can anything bad come from goodness?" Thea fears that she could harbor some evil which her conscious mind cannot detect, and when Mrs. St. Aubyn slips into a deathlike trance she honestly wonders, "Is it my fault?" In her troubled state, we again see reason's fragility, how easily it can be turned against the self, questioning all that is not consciousness.

If we recall the film's opening commentary on the degeneration of Aphrodite, the goddess of love and beauty, into the vorvolaka, a figure of life-draining evil, we can see how Thea helps underscore the mythic decay which haunts the narrative. Almost an embodiment of Aphrodite, Thea—whose very name means "goddess"—is a beautiful young girl who brings the possibility of love into this death-filled world; yet she is eyed suspiciously for those vibrant attributes. Here man has come to such a state that beauty can be thought a thing of evil, love can be denied, and the human spirit can be viewed as sinister and potentially threatening simply because man's fear of the unknown and his compulsion for rationalization remain strong. As Hillman reminds, love represents "a means for the return of soul through the human and by means of the human to the imaginal, the return of the human psyche to its nonhuman imaginal essence. Love, in this view, is one of the many modes of archetypal emotion and fantasy."[13] In this suspicion of Thea and the love she brings into this world, then, a deep psychic and hence mythic truth is denied; reason is ranked not simply against feeling, but against spirit—hence the demonic shape that, in its aberrance, it increasingly seems to take.

The name Aphrodite, we might also recall, derives from the Greek word for "foam" or "surf," and literally means "born from the foam." It is an appellation which helps to link a number of the film's themes, especially the mythic decay, suspicion of Thea, and the recurrent washings described earlier. After each victim of the plague is buried, for example, we see a ritualistic cleansing carried out, despite its obvious futility. Demonstrating how compulsive this action becomes, a series of symbolic shots is inserted at the height of the plague's onslaught; it is of many hands scrubbing in a pool of dark, swirling water, a montage of washing hands which is intercut with several shots of the surf crashing on the island's rocky cliffs. These shots evoke the association of Aphrodite to comment ironically on the urge for sanitation. While they signal the power of life which both she and the water from which she was born represent in the mythic consciousness, these shots of the surf also recall the loss of that association; water has become affiliated with sterility, violence, and destruction, as the people see their world as hostile to love, beauty, and life. Only after many deaths, including the doctor's, is the ineffectual nature of that washing made clear and the attitude behind it called into question. Appropriately, it is Albrecht, the scientist whose experience has converted him to a mythic consciousness, even spurred him to pray to Hermes, god of healers, who finally announces that "it would serve our purpose a great deal more to join in prayer." What he essentially affirms is the fundamental power of belief, especially a communal belief, to bring some fellow comfort into this threatened and threatening world—thus his comment that "to believe, to pray, even if only to some pagan god, so long as belief is there, it brings comfort." This simple philosophy hints at the essence of what I have termed mythic thinking, as it suggests man's need—and his inherent capacity—to locate some hope or assert a communal strength in the face of a disconcerting, even chaotic moment. At the same time it signals the fundamental desire of psyche to regain contact with the realm of spirit from which it feels sundered, and thus to travel that *via regia* which "makes meaning possible."[14]

The alternative to such an archetypal or imaginal perspective, it seems, is to remain solely within the nontranscendent dayworld, a psyche stuck within a materialistic and naturalistic view of the self and its environment. Rather than an accommodation to our fears of death, for instance, we may seek to counter the naturalistic menace of death with a like response, lodging this dangerous violence which haunts man solely within the self, and through reason or superstition effectively transforming the self into a similarly threatening presence. The Lewton films persistently demonstrate how, in attempting to exorcise monsters from our thoughts and world, we always risk becoming ourselves the monstrous, disintegrative forces we fear. And as the film *Forbidden Planet* phrased this problem, the uncontrollable "monsters from the Id" that stand ready to be loosed on the world can easily overwhelm our usual dayworld defenses. What *Isle of the Dead* underscores, then, are the two equally threatening forms this monstrousness may take: first, its inherently self-destructive nature and, second, its disintegrative influence on the larger community of which the self is a vital part.

General Pherides clearly demonstrates the former danger, as his authoritative, self-assured rationalism gradually gives way to a superstitious and manifestly dangerous mania. Of course, casting Boris Karloff in this role almost automatically prepares for such a frightening transformation, since he brings resonances of his earlier monster portrayals to the character of the General; his normal role simply seems doubled here, as if he were alternately playing both Frankenstein and his creation. After trying "everything—every *human* remedy," all to no avail, Pherides turns to Kyra's superstitious explanations; his reason, pushed to its limits in maintaining control over this situation, becomes a form of unreason. Consequently, when the plague strikes him and thus points up his helplessness, the General—keeper of "the laws"—can try to murder Thea as a solution. The particular form of the plague which has struck and precipitated his delirious state seems carefully selected to comment upon this situation. Bearing no visible sign other than a change in behavior which marks its final stages, the septicemic plague essentially eats away at the vitals, specifically the bloodstream. As its etymology suggests, it is a kind of cancerous rotting from within, hinting at an internal danger to which man is prone, a self-destructive violence or decay which he may set in motion with the abandonment of his mythic perspective.

A correlative danger also accrues from a degeneration of the mythic, a loss of community. The island society, like Pherides's army, is being gradually decimated by the plague, and with that decimation the very spirit of community is eroding. Each person, as we see, eyes the others suspiciously, wondering who might be carrying the sickness that could eventually bring him death. Mrs. St. Aubyn offers the most subtle example of this societal decay. She refrains from burdening the others with her fears of premature burial, which have their source in a long family history of catalepsy; thus only her husband and Drossos know of the problem. When both of them die, therefore, she is left alone with her fears, isolated from the others who have their own, more pressing anxieties to cope with. When she falls into just such a trance, it is mistaken for but another visitation of the plague, and Mrs. St. Aubyn is buried like the others—mute testimony to the frailty of the modernist view which cannot even discriminate between life and death. Her interment alive, of course, only completes the on-going pattern of isolation and eventual destruction of the ego which naturally follows a decay of the communal spirit.

Mrs. St. Aubyn's premature burial also points up one of the film's subtler revisions of the traditional horror formula. While the genre typically evokes some monstrous presence or external threat to embody its elemental dangers and drive home its cautionary messages, the consul's timid wife fills that role here. Driven mad by her interment, she is transformed into just the sort of murderous being that usually haunts such films. And if, as I have suggested, the plague and accompanying violence here correlate to a degeneration of mythic thinking, then the victims of her murderous rampage are most appropriate, in their ends demonstrating the sort of ironic pattern of justice which pervades classical legend and literature. Seizing one of the artifacts Albrecht has been studying, a version of Neptune's trident, Mrs. St. Aubyn stabs both Kyra and Pherides, the latter just as he attempts to kill Thea. This mad but timely wielding of Neptune's weapon accomplishes much: it visits the ultimate power of the archetypal world upon those who have gainsaid it, reaffirms its powerful presence in the face of its seeming absence, and demonstrates precisely how we often generate from within—not only from our innate capacity for violence but also from our fear of it—our own monsters, every bit as dangerous as those which typically haunt this genre.

The trident is traditionally employed by the great "earth-shaker" to stir the oceans, creating waves and storms which might buffet mankind—like we saw in the repeated shots of crashing waves on the island's coast. Its use here, then, hints at a continuing and powerful mythic presence in this world, although one which often goes unseen or denied by those who prefer to believe in what they "can feel, and see." Certainly it is a force which reserves the last say with those who, like the General, might see themselves as modern "earth-shakers."

Mrs. St. Aubyn's subsequent death elaborates on this mythic motif, for after killing Pherides and Kyra, she rushes outdoors, hair streaming in maenadlike frenzy, and plunges from a cliff into the sea, back to Neptune's world, as it were. We view this sudden climax in what is easily the film's most careful composition. Mrs. St. Aubyn enters a perfectly balanced frame, to the left the remains of an ancient temple, a single doric column marking its margin, and to the right a wooded area with an old, gnarled tree rising from its edge. Between these almost archetypal signs of culture and nature, she rushes to her death, demonstrating thereby the consequences of man's failure to unite these two realms. Without the unifying force of myth, we understand, the psyche cannot bind the natural and the human worlds, the wild and the cultured, the superstitious and the rational into a meaningful pattern. In effect, such a sundered world ultimately affords no place for man.

The film's closing images eloquently testify to a tentative reconciliation between man and his mythic heritage that this violent purging effects. A shot of Drossos's tell-tale pennant indicates the onset of the long-awaited sirocco and thus heralds the end of the plague along with the end of the General and his reign of reason. This sign of relief, however, gives way to a close-up of the General's dead face, frozen into a fearful stare which makes him seem all the more like a watchdog, a human and more disturbing version of the haunting figure of Cerberus. His image then dissolves into a long shot of Oliver and Thea leaving the island, their departure watched over by Albrecht on the left of the frame and the statue of Cerberus on the right; in a longer shot, Cerberus's image is next superimposed on that of the couple in their boat. These various images, especially the pairing of Albrecht and Cerberus, hint of a science brought back into harmony with myth and the possibility for life that this harmony engenders. The sense of mystery which the archetypal perspective acknowledges and the inexorable and unpredictable forces it recognizes have been affirmed with the beneficial effects that traditionally attend a culture's mythmaking. Although myth-haunted, as Cerberus's superimposed image attests, Oliver and Thea can depart from this "isle of the dead," and their love, proscribed by Pherides and Kyra, might now flourish. Love and life have replaced war; a couple united in mutual care, in a love that, as Hillman says, allows "for the return of soul through the human," replaces an isolated self who, in his hubris, washed his hands of human responsibility. In more archetypal terms, the Jungian shadow, the projected dark side of human nature, has been joined to a persona and anima in a proper psychic harmony; and this archetypal marriage has been effected and a renewed sense of community made possible by "stepping back into the mythic" and regaining a sense of its great power.

Isle of the Dead accomplishes this psychic and communal rejuvenation largely through the repetition of two central image patterns. We have traced out the developing imagery of washing in which water comes to suggest not only life but also sterilization and a denial of human complicity. This usage undercuts its archetypal life-affirming characteristics, as the powers of the sea god Poseidon are symbolically usurped by man. This particular repetition, therefore, emphasizes the human impulse for power and control in order to reveal its inevitable consequences. In the recurring image of Cerberus we see a pointedly unnatural presence which, in its stony stolidity and enigmatic otherness, clearly mocks the human desire for knowledge and control. Its recurrent appearances haunt this world with a reminder of something permanent, not subject to change, of a mythic realm whose influence modern man would like to deny or appropriate as his own but cannot.

In the two styles of repetition that these images demonstrate, we can discern a further commentary on the notions of change and permanence. As Bruce Kawin explains, these two forms of repetition—the developing image and the simple recurring image—correspond to our different ways of representing time. The former implies a "time that builds," what we might term a human sense of history, while the latter invokes a time "that is always present, time that continues," in fact, a sort of timelessness.[15] *Isle of the Dead* thus develops a necessary complementarity between these two time schemes—that of man and that of myth, that of change and of the truths which defy all change, ultimately that of life and of death as well. The film's opening epigraph describes a sense of historical development in which man gradually loses sight of the eternal verities. The film's final image, however, evokes a constant presence, one that casts the present in a new light, just as the knowledge of death does to the experience of life. From this broader perspective the single moment opens onto a vast horizon of mythic time, an eternity in which man finds himself immersed as he often frustratingly tries to sift some sense from his own short life. What *Isle of the Dead* demonstrates most pointedly, then, is how myth might energize the present with its presence, by transporting man from an isolated, dead world to which modern thought threatens to consign him, to a larger, if equally unsettling world of the living in which, with some pain and effort, he might reside. In this sense the film represents the most complex and complete formulation of the fantasy aesthetic that informs all of the works we have considered.

Dealing with Death: *The Body Snatcher*

> Knowledge does not slowly detach itself from its
> empirical roots, the initial needs from which it arose, to
> become pure speculation subject only to the demands of
> reason; its development is not tied to the constitution and
> affirmation of a free subject; rather, it creates a
> progressive enslavement to its instinctive violence.
> Where religions once demanded the sacrifice of bodies,
> knowledge now calls for experimentation on ourselves.
>
> —Michel Foucault
> *Language, Counter-Memory, Practice*

As *Isle of the Dead* demonstrates, the consciousness of modern man and the prospect of death seem bound together in
a paradoxical relationship. On the one hand, we persistently
try to deny the fact of death and its ultimate assertion of human
limitation; on the other, we seem fascinated by it and the extinction it promises—so much so that death has become a singularly
attractive subject of inquiry, as if it were the repository of some
life-giving secret which requires that reason exhume and carry out
an inquest on it. With its next film, *The Body Snatcher* (1945), the
Lewton unit undertook a detailed examination of this paradox. In
effect *The Body Snatcher* explores the deal we feel we might make
with death, whereby we try to take its measure and turn it to life's
account, all the while maintaining a firm footing in the realm of
the living and its dayworld perspective. It is a pact that, the film
suggests, only the rational mind with its insistence on its own controlling powers could conceive of. Instead of our common, archetypal attraction to an underworld such as James Hillman
describes, "the innate urge to go below appearances to the 'invisible connection' and hidden constitution" of psychic life,[1] then,

The Body Snatcher details a disturbing fascination with the underground, as man turns his attention to the depths of the grave in an effort to nourish physical life by, as it were, feeding upon death.

As its title implies, *The Body Snatcher* presents a proscribed desire for the human body and a compulsion to violate the depths to which it is usually consigned at death. By invoking a perverse sort of resurrection, it elaborates on the problem *Isle of the Dead* sketched in the Greek peasants who, lured by rewards for whatever artifacts they found, became despoilers of their island's graves. While the earlier film focuses on the causes of such violations, specifically the replacement of a mythic consciousness by a rationalist perspective, *The Body Snatcher* pointedly examines the terms of transgression. How is it, the film asks, that one can almost eagerly explore the depths of the grave yet deny the desire to do so? How can a concern for appearances offset a fascination with the hidden and culturally proscribed? And how might a professed care for human life and community justify a reduction of the human to the data of experimentation and analysis and a removal of the self from the world under examination? To answer these questions, the film carries out its own quite literal depth analysis, employing the central trope of snatching bodies from the grave's depths to signal a subtler exploration of the psyche's reaches. In this respect it clearly parallels Hillman's approach to depth psychology, which involves, as he explains, "moving from outside in . . . a process of interiorizing; moving from the surface of visibilities to the less visible, it is a process of deepening; moving from the data of impersonal events to their personification, it is a process of subjectivizing."[2] Interiorizing, deepening, and subjectivizing are the typical activities that we have observed in the Lewton films, which try to drive home the extent to which our world takes its shape from its occupants, and thus to clarify the individual, subjective responsibility we all bear in ensuring its human contours.

Like few other films in the series, *The Body Snatcher* draws the outline for this exploration from a well-known literary work, Robert Louis Stevenson's tale, "The Body Snatcher." In bringing this Victorian horror story to the screen, Lewton assumed the task of reworking its structure and characterizations himself, and his work was so extensive that, for one of the few times in his career, he took screen credit for the final script, using the pseudonym Carlos Keith, a name under which he had previously written several novels.[3] As Lewton explained, he accepted this writing credit only because "I had rewritten the script so completely that [the original screenwriter] Phil MacDonald, who did not trust my work, wanted someone to share the blame if it were a flop."[4] What he had to work with was by no means a simplistic horror tale; "The Body-Snatcher" is a multilevel story, structurally reminiscent of Henry James's *The Turn of the Screw.* It employs an anonymous narrator to introduce an acquaintance named Fettes and to recount this character's history as it was related to him. Distanced by time from the actions he reports, this narrator inexplicably breaks off his account with one horrific scene, a grotesque vision or visitation once experienced by Fettes.

Partly because of monetary restrictions and partly because he well understood the cinema's persistent and effective sense of "present tense," Lewton deleted the story's complex framing device, thereby avoiding the necessity of depicting two different time periods.[5] With this deletion there also went the anonymous narrator, whose characteristics were wedded to the figure of Fettes. Knowing, too, that grotesque visions, given their initial shock effect, cannot stand sustained scrutiny—by the camera or the human eye—that they tend to become "something to laugh at,"[6] Lewton and director Robert Wise altered the final horrific scene as well, giving it a more hallucinatory effect and joining it to a characteristically archetypal concluding image. In general the adaptation shares the typical structural distinctions of the other works in the series: complex recurring images, atmospheric and metaphoric settings, paired scenes to generate an ironic effect, and the use of characters to link scenes and plot elements.

What probably attracted Lewton and his colleagues to Stevenson's tale is its preeminent concern with the human psyche, rather than with the ghouls and monsters which so permeated the horror genre. Also, it offered the possibility of a doubling motif, less starkly stated than in Stevenson's more famous story, *Dr. Jekyll and Mr. Hyde*, yet similar to that developed in *The Seventh Victim* and *The Ghost Ship*. "The Body-Snatcher" focuses on a particular state of mind, that of Fettes who, while working in the dissecting laboratory at Mr. K____'s medical school, became "insensible to the impressions of a life thus passed among the ensigns of mortality."[7] In retrospect, a narrator tells of Fettes's medical schooling and of his association with a fellow student, "Toddy" MacFarlane, whose callous example spurred a psychic fall of sorts: "His mind . . . closed against all general considerations. He was incapable of interest in the fate and fortunes of another, the slave of his own desires and low ambitions" (p. 426). In this era the bodies used in medical study were often obtained illegally—through grave robbing or even murder—and Fettes does not shrink from such practices. With only slight prodding from his friend, he learned "to avert the eye from any evidence of crime" (p. 427), as long as he could obtain the right reward. Subsequently, Fettes even helps MacFarlane dispose of the body of Mr. Gray, a blackmailer whom he has murdered. Together they then plot to join in the lucrative "resurrection" business, digging up bodies to sell to the various medical schools. On their initial attempt, however, "some unnatural miracle," as Stevenson describes it, transforms the body of a local farmer's wife into that of Gray. With this discovery "a fear that was meaningless, a horror of what could not be" (pp. 440– 41) afflicts the grave robbers, and with this single shocking discovery and the sudden plunge into the supernatural it implies the narrative simply breaks off. Having transported us fully into this fantastic realm, Stevenson never returns to his narrator's privileged perspective and the frame of his frame-tale. Rather than belabor an obvious moral, he simply demonstrates how man's desires can lead him into that blindness and trap him within a haunting nightmare world largely of his own creation. The image of Gray stands as a striking cautionary note for the tale, a reminder of what we might "dig up" once we divorce scientific endeavor from ethical guidance.

While the Lewton unit's *The Body Snatcher* is visually rich, it holds few such grotesque images, and, as the previous films would lead us to expect, its attitude toward the world of science and reason is even more critical. True, it retains a version of the shock ending from Stevenson's tale; however, the apparition of Gray is bracketed within a subjective context, and this simple horrific confrontation does not conclude the narrative. The film is much less concerned with the details of individual degradation or the falling away from a properly scientific path than with a more complex psychic activity, especially the manner in which we try to deny, explain away, or mask the frightful aspects of our natures. Like the series' other entries, therefore, it develops a sense of incongruity and employs numerous ironic juxtapositions to criticize the rationality by which we often disguise or excuse the horrors around us. *The Body Snatcher* suggests that the grotesque and the fantastic lurk in our day-to-day activities, and we pass those experiences on from one person to another—in this case, from teacher to pupil, which is the new shape of the relationship between MacFarlane and Fettes. Rather than shocking viewers, the film develops an atmosphere in which horrors seem almost quotidian and the meaning of being human is left open to question.

As most of the earlier films in the series show, the Lewton team well understood that horror elements are most effective when a norm is established against which any aberrance can be measured. The film's opening conjures up such a commonplace context through a wealth of richly detailed images of daily life nowhere found in the original story. This visual detail drew some criticism for the film, several critics seeing it as an example of the unit's drift from pure horror to flamboyant period pieces. Joel Siegel, for one, finds the opening "too detailed to suit its function," and but one more demonstration of Lewton's need for a director with a visual sense to complement his writing, someone who "could select and graphically order the screenplay's abundant materials,"[8] as Jacques Tourneur did in the unit's first films. While director Robert Wise admits to being a "stickler for realism and honesty,"[9] he is hardly given, as Manny Farber slightingly suggests, to a "delirious . . . scenic camera work."[10] In fact, his theory is that careful attention to visual detail subtly enhances a film's effectiveness by evoking proper characterizations—even in films concerned with the fantastic. "Maybe some of the details could have been a little less thorough, might have been sloughed off a bit," he allows, "but I believe that the atmosphere that's created by some of those 'unregistering' bits of detail is very pervasive and gets to the actors; it influences them, therefore it influences the whole scene."[11] In truth, the highly detailed opening scenes, far from representing a simple fascination with the picturesque, actually lay the groundwork for the film's larger concerns, especially for its development of an interplay between a world of innocent appearances and the disturbing depths which they conceal.

Besides establishing a period setting, the opening montage—shots of a road leading to a castle, the cobbled streets of Edinburgh, and an avenue running by an imposing estate—and the following detailed scene of a single street establish several important motifs for the film. The initial static shots, with their roads running diagonally or horizontally across the frame, form tableaux with little depth; these picturesque surfaces simply suggest the various paths man takes in his everyday routine. Followed by the individual street scene, they also convey a solid sense of civilization, as the camera lingers to depict a bookstore, bootery, public house, police kiosk, and strolling shoppers, all of which imply that here "In Edinburgh in 1931," as an opening title notes, a sedate and civilized society routinely goes about its daily business, secure that reality is precisely as it is usually perceived. This serene atmosphere works to ironic effect as well, though, both by establishing a normalcy out of which the fantastic might later more strikingly emerge, and by preparing for a truly stark contrast with the film's closing scene which depicts another road, but one winding into a dark, craggy landscape as a storm rages. By means of this careful and parallel editing, the narrative takes its characters from order to chaos, from light to dark, and from all the appearances of civilization into a turbulent and disconcerting natural environment. At the same time it establishes a new direction for movement, the road in the last scene heading directly into the dark background, emphasizing the depth of this final composition and contrasting markedly with the flat, postcardlike images with which the film began. In this shift from surface to depth and the movement into a foreboding darkened frame, we should recognize the sort of vesperal journey that to some degree characterizes all of the films in the RKO series.

These opening scenes prepare us for a deeper and more complex perspective that will be developed more fully in succeeding images. *The Body Snatcher* places us within a world bustling with commerce, good intentioned and seemingly innocent, one initially evoking the typical Hollywood vision of a quaint Victorian England, Dickensian in atmosphere and attractive overall. Beneath this richly detailed surface, however, there stirs a world of frustration at the limits of human knowledge, of pain both treated and caused by the doctors of the day, and of murder for hire—although commissioned for the best of reasons. The infamous Burke and Hare, who obtained specimens for the medical schools simply by waylaying likely subjects, have been caught and punished, but their spirit lingers, as the dead and living alike still prove salable commodities in the lucrative business of aiding the advance of medical science. The film thus generates a tension between these first everyday images of civilization and the darker, blind depths which work upon it and with which it often unwittingly strikes a deal.

This complex relationship finds immediate representation in the introduction of the film's central character, Donald Fettes. In Stevenson's tale Fettes, lacking even a Christian name, is essentially a one-dimensional figure. Working in a dissection laboratory, he "understood his duty . . . to have three branches: to take what was brought, to pay the price, and to avert the eye from any evidence of crime" (p. 427). The manner in which the film introduces Fettes speaks much more ambiguously, even as it underscores his quite different naiveté. We first see him seated atop a fresh grave in the city cemetery, where he incongruously eats his lunch, heedless of those "ensigns of mortality" around him—just as of those depths beneath. This scene quickly underscores his dayworld perspective, which is important, since the same composition later recurs in a similar view of the cabman Gray—bringing Fettes together with an old lady visiting her son's grave, mindful of what lies beneath these surfaces. She tells Fettes of her fear that grave robbers might steal her son's body and of her disdain for the doctors who encourage that practice. Incredulous, he defends the medical profession he hopes to join and assures her that there is "not much danger here . . . I wouldn't think, not right here in the heart of Edinburgh." Rather than close the scene on this note of naive confidence, however, the narrative inserts a questioning image. In an extreme long shot of the cemetery, metaphorically a more encompassing perspective than that enjoyed by Fettes, we see a mysterious carriage slowly pass the gate. Although a commonplace image, even the sort which might be dismissed as atmospheric detail, it seems unnaturally eerie and subtly calls into question Fettes's confidence, due to its context and the oblique camera angle employed. This suspicion is quickly substantiated, as we learn that it is the coach of Gray, the "resurrectionist" who plagues this area and supplies bodies to the young man's teacher, the illustrious surgeon Dr. MacFarlane.

Gray's coach subsequently serves as a visual link between the introduction of Fettes and that of MacFarlane, while it also hints at just how much generally goes hidden in this world. The next scene opens with this coach pulling up in front of MacFarlane's magnificent house. It brings a crippled girl, Georgina Marsh, to request that the doctor operate on her crippling spinal injury. When he refuses to become involved in her plight, claiming to be "more dominie than doctor," the image of the helpless child provides an immediate emotional indictment of his cold, theoretical concerns. Even Gray, in contrast, initially seems more sympathetic, as we see him bearing Georgina in his arms, helping her from his carriage, and smiling as he lifts her up to pet his horse. Disarmed by such appearances and the seemingly genuine feelings on display, we inevitably find our next view of Gray quite jarring. That night, following Georgina's interview with MacFarlane, Gray appears as a silhouette against the cemetery wall—iconically suggesting his place in that shadowy realm whose existence Fettes has denied. There he unhesitatingly kills a small dog guarding its master's grave, which he then plunders, whistling while he "works"; ironically, it is the same grave whose security Fettes earlier affirmed. The shift from day to night, from light to shadows, and from manor house to graveyard marks a transformation in our perspective, which points up the complex and usually unseen interworkings between the dayworld and its shadow, and one fittingly embodied in the image of Gray disrupting the normal boundaries between these two realms, as he unnaturally draws the dead back into the world of the living. Gray's carriage by day transports the living and by night serves as a hearse for the corpses he has stolen, while Gray himself is disturbingly able to blend in with the world of common day, then prowl the cemeteries and streets at night, stealing or, if necessary, murdering to obtain the valuable specimens for his employers' dissecting tables.

The paradoxical nature of his character is most clearly expressed in a later scene which recalls Fettes's introduction. Gray murders MacFarlane's servant Joseph, who has attempted to blackmail him, and while straddling the corpse, he strokes his pet cat and speaks lovingly to it. This incongruous composition reminds us of Fettes eating his lunch atop the fresh grave, although in this instance all notion of naiveté is dispelled by the horrifying heedlessness implied. Gray's capacity for such demarcation, for gestures alternately monstrous and humane, strikes directly at our human desire for predictability and our normal tendency to judge the world on the basis of its appearances. This discordant image, consequently, affords a key to the film's fantasy strategy; it starts a fear not, like *Cat People*, that every shadow might hold some menace, but that every neutral or benevolent appearance might only be the temporary mask for some invisible, unimagined terror, that the clear, rational light of day might simply serve to disguise the dark, irrational elements of the human situation. And this sense of possible dissembling is ultimately much more debilitating, since it prompts us to question everything and everyone around. We "hestitate," as Tzvetan Todorov predicts, in interpreting even the most commonplace images and events, suspecting a most discomfiting paradox—that they actually conceal another, frightening truth, a depth beyond the promise of all surfaces.

Although less obviously, this disturbing capacity for demarcation marks MacFarlane's character as well, investing it with a similarly corrosive capacity. As the most eminent surgeon in Edinburgh, he presents an impeccable appearance, one which promises a most salutary effect. MacFarlane's house, though, which the camera seems to survey needlessly, hints at a different reality. Before he is introduced, we see several interior shots of his home as Georgina and Mrs. Marsh enter. Angled shots and a dimly lit interior create an eerie effect, and the high angle view of mother and daughter from atop the staircase, as if from MacFarlane's point of view, makes them seem small and insignificant. In fact, this composition foreshadows the condescension and air of detachment which the doctor subsequently displays, as he excuses himself from offering any help, holding himself aloof from their situation. The layout of the house corroborates MacFarlane's attitudes by demonstrating his tendency to compartmentalize his life. His lodgings occupy the second floor and part of the first, his office and examination rooms the remainder of the first, and his medical facility—including the dissection tables, lecture room, and storage facilities—is left to the basement. This arrangement suggests how McFarlane tries to shut out the more unpleasant aspects of his profession with the close of a door or figuratively hold himself above the grisly matters he has relegated to his basement school or delegated to Fettes as his assistant and Gray as his henchman.

This effort at demarcation, however, only further amplifies the nature of the paradox between the appearances which MacFarlane tries to maintain and the reality to which they correspond. Instead of winning for him a certain freedom from that dark realm, this compartmentalization contributes to a sense of entrapment which pervades the film. Even as he sleeps upstairs, for instance, Gray steals into his basement and leaves Joseph's corpse as a suitably shocking surprise, which the doctor must hurriedly dispose of to avoid a scandal. He finds himself in this position because, on the one hand, the pursuit of knowledge has brought him to traffic with men like Gray, with ghouls and murderers who obtain the bodies he needs for study. And, on the other, he is haunted by his own past, especially his associations with Gray when he was a young medical student like Fettes and forced into similarly unscrupulous methods to gain the specimens his teacher needed. As Mac-Farlane's mistress Meg explains, there has always been "the shame of the old ways and the old life to hold him back" from a glorious career. The house and Gray's frequent appearances visually affirm his entrapment in a round of sordid actions and explain his warning to Fettes that, given an initial accession to evil, one cannot easily turn back: "The more things are wrong, the more we must act as if everything is right." Gradually we recognize that the major difference between the esteemed Dr. MacFarlane and the lowly Gray is not a deeper understanding or moral sensibility, but a greater ability for maintaining this split within the self. The doctor's capacity for making things look right, for presenting a more natural and civilized appearance, despite reality, is simply more practiced and convincing evidence of his greater expertise at rationalizing every situation. The haunting presence of Gray thus points up the fault which runs through this façade, increasingly threatening to well up from the depths of his past, to burst through the fragile front of propriety, and to upset MacFarlane's delicately balanced dualism. In fact, the more that the doctor tries to deny Gray and relegate him to the dark side of his life, the more he seems to menace his carefully constructed world of appearances.

The complex relationship of MacFarlane and Gray is one of the film's major developments of Stevenson's story, as their interaction generates a constant tension between surfaces and depths and deploys it within a doubling formula reminiscent of *The Seventh Victim* and *The Ghost Ship*. In their contending alter egos these men resemble the skeletons which MacFarlane's students jokingly arrange in fighting postures in his laboratory. In fact, Gray calls attention to this relationship, reminding the doctor, "You and I have two bodies . . . very different sorts of bodies, but they're closer than if we were in the same skin." This closeness extends to the very pattern of their lives, which also seem doubled after a fashion and lead us to expect a doubled, equally tragic fate for them as well. Like MacFarlane, Gray is trapped by his situation, particularly by his past association with Burke and Hare, and he finds himself preyed upon by the blackmailing servant Joseph, even as he seeks to manipulate MacFarlane in the same way. Having accepted a bribe to hide MacFarlane's complicity in an earlier series of corpse snatchings, Gray now resents the seeming disparity between himself and his double, especially the doctor's appearance of respectability, which seems so much at odds with his own lowly state. Consequently, he turns this disparity back upon MacFarlane, using it to blackmail him and finding in this limited power some small consolation for his station: "I'm a small man, a humble man," he says, "and being poor, I've had to do so much that I did not want to do. But so long as the great Dr. MacFarlane jumps at my whistle, that long am I a man—and if I have not that, I have nothing. Then I am only a cabman and a grave-robber."

This motif of disparity finds further emphasis in Gray's lodgings which, located in the rear of a barn on a dead-end street, sharply contrast with MacFarlane's manor. In his dark, meager quarters he seems trapped and constantly reminded of his situation. When Fettes threads the bleak, labyrinthine avenues to bring Gray an urgent request for a body, this sense of hopelessness translates into a series of telling compositions in depth, underscoring both his entrapment and his figurative embodiment of the dark realms that seem typically to go denied here. After Fettes leaves, for instance, we see Gray in long shot, a small figure framed first in the doorway of his lodgings, then, as the camera tracks back, through a portal of his door. Diminished and confined by the multiple frames, bound within darkness, he seems both pitiable and menacing, firmly locked in by environmental pressures to a round of gruesome activities he has made his life. Fittingly, as Gray harnesses his horse in preparation for his mission, we view him through the bars lining the stall; it is a composition that affirms his imprisonment, even as it marks an internal tension as well, a reluctant resignation to the way of life he has entered. Moreover, as a denizen of this darkness and a human extension of the proscribed desires which MacFarlane and Fettes manifest, he reminds us how easily those discomfiting absences might insinuate their influence into the everyday world we inhabit.

From this tension between open and closed spaces and the visible and invisible, there arises a troubling atmosphere of moral ambiguity that distinguishes *The Body Snatcher* from a number of the earlier films in the series. It depicts a world in which the best intentions can lead to evil deeds, while those same frequent misdeeds are excused or covered up by the human penchant—and as this film suggests, perhaps even a need—for rationalization. In Stevenson's story Fettes and MacFarlane are simply fellow students brought to their crimes by the lure of easy money and pleasures. As in *The Ghost Ship*, however, the film's characters have a relationship that resembles that of father and son. It is a development that helps pose a greater moral dilemma by questioning the legacy of knowledge which the parent passes on to his offspring. Technically brilliant but lacking a humanistic sense, MacFarlane sharply contrasts with the idealistic young Fettes, although both display a similar failing. In his singleminded concern with the advance of medical knowledge, MacFarlane continually complains that "ignorant men have dammed the stream of medical progress with stupid and unjust laws. If that dam will not break, the men of medicine . . . have to find other courses." One such course is dealing with men like Gray and winking at their methods—including murder. In effect, it means developing a debilitating dualistic perspective on the self and the world. Lest we judge MacFarlane too harshly, seeing him as simply overly zealous, though, Fettes displays a similar weakness, which demonstrates how easily and unwittingly one might accept that unsettling legacy under the pressures of necessity. In his desire to help the crippled Georgina, for instance, Fettes presses MacFarlane to operate and asks Gray for a specimen to study in preparation for the delicate surgery. His urgings, however, precipitate Gray's murder of a young street singer, whose body Fettes immediately recognizes. Her corpse visually drives home the moral complexity of Fettes's world, as well as a basic paradox with which the film is concerned. The easiest way to advance human knowledge, it seems, is to set aside one's humanity, and one aid in promoting life is murder. In this case we see most clearly how even the most humanitarian concerns may be twisted into rationales for a denial of life and the violation of the dead, although the cost of embracing such a paradox, of inscribing such a duality in the psyche, remains to be shown.

As in the earlier Lewton films, it is the voice of reason which speaks in favor of this disturbing dualism, and the force of its rhetoric drives home its threatening aspect. Stevenson's original character lacks this complex dimension which MacFarlane shows in the film. The literary figure's philosophy is simple and straightforwardly naturalistic: "There are two squads of us," he explains, "the lions and the lambs. If you're a lamb, you'll come to lie upon these tables . . .; if you're a lion, you'll live and drive a horse like me, . . . like all the world with any wit or courage" (p. 434). In the film, however, MacFarlane is obsessed with his sense of right, as he consistently feels compelled to explain himself to Fettes and to rationalize his every descent into darkness. On three occasions he reasons his assistant out of quitting the medical profession and into helping him with his work—in spite of its increasingly foul nature—pointing to "the stupidity of the people, the idiocy of their laws" as a suitable rationale for continuing in their questionable activities. His ease in turning reason to such ends, however, is itself unsettling, as the murder of the young street singer demonstrates. In one of *The Body Snatcher*'s most effective scenes she disappears into a dark alley, a field of absence in the rear of the frame, and is followed by Gray and his coach; after some moments her singing abruptly stops, suggesting the completion of the cabman's work. When she turns up on his dissection table, MacFarlane tries to explain her sudden death by surmising that she may have been an epileptic who, in a fit, fell and hit her head. "All the pieces fit," he asserts, but his implausible explanation hardly convinces even the gullible Fettes. It simply gives the lie to MacFarlane's continuing pretense of a truly humanitarian concern and underscores how indiscriminately reason's discourse may be employed. Just as the earlier scene of a dark alley in the middle of a lighted frame served to visualize the tension between the seen and unseen here, so does the doctor's explanation in the face of this murdered girl express the duality which so deeply marks his character.

An even more pointed indictment of MacFarlane results from the operation on Georgina Marsh. It is painted as a kind of performance in which the doctor demonstrates correct surgical procedure to his admiring students. After the surgery, however, the child still cannot walk, despite MacFarlane's avowals that "everything is in place," and everything looks "right." This result affirms that there are things which defy his science, which he "can't define, can't diagnose." Under the force of this blow to his philosophy and public image, MacFarlane freely acknowledges the double he has sought to deny, seeking the company of Gray, as if that embodiment of his darker self might shed some light on his dayworld failure. Appropriately, Gray delivers an important lesson, which underscores the limits of the doctor's rational, mechanistic approach and his deep-rooted duality. "You can't build life the way you put blocks together," Gray reminds him, noting that while MacFarlane indeed has "a lot of knowledge," he has "no understanding," since it is only "the dead ones" he truly knows.

The failure to heal Georgina disillusions Fettes, who realizes that MacFarlane "taught me the mathematics of anatomy, but he couldn't teach me the poetry of medicine." The union of two seemingly disparate ways of understanding—the scientific and the poetic—that he cites underscores his mentor's psychic schism, which sees in the world around him not a harmony but an inevitable duality, in effect—and paradoxically—an ultimate cleft between the self and true knowledge. His perspective can distinguish a world of appearance and one of reality, an individual depth of desire and a surface of societal limitations, but he simply tries to lay claim first to the one and then the other, all the while asserting the fact of their mutually exclusive nature. It is a perspective clearly shot through with contradiction, yet it is precisely the sort of vision which, the film implies, informs the consciousness that feels it can indeed snatch life from death.

With the rejection of this legacy, the film's father-son relationship quickly disintegrates, thus suggesting how human relations have here become quite dependent on a questionable epistemology. MacFarlane has from the first sought more than just approval from his student; childless and with a low-born mistress he refuses to acknowledge as his wife, the doctor desires an extension of himself and his beliefs. Like *The Ghost Ship*'s Captain Stone, he seeks someone who will continue his work—"see it as I see it." And as we have seen, he has already laid the groundwork for a duplication of his dualistic perspective by delegating much of his necessary dealings in death to young Fettes.

The possible consequences of such a doubling are outlined in a climactic scene that echoes another failed father-child relation described earlier. Three years before, Georgina Marsh was crippled and her father killed when his reckless driving caused their coach to overturn. The film's conclusion puts MacFarlane and Fettes in a similar situation. After murdering Gray, MacFarlane tries to strike a deal with Fettes, promising to become "a new man and a better teacher," and asking Fettes to help him dig up corpses to supply the school and thus once again work toward the "advancement" of knowledge. Having begun his "new life" so paradoxically, by again delving into the dark and generating a "new man" from a murdered one, he sets the stage for his own destruction— a final and fatal doubling of Gray. Teacher and pupil drive wildly through a suddenly stormy night with the body they have retrieved propped between them. In effect, we see that Fettes, at the mercy of a morally reckless "father," faces a fall like Georgina, but he risks a far less remediable injury, less a physical than a spiritual crippling, if he follows the path laid out by MacFarlane. In this context, Hillman's description of spirit as essentially "a perspective rather than a substance, a viewpoint toward things rather than a thing itself"[12] clearly echoes. Since Fettes's viewpoint is already

Doubling patterns: the antagonistic alter egos—the scientist MacFarlane (Henry Daniell) and his murderous assistant Gray (Boris Karloff); MacFarlane's mistress Meg (Edith Atwater) meets the similarly "husband-less" Mrs. Marsh (Rita Corday).

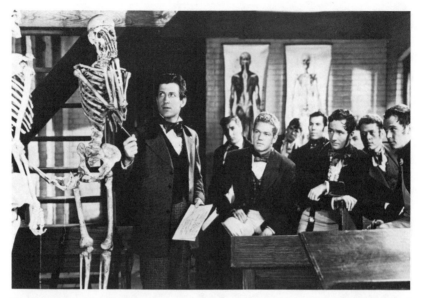

Fettes (Russell Wade) passes on the "mathematics of anatomy" learned from MacFarlane.

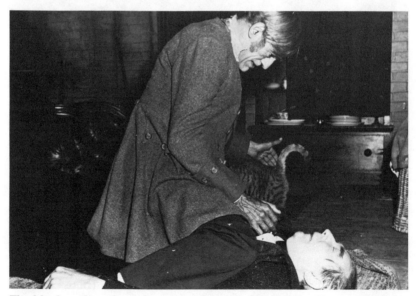

The blackmailing Gray dispatches his own blackmailer Joseph (Bela Lugosi).

perilously close to that of his mentor, it is especially fitting that the final break between them is dramatized in their differing perspectives on the body they carry. As the corpse repeatedly falls onto his shoulder, MacFarlane begins hallucinating that it is, in fact, Gray, who has returned to haunt him. While Stevenson's story attributes this vision to both MacFarlane and Fettes, the film limits it to the doctor, who is then killed as the coach lurches out of control and over a precipice, while his student is thrown clear and saved. The lamp which Fettes holds up to inspect the accident symbolizes his undistorted perspective—one which sees in the corpse that effectively frightened MacFarlane to death nothing more than the body of an old woman. That fantastic vision was simply a product of the doctor's disordered mind, a projected image of an internal horror which he long tried to repress or mask under a guise of respectability and scientific purpose.

A final addition to Stevenson's story underlines this pattern of visual revelations, of absences which persistently intrude upon a world of commonplace presences. In an extreme long shot we see Fettes leaving the accident; as he walks into the dark background, he lights his way with the lamp he used to inspect the bodies. Over this image a heavily—almost clumsily—didactic title is superimposed, stating, "It is through error that man tries and rises. It is through tragedy he learns. All the roads of learning begin in darkness and go out into the light." This awkward bit of moralizing implies that the cycle of grave robbings and murders in the name of science is over and that Fettes at least will not follow the path laid out by his strange father figure. The image which these words interpret so moralistically, however, conveys a much more complex message. On the one hand, it recalls the opening shots of the cobbled, well-lit, bustling streets of Edinburgh, so that the two scenes form a frame that comments upon the story of MacFarlane and Fettes. The paired scenes remind us of the two paths open to man: the common, dayworld avenue of picturesque surfaces, and the darker, vesperal road—or *via regia*—which leads, like the rough path in the final shot, into our own dark background, but which thereby serves to connect absence and presence, binding them into a broader, more extensive, and finally more challenging environment for man to inhabit.

At the same time the final shot comments on the narrative's own effort at a kind of depth analysis. While the body of the film demonstrates the deceptive nature of those initial images of civilization, the last scene, in its emphasis on a dirt road dimly winding through a rough, natural landscape, suggests a necessary vesperal complement. Within this vista, Fettes seems a small, fragile figure, although one who now carries a deeper understanding of both his world and himself. It is this sort of "revival" of life which, Hillman asserts, typically "emerges from the threat to survival," just as a sense of the soul can grow out of our frequent fantasies about death.[13] Having survived this encounter, Fettes takes with him a larger knowledge than he could ever have gained from MacFarlane and his scientific expertise, which, like the lamp he carries, might light his way along the hazardous paths he has yet to travel.[14] This suggestive combination of light and dark, man and nature, direction and disorder makes for a particularly striking image, one paradigmatic of the larger thrust of the Lewton films. In it we can discern a movement into the psyche's depths, although one accompanied by the light of understanding, as man seeks therein a more encompassing vision and more fundamental truth than science's mechanistic explanations of life and death afford. Literally, we might speculate that Fettes is returning to his true father, a minister who, we were earlier told, resides in the country, deliberately apart from the modern society which MacFarlane seems to represent. In such a scenario Fettes enacts precisely the sort of spiritual return that *Isle of the Dead* advocated in its plea for belief from mankind. With his secular faith undermined, his belief solely in, as General Pherides put it, "what I can feel, and see, and know about" called into question, Fettes returns to a world in which the enigmatic and indeed the spiritual still hold a place, still speak to man of that which finds little or no expression in his everyday world.

In depicting the interrelationship of these surfaces we term reality and the depths we commonly deny or explain away, *The Body*

Snatcher offers a complex vision of the world and a reminder of our complicity in its make-up. In this respect alone it is a considerable development of Stevenson's hardly subtle story. What makes the film all the more effective, however, is the manner in which it permits the fantastic to surface quietly from beneath a veneer of normalcy, thus revealing not only the weakness of our rational perspective, but also a certain horror that lurks within it. Consequently, *The Body Snatcher* offers a vision of grotesquery more subtle, yet also more truly photogenic than that found among the ghouls and monsters which so populated the horror genre during the 1940s. In focusing our attention beneath the surface, on man and his actions in all their ambiguity of motivation and unintended effect, this film, like its predecessors, revealed those more unsettling horrors that come from within, manifestations of the ghosts with which we commonly haunt our own lives as a result of the deals we try to work with death itself.

In the process *The Body Snatcher* also affords an insight into the fundamental attraction of fantasy films. In its examination of the desire for both experience and demarcation, we see mirrored our own fascination with the horror form, which permits us to unearth our darkest desires or fears, but also to stand apart from them, fascinated yet detached from the full implications of our fascination. With the consequences of such a perspective dramatically made clear, however, we are snatched back, saved from a fall to which we indeed seem prone. In effect, a film like *The Body Snatcher* saves us from this dualism, this separation of mind and body which prompts a deal with death; instead, we are granted a more comprehensive perspective, which allows us to see not just underground but into that underworld realm where the psyche finds its meaning.

10 Bedlam's Walls and the Age of Reason

What the classical period had confined was not only an
abstract unreason which mingled madmen and libertines,
invalids, and criminals, but also an enormous reservoir of
the fantastic, a dormant world of monsters supposedly
engulfed in the darkness of Hieronymus Bosch which had
once spewed them forth. One might say that the fortresses
of confinement added to their social role of segregation
and purification a quite opposite cultural function. Even
as they separated reason from unreason on society's
surface, they preserved in depth the images where they
mingled and exchanged properties.

—Michel Foucault
Madness and Civilization

Along the vesperal path of dream and fantasy which James
Hillman describes, the psyche encounters significant and
even salutary images usually obscured from consciousness.
These are "the necessary" and also "axiomatic, self-evident images to which psychic life and our theories about it ever return,"[1]
as well as what the modern world and its everyday perspective
admonish us to overlook or dismiss from consciousness. Because
they seem to speak in another, disconcerting voice, in a language—that of the imagination—which challenges the rational
system by which we ordinarily conceive of our world, we allow
them to remain separated or walled off from us; thus we need the
special return found in dreams and fantasizing. The animal imagery in *Cat People* and *The Leopard Man*, that of the sea in *I
Walked with a Zombie* and *The Ghost Ship*, or the images of ancient
Greece and its mythic heritage which dominate *Isle of the Dead*
show how the Lewton films draw upon this fantasy language, granting it a say on the commonplace and thoroughly rational worlds

that their surfaces describe. It is in the last film of the RKO series, *Bedlam* (1946), however, that this imaginal realm was tapped for its most disconcerting challenge to the modern world and its rule of reason. This film's examination of the Age of Reason focuses on one of the period's most telling creations, the mental asylum, to lay bare a most feared image, that of unreason in its undeniably human aspect.

The force of reason and the perspective which it affords on man and his world are recurrent concerns of the Lewton films. In fact, these motifs drive their examinations of power or authority in modern society, especially the power which we unwittingly exert upon ourselves, as we haunt the self and the human environment with specters that effectively shape our lives. By juxtaposing the potent forms of reason with the threatening otherness of unreason, therefore, a film like *Bedlam* can point up an underlying fragility in the former, and thus accomplish an important reflexive task, characteristic of fantasy. Like the dreams and fantasizing of which Hillman speaks, it holds a mirror up to the psyche, showing a consciousness which "is reflective, watching not just the physical reality in front of the eyeballs and by means of them, but seeing into the flickering patterns within that physical reality, and within the eyes themselves," within to those often denied depths where reason and unreason indeed meet and become one.[2]

In conjunction with this imaginal perspective, *Bedlam*'s narrative structure illustrates the kind of deconstructive process which the Lewton films produce on our normal vision of the self and society. Several of the later films were criticized because they seemed to stray from a successful fantasy formula in favor of the melodramatic. James Agee, for instance, the most insistent champion of the Lewton productions, found both *The Body Snatcher* and *Bedlam* to demonstrate their producer's "interest in costume movies, which seem to draw on his romantic-literary weaknesses more than on his best abilities."[3] In similar fashion the *New York Times* found *Bedlam* unsatisfactory, seeing it as a misbegotten sociological study, handicapped by elaborate period detailing.[4] This ornateness and intricate plotting, however, have apparently led critics to overlook the film's pervasive ironies. While clearly drawing on a tradition of melodramatic narrative, as even director Mark Robson admits,[5] *Bedlam* ultimately undercuts that formula in a way that recalls *The Leopard Man*'s manipulation of classical narrative. As a result, it forms a most fitting coda for the RKO fantasy series, attesting to the complexity with which the films carried out their vesperal exploration.

Like most investigations of society's institutions, *Bedlam*'s narrative is superficially melodramatic, but it treats this formula ironically. The film focuses on the linkage of madness and criminality, of reason and social order which Michel Foucault describes; and it juxtaposes these pairings in order to underscore the paradoxical manner in which society maintains its civilized surface and also to reveal the deeper links with unreason which it persistently tries to deny. This strategy, however, is at odds with what John Cawelti sees as melodrama's "characteristic purpose," differentiating it "from the other major formulaic types. This type has at its center the moral fantasy of showing forth the essential 'rightness' of the world order."[6] It accomplishes this by presenting "the trials and tribulations that the good are subjected to by the wicked together with the final triumph of the good and the punishment of the wicked," and in its most common form, as "social melodrama," the genre examines a particular institution into which it "claims a special insight." Despite its subject and a conclusion which comfortingly combines triumph and punishment, *Bedlam* is haunted by a dark shadow, a fundamental questioning of both the "world order" and the voice of reason upon which it is predicated. An opening title card hints at this strategy, noting that the film is set in "London—1761," and reminding us that "the people of the Eighteenth Century called their period 'The Age of Reason.'" An unusual narrative device complements this initial stance; drawings from William Hogarth's *Rake's Progress* are interspersed in the film to lend their bitterly satiric tone to all that we see.[7] In fact, the movie's tone might be termed Hogarthian, for *Bedlam* casts a similarly ironic and jaundiced eye on each character and event with which the engravings are juxtaposed. The effect is to suggest a larger, commentative intelligence speaking through the film's images about the façade of reason behind which society and its institutions hide their disconcerting contradictions. Rather than revealing the ultimate rightness and intelligibility of the social order, then, *Bedlam* puts these appearances to question by revealing the deeper unreason upon which man so often founds his rational structures.

To the extent that the film does resemble melodrama, it follows the mythic pattern Frank McConnell describes in his exploration of the archetypal roots of this genre. His analysis sees in melodrama a fundamental story of established civilization, with the city providing "the scene of a conflict between its ostensive morality and its hidden violation of its own laws."[8] The hero of this mythic tale is an "agent . . . who strives to understand the real rules governing the operation of his society, and to bring them, even if by violence, into alignment with the precepts according to which the City was founded." Compounding his task is that the modern city is "unwalled," that is, it lacks the original physical boundaries which modeled a kind of moral architecture for its inhabitants and imparted an important cohesiveness. Much like the hero of the monomyth outlined by Joseph Campbell, therefore, this figure looks to retrieve or reassert some hidden truth or pattern of meaningful existence for his society.[9] In the case of *Bedlam*, the task of understanding is linked to an unexpected prevalence of walls, and the act of retrieval or moral assertion is shown to rely upon an understanding of how flimsy such structures are for constructing a truly humane world.

This mythic perspective also sheds light on *Bedlam*'s historical reconstructions, particularly the charges that too much attention was paid to period detailing. Actually, the Lewton team took a number of liberties with the film's setting, fashioning a historically questionable background, but one conducive to its mythic subtext. Even though the Tories were out of power in England after 1714, they are shown in control of the government, running it for their own selfish ends and in opposition to the Whigs, who are depicted as the champions of a public or social consciousness. The Tories are personified in the fat, buffonish Lord Mortimer, who spends his days seeking amusement from any source, while the Whigs are represented by the historical figure John Wilkes, a liberal reformer of the era. The film early codifies its fictive distinction between these two characters and their parties on the occasion of an entertainment that Lord Mortimer stages at Vauxhall. When the Whigs find distasteful his use of Bedlam's "loonies" for entertainment, he accuses them of having no sense of humor, to which Wilkes responds, "The Tories care only for the jest, but we Whigs have some concern for the humanities." If this dialectic is historically suspect, it serves an effective rhetorical purpose, precisely establishing the nature of that subtle "violation" McConnell describes—ostensibly of others, ultimately of the self and its most humane instincts—with which the narrative is concerned.

The primary scene of this violation and chief image of the conjunction of reason and unreason here is St. Mary's of Bethlehem Hospital, or Bedlam, as it was popularly called. While set in the Age of Reason and in the great metropolis of London, then flourishing under "enlightened" English law, the film emphasizes from the start the lack of a rational or enlightened approach to the problems of the mad. Bedlam's high brick walls shut up into a separate, brutish world of darkness those with whom society chose not to deal. As Foucault has shown, during this era segregation and confinement became the major cultural responses to the threat which madness was thought to pose. This recourse "had nothing to do with any medical concept"; as Foucault explains, it was simply "an instance of order" being asserted in an age which highly valued the appearance of order.[10] By creating such institutions and a policy of confinement, "classical rationalism could watch out for and guard against the subterranean danger of unreason, that threatening space of absolute freedom."[11] Thus, all who failed to conform to society's notion of order—invalids, criminals, and the poor, along with the insane—were equally subject to incarceration and segregation from the rational world. In some instances, as the film notes, husbands wishing their freedom committed their unwanted wives. In the case of the writer Oliver Todd, a fondness for drink prompts his family to have him shut away from temptation so that he may work. And the poet Colby has fallen victim to the jealousy of the asylum's head, the poetaster Sims, who has first had his rival confined and then caused his death. The picture which *Bedlam* offers, then, is much like that which Foucault describes, especially when he explains how the period perceived "indigence, laziness, vice, and madness mingled in an equal guilt within unreason; madmen were caught in the great confinement of poverty and unemployment, but all had been promoted, in the proximity of transgression, to the essence of a Fall."[12] Because the fall from sanity was linked to a moral fall as well, any human concern or responsibility could easily be denied. Consequently, those judged insane found themselves not subject to an enlightened treatment or compassion, but bound to a dark world for the sake of convenience or ill will, as society learned to use its powerful voice of repression and assert its normative dayworld perspective.

The narrative fittingly opens on this note of confinement and repression, joined to the motif of a fall, as a long shot shows Colby dangling from Bedlam's heights, where a warder pries loose his grip and sends him plunging to his death. This scene serves as a signpost for the rest of the narrative, indicating not so much an individual flaw or sickness as a social ill, signaling that we have here entered essentially a fallen world. As symbolized by Colby, the imagination itself seems to have fallen, with its place being usurped by reason and its self-flattering creations. Thus Colby is replaced by the poetaster Sims, poetry by the pretentious display of wit, and art by the mindless "entertainments" of the wealthy, here represented by the buffoonish Lord Mortimer, a "patron of the arts" who has also taken a special interest in Bedlam.

In this Age of Reason man has enthroned his rational capacities and set about imposing an artificial order on his world, and he has begun by casting out those whose claims to reason are suspect. Sims, consequently, treats his charges at Bedlam as exhibits, as nonhuman things visitors can glimpse for tuppence. At Mortimer's entertainment Sims has a boy painted gold to portray Reason, although he well knows that gilding his body in this way will kill him. Like many others in his society, however, Sims believes that his "loonies" have no claim to the human realm and that they are an embarrassment to a culture which prides itself on the show of reason: "They have their world and we have ours. . . . Ours is a human world; theirs is a bestial world, without reason, without soul. They're animals. Some are dogs; these I beat. Some are pigs; these I let wallow in their own filth. Some are tigers; these I cage." The link he makes—"without reason, without soul"—reveals the sharp schism a controlling reason can inflict on the human world, while it also points up the contrast between this perspective and the imaginal one which Hillman sees as necessary to psychic health. The images the imagination apprehends, he explains, "are both the raw materials and finished products of psyche, and they are the privileged mode of access to knowledge of soul. Nothing is more primary."[13] With this imaginative realm proscribed, man can easily be denied a soul and even be cast among the animals, since once relegated to the animal, the madman no longer casts his disturbing shadow on the sane, to call into question the foundation of their world by demonstrating its frailty. The fall envisioned by *Bedlam,* then, is a descent into the same rational, egocentric perspective which characterizes modern man and constantly threatens, despite pretensions otherwise, to render him less than human, even to deprive him of a soul.

In keeping with the elevation of reason over the imagination, society here seems more concerned with maintaining appearances than with the welfare of those locked-away specters of madness. In particular, the narrative repeatedly emphasizes the characters' concern with the way they look in the eyes of the world. For this reason, two seemingly inconsequential scenes are paralleled: in one, Lord Mortimer has his elaborate wig powdered, after the fashion of the day, while in the other, Sims hurriedly dons his worn headpiece to receive Nell Bowen, so that he might properly impress her. Although from different social levels, the lord and commoner are similarly preoccupied with their images, a trait later prompting their conspiracy to commit Nell to Bedlam when she publicly ridicules them. In fact, the manner in which Nell is committed points up the full extent of this concern with surfaces and how they might be interpreted. When Nell first suggests that Mortimer increase government appropriations for the care and treatment of Bedlam's inmates, Sims quickly dissuades Mortimer by noting that such an action would increase the latter's taxes and thus make it more difficult for him "to keep up appearances." The charge of insanity subsequently lodged against Nell is couched in similar terms, as she is accused of eating a £300 note which Mortimer offered her as a bribe to cease her public gibes at him. The explanation that she simply wished to show her contempt for his wealth and its abuses carries little weight with those who hear her case, however, since they customarily judge such proceedings solely on their appearances. In light of the prevailing belief that wealth was a sign of divine favor and thus of righteousness, Nell's action seems all the more disturbing and inexplicable to these upholders of the status quo.

As Nell's trial amply illustrates, anyone can be declared mad in this society, although especially vulnerable are those who threaten to disturb its normal appearance. Rational man can simply and easily twist a term like "insane" so that it might describe almost any action or denote a dangerous opposite to any social canon. Through such semantic manipulations, language itself becomes a force of confinement, effectively shutting off whatever it labels from further consideration. Hillman speaks to this danger when he explains how "once experiences have been labeled and declared abnormal, we cannot learn from them or let them carry us beyond their immediate actuality."[14] Colby's death pointedly dramatizes this problem. When forced to account for his rival's death, the glib Sims simply repudiates the charges against him with a quibble: "That was no murder," he equivocates, merely "an accident," "a misadventure contrived by the victim and executed by nature's law that all who lose their grip on gutters must fall." When Nell later accuses Sims of murdering the boy who played Reason by blocking his pores with gilt, Sims similarly excuses his culpability, using the sort of pseudoscientific phrasings which Swift so harshly satirized, as he protests that, to be precise, the boy "killed himself . . . by his own exhalations." In like fashion what Sims terms his "treatment" for the insane, which he plans to use on Nell before releasing her, is actually a form of torture, a calculated display of madness itself that in the past has only worsened the condition of its recipients, reducing them to an animal level by wrenching them loose from what reason they still cling to—as Colby was pulled loose from the asylum's gutters. While language is usually thought to signal man's rationality and permit him to communicate with others, it has here been perverted into a means of confusion and human isolation, a method of maintaining society's appearances by restricting its undesirable or threatening elements behind a façade of words or confining them within a realm of silence.

For this world to be put right, according to most mythic formulations, someone must pierce through these appearances and breach the walls of confinement and rationality. As Campbell in his *Hero with a Thousand Faces* describes the normal pattern, it involves "a penetration" into a realm of "darkness, the unknown, and danger," which results in "a life-enhancing return" and a new perspective on this world.[15] In the kind of irony which typifies the Lewton films, that task is here entrusted to an actress, someone accustomed to trafficking in illusion. Nell Bowen, we learn, once played Aurora in *The Rivals*, and apparently it is her function to bring a dawn of sorts to the dark world of the insane.[16] To underscore the archetypal task of bringing light into this realm, the film employs a pattern of association, whereby Nell is consistently juxtaposed with or framed amid lights or candles. During Mortimer's Vauxhall entertainment, for example, reaction shots of Nell and her patron are intercut with those depicting Sims's abuse of his charges, contrasting the former's horror at these events with the latter's mindless enjoyment of the proceedings. By way of emphasis two large candles frame Nell's face and flicker as her rage builds. When she eventually turns her wrath on Sims, we see her face in close-up, while in the background a three-tined candelabra burns brightly. Turning back to Mortimer to register her disapproval, Nell is again framed between two large candles while he sits alone against a dark background. This visual pattern then links this scene to the following one, as she searches for her

Nell Bowen (Anna Lee) and the light motif.

Nell surveys Sims's (Boris Karloff) "enlightened" methods.

Bedlam's interior, modeled on a print from Hogarth.

Hannay (Richard Fraser) threads the human labyrinth of Bedlam.

Like *Cat People*'s Irena, Nell finds herself trapped by the walls of reason.

Quaker friend Hannay, who earlier remarked on her obvious concern for those whom Sims mistreated.[17] They meet in a darkness emblematic of the bleak and uncaring world they inhabit, and she asks him if he indeed thinks her "a person of kind heart." Behind them, meanwhile, a barber's window shines brightly in the night, its twelve panes each lit by a burning candle, the sum of which metaphorically answers her question.

After Nell is confined to Bedlam, this motif reappears to suggest the mercy and human concern she brings into this world. Most of the inmates are not permitted to have a candle or lamp for fear they might start a fire in their straw bedding; as a result, they live in a darkness that signals their segregated status. A select group, "the people of the pillar," considered to be "the safe ones, the good ones, the wisest," however, share a single candle as a mark of their near normalcy. Nell initially aligns herself with this elite group, seeking the security and haven of reason their candle signifies; however, the groans of another patient, suffering from one of Sims's treatments, move her and reaffirm her compassion. Nell appropriates the single candle to light her way in Bedlam's dark recesses and, when she finds the sufferer, dresses his wounds with strips torn from her petticoat. The light of reason thus joins with the flame of human compassion to penetrate the asylum's foreboding darkness and locate a new possibility for community in its chaotic interior. Shortly afterward, Nell practically transforms the world of Bedlam, prompting one inmate to describe her to a visitor as "an angel in this darkness."

One of the more subtle links to *Bedlam*'s mythic underpinnings is this angel's reluctance to undertake the task of exploring the deceptive appearances of her world and penetrating to its dark core. A common element of the heroic monomyth, as Campbell explains, is a "refusal of the call," stemming from "a refusal to give up what one takes to be one's own interest."[18] As Lord Mortimer's "protégée," Nell certainly has much to give up; she enjoys a privileged life, her apartment, furnishings, clothes, and sundry pleasures all the result of his largesse, while in recompense she only needs to amuse her patron with her ready wit. Consequently, she hesitates to question a world that grants her privilege or to admit the flaws in its glittering mirror of modern society.

Her temporary hesitation, however, reminds us of how the visible, rational world maintains its own system and effectively thwarts any questioning. In a speech that reinterprets the pervasive wall and confinement motifs here, the Quaker Hannay puts the moral challenge to Nell. He explains how, as a stone mason, he attempts to construct a moral framework for his world: "I build well. Let others build as well and soon this city will become a clean and decent habitation." His implication is that Nell, too, must begin with herself, conquering her fear of being mocked for her compassion and her dread of those needing help. When she first visits Bedlam to investigate the plight of the "loonies," an unusually elaborate shot sequence dramatizes the start of her shift in attitude. Walking along an outer corridor, Nell is shot in close-up, the camera tracking with her, but as she enters the inmates' chambers, the camera quickly tracks back from a reaction shot of her face to a long boom shot of her surroundings. From the small, subjective world of her own thoughts and concerns, Nell's perspective is abruptly expanded, as she must confront this other, usually walled-off human dimension. Reacting in a predictable human fashion, she recoils in horror at both the inmates themselves and Sims's mistreatment of them. Outside of Bedlam's walls, though, with that threat to her normal perspective again confined in its darkness, Nell readily denies any care, unwittingly echoing Sims as she tells Hannay, "I have no pity for them—animals without souls." And in a remark which ironically reintroduces the candle/light motif, she protests her disinterest: "My heart is like a flint, sir. It may strike sparks, but they're not warm enough to burn." Of course, a quite opposite attitude leads to her own imprisonment and puts her character to the ultimate test. When forced to live among the insane, without society's walls to segregate their unreason from her, Nell sounds even more like Sims, as she tells Hannay that "these people are like beasts" and pleads for "a weapon to defend myself with." If human sympathy was difficult to evoke from a secure, civilized distance, the film implies, it may be al-

most impossible from the other side of those walls. Nell's protest—
"I still want to aid them, but I cannot here, not here where they're
all about me"—thrusts home the paradox implicit in the walls
which society erects to confine unreason, hold it at a safe distance,
and thus maintain, unchallenged, the purity of its own rational
order.

Placed behind those walls, however, one does see things differ-
ently, especially the self. As Hillman says, the process of "entering the underworld is like entering the mode of reflection."[19] In
Campbell's mythic view, exploring this other dimension involves
"the agony of breaking through personal limitation," or more precisely, "the agony of spiritual growth."[20] In keeping with this pattern, Sims repeatedly taunts Nell for her fears of those she planned
to help, as he tries to demonstrate "that all those mawkish theories
you've learned from the Quaker are lies. . . . Men are not brothers; men are not born good and kind. Even the mindless ones are
savage and must be ruled with force." When he tests Nell, offering
her a place with one of his caged maniacs and fully expecting her
to refuse and thus admit the correctness of his brutish views, then,
she faces an either/or proposition: as Sims puts it, to "enter the
cage; gentle him with a word, conquer him with kindness, or admit
that your Quaker lies." By treading this vesperal path, entering
the madman's cage and speaking to him in a humane, understanding way, however, she succeeds in casting off her old, fearful self
which dreaded all that was abnormal and a threat to her rational
world. What Nell's passage emphasizes is the full extent to which
reason and unreason have actually "mingled and exchanged properties" here. As we see, people like Sims are really more dangerous than the caged inmates, precisely because they try hardest to
maintain a sharp demarcation between themselves and the otherness of unreason, to hold fast to their division of men into human
and animal categories, to grant a soul to some and deny it to others. Fittingly, this scene concludes with the camera inside the cage
with Nell, showing Sims in medium shot through the bars and
ironically making him look like the imprisoned one.

To reform such a society, according to the formula mapped out by McConnell, the mythic figure must "locate the clue, the fact, the essential bit of information which will resolve the seeming contradictions and chaos of its life into a fundamental continuity with . . . the past of its own best ideas of nobility, dignity, and decency."[21] In the melodramatic tradition, this movement translates into an attempt to establish a continuity between the present and an older, forgotten or ignored system of values in which a ground for retribution or justice might be located. Hannay's appeal to John Wilkes, that he intercede for Nell, hints at such a reassertion of order, particularly when Wilkes remarks that "this is still England . . . and we have laws here, laws of right and justice, and I shall see that Sims feels their full weight." From the start, however, the narrative has established an ironic view on the past and its "laws," so it is appropriate that Sims meets with justice at the hands of those he has tormented, as Bedlam's inmates seize their keeper and, doubling the earlier mock trial in which Nell was committed, conduct their own trial to determine, on the evidence of his mistreatment of them, whether Sims is himself insane. With a prosecutor repeatedly shouting, "Split him in two," the trial mocks the "laws of right and justice" that Wilkes lauds, while also reminding us of the dualistic vision Sims has so violently visited upon his charges. More important, though, it testifies to a fundamental sense of justice inhering not so much in the laws as in human nature—a nature marked by the same mixture of reason and unreason Foucault describes. Consequently, the mock trial points up the flaws in Sims's character, which becomes a mirror of his society, its faults, and especially its great concern for appearances. Like Boris Karloff's character of Gray in *The Body Snatcher,* he is shown as a pathetic figure, slavishly following the example of his "enlightened" age and acting largely from fear of losing the position that gives him some standing in society. Thus he confesses to his inmate jury that he "was frightened . . . of the great world, the great world of this age that gave me my place, the comforts and the authority, what little I have of riches. . . . What that world thinks, I must think; what they do, I must do." Recognizing an elemental kinship in this admission of fear and compulsive conformity to society's unspoken rules, those whom Sims previously described as "beasts" ironically find reason in his plea, understand despite their segregation from all understanding, and finally acquit him. The only trace of a melodramatic justice occurs when Sims, just as his captors are about to release him, is stabbed by one of the inmates he has most harshly abused and, while still alive, is entombed in the walls of his asylum—buried behind the boundaries which have symbolized his power.

The wall in which Sims is immured subsequently becomes a key image of justice's ironic operation, as well as of the culture's efforts to segregate reason and unreason into mutually exclusive realms. First, this structure symbolizes Sims's venality and corruption. Before contracting for its construction, he demanded a bribe—one which Hannay refused to pay; so by being entombed in this emblem of his dishonesty, Sims receives a terrible and most ironic justice. Second, this image links the recurrent wall motif to the theme of confinement, and thus to the era's basic approach to the problem posed by unreason in its various shapes. In this context we might recall the film's opening shot of Colby dangling against Bedlam's outer wall. Every exterior scene of the asylum begins with such a long shot, emphasizing its stark brick walls rising above the busily heedless pedestrians of London, or the spiked fence across the street, intruding its menacing points into the lower portion of the frame. Inside the asylum the emphasis is similarly on the dark walls, doors, and cages which partition off the inmates from each other and from the outside world, forming both their torment and their protection. With Sims's entombment, the principle of confinement and exclusion is visited upon its practitioner, who, in his last, half-maddened glimpse before the final stone is set in place, reminds us how easily these positions might be reversed and, in effect, how unreason or madness inheres in the walls themselves and the impulse of confinement they signify. Finally, the wall recalls McConnell's description of the melodramatic world as essentially a sort of "unwalled city," a place lacking the physical boundaries that once would have identified it as the locus of social order. We can now discern how prevalent these walls still are and at the same time how inadequate for ensuring a real social cohesion or order. In fact, *Bedlam* reveals the danger of creating such a "walled" world without the prior "construction" of which Hannay speaks: a human commitment to that order it signifies. In more modern terms the problem essentially consists of creating an institution to deal with the human psyche before we have a clear sense of the nature of the psyche. Through this recurrent wall imagery, then, the film dramatizes the danger of substituting real walls, or the hard, uncaring, and heedless attitudes they suggest, for what in the modern world must take their place, self-understanding and fellow concern.

Another occurrence of the wall motif deserves mention for the way it places these various themes in the context of the narrative's larger vesperal movement. The psychic activity of dream and fantasy, Hillman explains, evokes important archetypal images which offer a new perspective on the self. In Hannay's search of Bedlam's dark halls for Nell, we see a clear model of this notion. To gain entrance to the asylum, the Quaker helps some fellow masons carry the stones for Bedlam's new basement wall. Once inside, Hannay is told he can gain a free glimpse of the "loonies" by following a long, unlighted hallway: "It's a little dark, but if you get to the end of it, you'll get an eyeful." As he inches along the dark corridor, the Quaker is suddenly startled, in the sort of bus effect which is a trademark of the Lewton films, by an arm thrusting out from one of the seemingly solid walls; and as he recoils in fright to the other side of the hall, another arm grabs for him from that area. Subsequently—and almost surrealistically—those arms quickly multiply, spasmodically waving and grasping at Hannay from both sides, forcing him into a small, lighted space in the corridor's center, away from either wall. What the darkness had obscured is that the hall was simply a passage between two rows of cages in which Sims locks his most disturbed patients, those dark "walls" no more than the bars confining and segregating the world of unreason from a rational society that finds its existence so threatening. Hannay's dark passage frightens but does not harm him, and it indeed affords the predicted "eyeful," a perspective on darkness itself. A world which depends on such walls and on institutions like Bedlam must inevitably seem a menacing place; and in such a world man will always feel compelled to walk a very narrow and frightening path.

The film ends on a scene which again emphasizes Bedlam's basement wall, and which further comments on the narrative's departure from the melodramatic. As the authorities arrive to rescue and, at Wilkes's insistence, punish Sims according to the "laws of right," the mysterious disappearance of the Apothecary General stalls any resolution. Society can hardly reassert its own system of justice in the absence of either criminal or crime. The officers of the court simply meet a wall of silence from Bedlam's inmates, and from Hannay and Nell as well—a wall as impenetrable as the newly constructed one which stands, unexamined, before them. Consequently, the film leaves us with not a simple restoration of order, a making right of all that had been wrong in this world, but a society which still has its walls, its depths to be penetrated, and a horror behind those surfaces that even the mad, in their fear of the rational world's retribution, have felt compelled to erect.

This combination of the telling image and the blank surface it presents to the world, like the mixture here of a justice accomplished almost in spite of society's official rules of order, should argue against dismissing *Bedlam* as a simple costume melodrama, as a number of critics have done. Like the other films in the Lewton series, it follows a pointedly archetypal formula, detailing a heroic penetration and return, while also disclosing an image so troubling that modern man has sought to segregate it from his world, confine it behind walls, and deny its human visage. As Campbell says, though, in the mythic, as in our fantasizings and dreams, we can glimpse "the dynamics of the psyche" at work.[22] What *Bedlam* particularly reveals is the manner in which the psyche shows itself, fashioning in its depths images of reason and unreason as they mingle and exchange properties. Because of our traditional proscriptions against madness, arising not only from a fear that it might prove contagious like a disease, but also from the challenge it poses to our normal perspective, such images prove especially effective material for fantasy and horror. In addition, they contribute to make *Bedlam* a singularly appropriate conclusion for the RKO fantasy series. It effectively sums up the ongoing project of these films: a questioning of the various forms and rationales we typically employ to structure and control our world at the cost of shutting out a part of the self.

At one point in the narrative the inmate Long reveals to a visitor a picture flip-book he has created, its illusion of motion astounding the onlooker. The visitor sees a commercial potential in this invention and proposes that they use the stories of the writer Todd as the basis for additional moving picture books. Long goes a step further, outlining his idea of illuminating the pictures and projecting them upon a wall, but he quickly halts his scheming, as he recalls, "It's because of these pictures that I'm here." More than simply a movie "inside" joke, perhaps a comment on the Lewton group's view of their work, this scene also remarks on the larger strategy of the fantasy film. With a filmmaker, scriptwriter, and even an actress locked behind the asylum's walls, their imaginative perspectives confirming their madness to a rational world, *Bedlam* speaks in a momentarily direct way of the sort of indirection by which such films have to work their challenge to the commonplace. It is, in fact, their seeming madness which attracts us, as they project on a movie screen—or a wall—images which reason normally keeps immured, segregated, and confined from daily life, but which persistently move in the psyche's depths and ultimately cast their disturbing shadows on our everyday world, reminding us of how much our rational perspective implies its often denied opposite.

11 The Redemption of Nonphysical Reality

> Fantasy is the primordial force of the soul that would take
> everything back into its prior condition, ritualizing all
> occurrences, turning events into mythemes, fixing the
> trivia of each case history into the precise details,
> seemingly so irrelevant, of a legend, continually
> confabulating our lives into patterns that we can neither
> understand with our minds nor manage with our wills but
> which we can love with an *amor fati.*
>
> —James Hillman
> *The Myth of Analysis*

In both its literary and cinematic forms, a certain dualism or
tension commonly haunts our encounter with fantasy, as James
Hillman's comment implies.[1] This complex response, speaking
simultaneously of our anxieties and our unspoken desires, should
suggest the difficulty which can be expected to attend any study of
the form. Critical attention has usually focused either on the fear
and unease the fantastic generates or on the curious attraction it
holds for audiences—an attraction seen especially in recent years,
as the dominant film genres of horror, science fiction, and heroic
adventure have so successfully sprung from the fantasy impulse.
By grounding this study in a specific body of fantasy material, the
films produced by Val Lewton's unit at RKO Pictures, I have tried
to join these perspectives into a single focus on the larger topic of
cinematic fantasy. In addition to their quality as film narratives
and effectiveness as fantasy texts, these works offer a singularly
appropriate field for such investigation because their emphasis is
also twofold: first, they explore the potential for creating unease
not with grotesquery, but with archetypal images and a sense of
absence—what Lewton described as "dark patches"; second, they

locate a beneficial effect in this encounter with darkness, absence, and the mythic which seems paradigmatic of the best work in fantasy. These films thereby illustrate both a particular development of cinematic fantasy, what I have termed, borrowing from Hillman, "vesperal film," and a larger perspective that we might take to the entire form—one which links the usual matter and manner of the fantastic to an abiding dream which energizes film itself. The persistent human desire to create lifelike illusions, to fix life's flux and assert control over it, operates in fantastic no less than in realistic cinema, as we look to "redeem" not just "physical reality," as a theorist like Siegfried Kracauer would have it, but the nonphysical as well, especially the human psyche as it helps to shape the world of which it is a part.

Following the dualistic nature of its subject, this study has employed the term "vesperal film" in a manifestly double sense as well. First, and most important, it has served to designate a particular type of film, the form that preeminently took shape in the Lewton series during the 1940s. In this sense it refers to the labyrinthine, indeterminate, and dark perspective on the modern world and its rule of reason which these works offered, as they repeatedly deconstructed our normal vision of things and our usual methods of formulating or narrating the complexities of human experience. Second, the term describes a different mode of vision which fantasy films generally try to evoke. In their disconcerting interplay of absences and imagery, we encounter a kind of psychological language, speaking from within in recurrent figures and patterns, urging us to a larger, archetypal vision of the self and its role in the world. In sum, the phrase designates the manner in which certain films have developed this important psychological perspective and the various ways in which this perspective—through the mechanism of the movies—continues to impress itself upon us.

As developed by the Lewton unit, the vesperal film describes a vivid movement within—a penetration of the forms of society, of the patterns in which we typically conceive of and narrate our lives, and of the psyche itself as it interprets all around. The empty spaces and menacing shadows abounding in such films signal the various depths awaiting penetration, while they also hint of a danger implicit in this activity. We can discern a model of this process in one of the most prominent and recurrent images of the series, that of an individual attempting to thread his way along a dark and uninviting passage or street. Alice's hurried walk down the deserted streets of New York in *Cat People*, Betsy's passage through the cane fields to the voodoo houmfort in *I Walked with a Zombie*, Amy Reed's frightened wandering amid the snows in *Curse of the Cat People*, and Hannay's exploration of Bedlam's dark corridors all evoke a frightening prospect in their suggestion of a menacing, even brutally naturalistic world through which an individual must make his way. The primary emphasis of such scenes, however, is less on what lurks in the dark mazes of city streets, back alleys, and building corridors than on how one perceives and responds to these enigmatic passages—whether they contribute to the ongoing psychic process of what Hillman terms "re-mythologizing consciousness."[2] By this motif, then, we are reminded of a subtler narrative at work in the Lewton films, a story of the human psyche and its difficult but necessary self-creating journey through life.

Another recurrent image we have described, that of the double, comments on the manner in which this fundamental psychic development occurs. The frequent doublings in these films, such as Irena and Alice in *Cat People*, Mary and her sister Jacqueline in *The Seventh Victim*, and *The Body Snatcher*'s MacFarlane and Gray, hint at a necessary encounter with the self, as these paired figures literally embody the psyche's various urgings and the individual's best and worst potentials. Such a confrontation almost forcibly shifts the individual's perspective away from the ego as a center of consciousness and primary measure of the world by calling attention to the self's other possible shapes and its normally repressed or denied desires. In the process it also reminds the psyche of its possible roots in another realm, an archetypal region where every aspect of consciousness finds its source and from which spring the images that move us so deeply yet incomprehensibly. The focus on man's rationality and his reliance on it to measure both the self and the world—that which culminates in *Bedlam*'s scrutiny of the Age of Reason and its pretenses—attests to modern man's lost perspective on the vast realm of mythic patterns and archetypal images, as well as to the tendency of his ego-consciousness to hold any such discomfiting matter beyond the pale, proscribed within a darkness that symbolizes his own inability to manage or understand it. By this focus, however, the Lewton films help to counter such an attitude; by reflecting the ego's distorted image of itself, they permit us to view the effects of a denial or subordination of the psyche's own underworld. They thereby take us along what Hillman—after Freud—terms the *via regia* or royal road into the unconscious, where we might glimpse the depths which underlie normal consciousness and give a most fundamental meaning to it.

Viewed in this light, the films discussed here offer a basic challenge to the manner in which we typically think of the fantasy form and its audience-related function. For example, Rosemary Jackson, echoing Tzvetan Todorov's commentary on the genre, describes the fantastic as being "preoccupied with limits," although she identifies in that sense of limitation an important subversive function.[3] "All that the modern fantastic suggests," she contends, "is the *impotence* of mind to transcend matter—and the grotesque victory of the latter."[4] By revealing and isolating this "impotence," fantasy in her view subverts our implicit faith in reason, in representations, and in the individual's power to impose a personal order on his world, while it also expresses a typically unspoken desire for different social and historical circumstances, that is, an alternative ideology. While in general agreement with the initial terms of her "subversive" interpretation, I find its conclusion more troubling. In analyzing the psychic activity of fantasy, Jackson arrives at a materialistic explanation, which sees in our fantasizings an unconscious mechanism for questioning or protesting against repressive material conditions. Seen from this perspective, fantasy effectively becomes a modeling of the individual's plight in society, as he is immersed in an exploitative or repressive society and longs for something other than this limited and limiting world.

Carl Jung sought to reverse the common belief which underlies such theories, that which "holds reality to be external, images to be the imprint of externals, and fantasies to be decayed or distorted impressions."[5] He saw in such a notion a fundamental devaluation of the psyche, interpreting it largely as a mirror of the material world and as dominated by its substance. Following Jung's lead and the subsequent work of archetypal psychology, one may see in the psychic activity of fantasy the mirror of a decidedly psychic concern. Hillman's seemingly radical assertion, that "only fantasies are utterly, incontrovertibly real,"[6] exemplifies such an approach, as it implies that the fundamental substance of reality derives from man's psychic participation in his world, that the psyche precedes the material world and not vice versa. Instead of discerning in our dreams and fantasizings a psychic "impotence" or a "decayed" version of reality—a second-hand access to our world and ourselves—we might find in them the clearest indication of the psyche's potency, and especially its capacity to overcome a material domination. If we must take a dialectical approach to the form at all, it should not be one which devolves into a contention between mind and matter, the self and some repressive or threatening otherness external to man. Rather, we should think in terms of the differing ways in which we may view our world, to employ Hillman's words once more, in terms of the contrast between our "dayworld" and "vesperal" perspectives.

Unfortunately, modern man seldom achieves this crucial perspective on the manner in which he views the self and all around him. As a result, Owen Barfield has argued, man is today in great need of "saving the appearances" of his world, that is, of striving against a "gradual disappearance of participation" in the phenomenal realm he inhabits, which results in a devitalization of the material world.[7] The problem facing modern consciousness, he explains, "can best be understood as a . . . continuous progress from a vague but immediate awareness of the 'meaning' of phenomena towards an increasing preoccupation with the phenomena themselves"; and the consequence of such "progress" is a kind of modern-day "idolatry," as we come to envision the phenomena of the world as objects separate from man, possessed of a mysterious life all their own, and capable of possessing our imaginations and desires.[8] To counter a lapse into such idolatry and to avoid eventually reducing the self in a similar manner to the status of yet another object in a field of objects, Barfield suggests, we need to subordinate the material and literal to the imagination, give the psyche primacy once more. In this way we might reinfuse appearances—"save" them—with a renewed sense of our own mysterious participation in their reality.[9]

This process of participation finds special emphasis in the Lewton films, as they repeatedly sketch out the manner in which we project into the abounding darkness and undefined presences around us various shapes drawn from our psyches, and ultimately from the archetypal reservoir of images on which all psyche draws. Besides establishing the enigmatic as an alluring external force or a threatening potential, though, they insist on "saving" the dark, defining it as an essential part of us. Despite their somber and, in the case of *The Seventh Victim*, sometimes even bleak surfaces, then, these films are never quite nihilistic. In the blind spaces of our normal vision, the limitations which characterize our verbal lexicon, and the aporia which inevitably mark even the stories we fashion, they locate not just a sense of human limitation, as Jackson or Todorov might argue, but also a passage into the enigmatic and thus a place for man within that darkness. Such a passage naturally evokes a level of anxiety, at least the common fears of what usually resides outside of our experience and conceptualizations and beyond our conscious control. Whatever fright or mystification we experience, however, is to good effect, since a psychic growth can follow only from this experience of unknowing and from our encounters with the disconcerting images to which the self gives rise. It is from such reflective experiences that we gain a new perspective on our role—and our responsibility—in shaping the human realm.

By investigating the particular strategy of the Lewton films, we can also gain a better understanding of how cinematic fantasy— and preeminently the vesperal form they pioneered—serves a re-

demptive function in keeping with a notion long held by film theo-
rists. In spite of its seeming remove from the commonplace, the
form does "redeem" reality, although hardly in the manner that
Kracauer, for example, envisioned. Film fantasy accomplishes this
redemption by extending the reach of the real, by embracing rather
than cordoning off the nonphysical into a separate and underval-
ued realm. Consequently, the mythic, the archetypal, and the imaginal—that which moves in the depths of the human psyche and
infuses the phenomenal world around us—find a place, not just
as additions to, but as the necessary foundation for what we term
physical reality. If the Lewton series established a substantial
backdrop of the mundane and supremely natural out of which fantastic and disturbing elements could unexpectedly arise, the purpose was not simply to enhance the shock effect or to demonstrate,
as one critic suggests, "the legitimacy of fear" in modern society.[10]
Rather, these films sought to mark the full, if often unperceived,
range of the real by making us mindful, as Hillman puts it, that
"there is no place we can stand . . . beyond the reach" of the
fantastic.[11]

The perspective afforded by vesperal films holds the key to this
redemption and, in fact, provides the fullest justification for our
use of the term. Their point of view is fundamentally reflective,
although the images with which we are confronted are unfamiliar,
not the figurations of the ego we might expect, but visions of the
psyche's participation in the world. In the normal human development of this perspective through the commonplace activities of
dreaming and fantasizing, Hillman sees an ongoing process of
"soul-making," as the psyche speaks in its own, often misunder-
stood language of a state of understanding and being for which the
self secretly longs and toward which it naturally if almost imper-
ceptibly moves. In vesperal films we can detect a similarly "spiritual" function, at least in their attempt to transcend a purely
material or physical perspective. Films like those produced by the
Lewton unit effectively save reality from itself, from the baser,
more barren pull of the purely physical, and by doing so they
achieve a certain human redemption as well, saving man from his

persistent materialist and rationalist vision—from all that ties him to the less than human. Like the "dark patches [which] interrupt the light," as Plato described our dream images, these works discomfit us by disrupting our normal perspective, which in the light of day seems perfectly coherent and satisfactory. However, they thereby serve a fundamental need, even feed a hunger by finding for us a place in the dark, beyond our normal limitations. There our lives are indeed confabulated, the real and the fantastic joined to make best sense, a psychic sense, of human experience.

Notes

Notes to "Seeing in the Dark"

1. David Thomson, *America in the Dark* (New York: Random House, 1977), p. 18.

2. Tzvetan Todorov, *The Fantastic*, trans. Richard Howard (Ithaca, N.Y.: Cornell University Press, 1975), p. 120.

3. Eric S. Rabkin, *The Fantastic in Literature* (Princeton: Princeton University Press, 1976), p. 4, and Rosemary Jackson, *Fantasy* (London: Methuen, 1981), p. 30.

4. Jackson, *Fantasy*, p. 3.

5. See Siegfried Kracauer's *Theory of Film* (New York: Oxford University Press, 1960), particularly p. 46. In Kracauer's view films "assume three kinds of revealing functions. They tend to reveal things normally unseen; phenomena overwhelming consciousness; and certain aspects of the outer world which may be called 'special modes of reality.'" All three divisions presuppose that film's primary function is to make things *visible* for us and thereby "redeem" what must be otherwise a "fallen"—because unseen—world.

6. Mark Nash, "*Vampyr* and the Fantastic," *Screen* 17 (Autumn 1976), 34.

7. See William Troy's review of *King Kong*, reprinted in *American Film Criticism*, ed. Stanley Kauffmann and Bruce Henstell (New York: Liveright, 1972), p. 282.

8. Andrew Bergman, *We're in the Money* (New York: Harper & Row, 1972), p. 70.

9. Frank McConnell, "Rough Beasts Slouching," in *Focus on the Horror Film*, ed. Roy Huss and T. J. Ross (Englewood Cliffs, N.J.: Prentice-Hall, 1972), p. 31.

10. James Hillman, *Re-Visioning Psychology* (New York: Harper & Row, 1975), p. x. This point hints at an important kinship between Hillman's "imaginal" psychology and the phenomenological school of philosophy, as we can see even more clearly in his later comment: "Between

us and events, between the doer and the deed, there is a reflective moment."

11. The distinction implied by the term "vesperal" is essentially that between the perspective offered by a traditional Freudian model of psychology and that of Hillman's imaginal or archetypal approach. While most of our understanding of the psyche and its dreamwork derives from an effort to move our dreams into the light of day where they might be analyzed and, in effect, deprived of their troubling force, there is also the potential, Hillman explains, for an opposite kind of motion, "vesperal, into the dark" itself where our dreaming and fantasizing go on. See his *The Dream and the Underworld* (New York: Harper & Row, 1979), p. 1.

12. Quoted by Manny Farber in "Val Lewton: Unorthodox Artistry at RKO," *Kings of the B's,* ed. Todd McCarthy and Charles Flynn (New York: E. P. Dutton, 1975), p. 106.

13. John Houseman, *Run-Through* (New York: Simon and Schuster, 1972), p. 478. A more detailed account of Houseman's relationship to Lewton can be found in the second volume of his memoirs, *Front and Center* (New York: Simon and Schuster, 1979).

14. Joel Siegel, "Tourneur Remembers," *Cinefantastique* 2, no. 4 (1973), 25. Tourneur's comments on this partnership are worth quoting in full, particularly since the relationship he describes seems akin to that between the waking and dreaming self, upon which I put much weight in the interpretation of the films themselves: "Val was the dreamer and I was the materialist. I always had both feet on the ground. We complemented each other. By himself, Val might go off the deep end and I, by myself, might lose a certain poetry."

15. "RKO Radio: An Overview," *Velvet Light Trap* no. 10 (Fall 1973), 3.

16. Joel Siegel, *Val Lewton* (New York: Viking Press, 1973), p. 21. I am indebted to Siegel's study of Lewton's career for much of my background commentary.

17. "Tourneur Remembers," p. 25.

18. Dannis Peary, "Mark Robson Remembers RKO, Welles, and Val Lewton," *Velvet Light Trap* no. 10 (Fall 1973), 35.

19. Quoted by Siegel in *Val Lewton,* p. 25.

20. The extent to which this sense of collaboration filtered down into the various levels of the Lewton unit might be seen in another comment

offered by secretary Jessie Ponitz, who recalls that Lewton "often asked me for my advice, making me feel as though I was contributing much more than I actually was. When he asked for your opinion, you felt that he seriously wanted to hear what you had to say. You felt so much a part of the picture he was making. It was the same with everybody else; there was a great sense of collaboration, although it was really, and finally, Val's work. Afterwards, when you saw the finished movie on the screen, you felt that it all had something to do with you." Ibid.

21. See DeWitt Bodeen's lengthy discussion of this preproduction procedure in "Val Lewton," *More from Hollywood* (New York: A. S. Barnes, 1977), p. 310.

22. Rui Nogueira, "Robert Wise at RKO," *Focus on Film* no. 12 (Summer 1972), 45.

23. In a letter to his mother and sister, Lewton explains his reluctance to accept writing credit, under either his own or an assumed name, on his pictures: "I am and have always been a writer-producer. . . . The reason I do not ordinarily take credit for my very considerable work on my own scripts is that I have a theory that if I take credit, whenever I rewrite another's work, I can very properly be suspected of rewriting merely to get such credit." Quoted in Siegel, *Val Lewton*, p. 23.

24. For further discussion of this approach to the question of authorship, see Michel Foucault's "What is an Author?" in *Textual Strategies*, ed. Josué Harari (Ithaca, N.Y.: Cornell University Press, 1979), pp. 141–60.

25. "Notes Towards the Construction of Readings of Tourneur," in *Jacques Tourneur*, ed. Claire Johnston and Paul Willemen (Edinburgh: Edinburgh Film Festival, 1975), p. 16.

26. Even the two films which the Lewton unit produced that do not readily fall into the category of the fantastic, *Youth Runs Wild* and *Mademoiselle Fifi*, show a clear continuity with the fantasy themes and approach which characterize the larger body of films. My discussion of *Curse of the Cat People* traces several similarities to *Youth Runs Wild*. Like numerous other films in the series, *Mademoiselle Fifi* opens with an epigraph which establishes the story's setting and tone: "1870—The Franco-Prussian War—Then as in our own time, there was Occupied and Unoccupied Territory"; in the notion of "Occupied and Unoccupied Territory," we should discern an analogy to the demarcation of dayworld and fantasy realms which the other films develop in great detail.

27. Farber, "Val Lewton: Unorthodox Artistry at RKO," p. 107.

28. André Bazin, *What is Cinema?* trans. Hugh Gray (Berkeley: University of California Press, 1967), 1:20.

29. Peary, "Mark Robson Remembers," p. 35.

30. Bodeen, *More from Hollywood*, p. 310.

31. Peary, "Mark Robson Remembers," p. 36.

32. Ibid.

33. Quoted by Siegel in *Val Lewton*, p. 32.

34. See Richard Schmitt's discussion of phenomenological bracketing in his "Husserl's Transcendental-Phenomenological Reduction," in *Phenomenology*, ed. Joseph J. Kockelmans (Garden City, N.Y.: Doubleday, 1967), p. 59.

35. Todorov, *The Fantastic*, p. 122.

36. See Robin Wood's essay "Return of the Repressed," *Film Comment* 14 (July-Aug. 1978), 26.

37. Cited by Hillman in *Re-Visioning Psychology*, p. 23.

38. Ibid., p. xvi.

39. Hillman, *The Dream and the Underworld*, p. 53.

40. Quoted by Siegel in *Val Lewton*, p. 32.

41. See *Plato's Theory of Knowledge*, ed. and trans. F. M. Cornford (London: Routledge & Kegan Paul, 1935), p. 327.

Notes to "Structures of Absence: *Cat People*"

1. Curtis Harrington, "Ghoulies and Ghosties," *The Quarterly of Film, Radio and Television* 7 (1952–53), 195.

2. Quoted in Joseph McBride's "Val Lewton, Director's Producer," *Action* 11 (Jan.-Feb. 1976), 12.

3. Hillman, *The Dream and the Underworld*, p. 119.

4. Jacques Derrida, *Speech and Phenomena and Other Essays on Husserl's Theory of Signs*, trans. David B. Allison (Evanston: Northwestern University Press, 1973), p. 138.

5. Siegel, *Val Lewton*, p. 102.

6. Paul Willemen, "Notes Towards the Construction of Readings of Tourneur," in *Jacques Tourneur*, ed. Johnston and Willemen, p. 26.

7. Robin Wood, "The Shadow Worlds of Jacques Tourneur," *Film Comment* 8, no. 2 (1972), 67.

8. Siegel, *Val Lewton*, p. 29.

9. Hillman, *The Dream and the Underworld*, p. 10.

10. See Clarens's *An Illustrated History of the Horror Film* (New York: Capricorn Books, 1968), p. 113, and Siegel's *Val Lewton*, p. 102.

11. Hillman, *The Dream and the Underworld*, p. 11.

12. Although Siegel asserts that the epigraph is taken from Freud's work, I am unable to locate a precise source, particularly since Freud seldom uses the key term here, "sin," which seems more like an injection of that religious element that recurs throughout the Lewton films. In Freud's discussion of the relationship between religion and conscience, however, we might discern the broad outlines of this passage. See his *Civilization and Its Discontents*, trans. James Strachey (New York: W. W. Norton, 1961), pp. 31–32.

13. Carl Jung, *Modern Man in Search of a Soul*, trans. W. S. Dell and Cary F. Baynes (New York: Harcourt, Brace & World, 1953), p. 240.

14. See Aniela Jaffe's explanation of this motif in "Symbolism in the Visual Arts," *Man and His Symbols*, ed. Carl G. Jung (New York: Dell, 1968), p. 266.

15. That Lewton's own attitude was substantially different from this common perspective can be seen in his journal entry recording a particularly vivid and disturbing dream he had—one which also suggests the extent of his own contributions to *Cat People:* "I dreamt that a house cat jumped on my shoulders and began to claw me. I woke. The person in the berth above was stirring. Evidently some atavistic instinct to guard against a beast leaping from above brought on the dream and had awakened me." Quoted in Siegel's *Val Lewton*, p. 28.

16. Jung, *Modern Man in Search of a Soul*, p. 225.

17. Søren Kierkegaard, *The Sickness Unto Death*, in *Fear and Trembling* and *The Sickness unto Death*, trans. Walter Lowrie (Garden City, N.Y.: Doubleday, 1954), pp. 147–48.

18. Derrida, *Speech and Phenomena*, pp. 91–92.

19. See Joel Siegel's interview, "Tourneur Remembers," *Cinefantastique* 2, no. 4 (1973), 24.

Notes to "Narration and Incarnation: *I Walked with a Zombie*"

1. Jackson, *Fantasy*, pp. 45–46.

2. James Naremore, *The Magic World of Orson Welles* (New York: Oxford University Press, 1978), p. 26. For an additional discussion of RKO's status in the film industry at this time and its method of operation, see Tim Onosko's "RKO Radio: An Overview," *Velvet Light Trap* no. 10 (Fall 1973), 2–5.

3. Siegel, *Val Lewton*, p. 108.

4. Wood, "The Shadow Worlds of Jacques Tourneur," p. 70.

5. Jean-Paul Sartre, "'Aminadab' or The Fantastic Considered as a Language," in *Literary and Philosophical Essays*, trans. Annette Michelson (New York: Philosophical Library, 1957), p. 57.

6. Bruce Kawin, *Mindscreen* (Princeton: Princeton University Press, 1978), p. 6.

7. Ibid., p. 22.

8. Hillman, *Re-Visioning Psychology*, p. 90.

9. J. Hillis Miller, "Ariachne's Broken Woof," *Georgia Review* 31 (Spring 1977), 55.

10. In *The Fantastic in Literature* (Princeton: Princeton University Press, 1976), p. 197, Eric Rabkin argues that fantasy derives its epistemological content from its operation "against a background to which it offers a direct reversal." Consequently, it necessitates that we revise our usual perspective on that background, reconsider its significance. This formulation suggests as well that fantasy is, in fact, a method of redeeming reality by means of this structural contrast which we fashion for our world and which enables that world to have its own say.

11. Siegel, *Val Lewton*, p. 109.

12. "The Beauty of the Sea," in *Jacques Tourneur*, ed. Johnston and Willemen, p. 46.

13. Todorov, *The Fantastic*, p. 25.

14. According to Siegel, this last voice simply intones "the Christian funeral service" (*Val Lewton*, p. 114). This interpretation clearly misreads the last lines of the film and ill squares with what is occurring at this final point. Moreover, it suggests that he has missed the essential thrust of the narrative, which is to establish that mystery which cannot be explained away or excused. At the very least the narrative suggests that Christianity and voodoo are equally incommensurate when faced with such situations and that some combination of these perspectives might be more appropriate, as in the case of the injured child whom Mrs. Rand tends, he who has "one foot in the church and the other in the voodoo houmfort."

15. Kawin, *Mindscreen*, p. 50.

16. Todorov, *The Fantastic*, p. 31.

17. See Foucault's *Power/Knowledge*, ed. Colin Gordon (New York: Pantheon Books, 1980), p. 83, wherein he discusses the necessity to attempt to join the "erudite knowledge" of civilization and rationality to

"a popular knowledge" or "local memory" of fundamental truths which civilized man has largely forgotten or even ignored. It is a project that seems closely allied to the fantasy work we find in the Lewton unit's films.

Notes to "Formulas and Labyrinths: Tracking *The Leopard Man*

1. Review of *The Leopard Man, New York Times*, 20 May 1943, p. 26, col. 4.

2. See Clarens, *An Illustrated History of the Horror Film*, p. 113, and Siegel, *Val Lewton*, p. 116.

3. Quoted from Siegel's interview with Tourneur, "Tourneur Remembers," p. 25. Tourneur makes essentially the same assessment of the film in an interview published in *The Celluloid Muse*, ed. Charles Higham and Joel Greenberg (Chicago: Henry Regnery Co., 1971), p. 219, as he describes *The Leopard Man* as "too exotic, it was neither fish nor fowl: a series of vignettes, and it didn't hold together."

4. Manny Farber, "Val Lewton: Unorthodox Artistry at RKO," in *Kings of the B's*, ed. McCarthy and Flynn, pp. 107–8.

5. Jackson, *Fantasy*, p. 84. This structural approach is, of course, the basic thrust of Todorov's study of the genre, *The Fantastic*.

6. This discussion of classical narrative and its distinction from modern film style and structure derives from David Bordwell's essay, "The Art Cinema as a Mode of Film Practice," *Film Criticism* 4 (Fall 1979), 57, 61.

7. J. Hillis Miller, "Narrative Middles: A Preliminary Outline," *Genre* 9 (Fall 1978), 375.

8. J. Hillis Miller, "Ariadne's Thread: Repetition and the Narrative Line," *Critical Inquiry* 3 (Autumn 1976), 68–69.

9. Bordwell, "The Art Cinema as a Mode of Film Practice," p. 58.

10. Todorov, *The Fantastic*, p. 41. This hesitation, as Todorov says, hinting at a participatory component of the genre, is in literature "common to reader and character, who must decide whether or not what they perceive derives from 'reality' as it exists in the common opinion."

11. See Frank McConnell's discussion of justice and the melodramatic formula in his study of myth and narrative, *Storytelling and Mythmaking* (New York: Oxford University Press, 1979), pp. 138–99.

12. A commonplace notion of fantasy criticism is that, as Todorov puts it, the genre "represents an experience of limits" (*The Fantastic*, p. 93). In the Lewton films death itself becomes the ultimate limit toward which

the characters feel themselves inexorably moving and with which they must, usually for the first time, learn to cope. Hillman's linking of death and fantasy thus all the more firmly ties the Lewton works to the larger structures of the genre. As Hillman explains, "When we search for the most revelatory meaning in an experience, we get it most starkly by letting it go to Hades," for in that end is contained a sense of "the very *telos* of every soul"; dreams and fantasies, especially of the sort represented by the Lewton films, therefore, aid the life process by granting a more comprehensive perspective, a "finalistic view." See *The Dream and the Underworld*, pp. 30–31.

13. R. H. W. Dillard, "The Pageantry of Death," in *Focus on the Horror Film*, ed. Huss and Ross, p. 37.

14. John Cawelti, *Adventure, Mystery, and Romance* (Chicago: University of Chicago Press, 1976), pp. 106–7.

15. We might compare Galbraith's pleading confession to the speeches mouthed by other antagonists in the Lewton films, especially by Boris Karloff's character in both *The Body Snatcher* and *Bedlam*. In the latter film Master Sims is captured by the inmates of his asylum whom he has mistreated and, in pleading with them for his life, explains that he "was frightened . . . of the great world, the great world of this age that gave me my place. . . . What that world thinks, I must think; what they do, I must do." The recurring theme is that man's actions—and indeed his thoughts—are never totally self-determined, that larger forces, psychic, environmental, and cultural, constantly move him about, despite his ego's belief in and desire for control.

Notes to "Repetition and the Experience of Limitation: *The Seventh Victim*"

1. Siegel, *Val Lewton*, pp. 120–21.

2. Todorov, *The Fantastic*, p. 93.

3. Hillman, *The Dream and the Underworld*, p. 4. Hillman's notion of "the return through likeness" also suggests the paradoxical nature of repetition, for, on the one hand, a likeness, double, or repetition is seen as leading us back into the dark, often frightening depths of the psyche, while, on the other, it might open onto "multiple possibilities" and a new perspective on the self (p. 4).

4. For a discussion of the paradoxical nature of the repetition compulsion, see Freud's *Beyond the Pleasure Principle*, trans. James

Strachey (New York: Liveright, 1961), pp. 30–33. Before relating this compulsion to the death instinct, Freud notes a similar paradox which attaches to repetition in terms of the "pleasure principle": "the greater part of what is re-experienced under the compulsion to repeat must cause the ego unpleasure," but it is of a sort which "does not contradict the pleasure principle" itself (p. 14).

5. Miller, "Narrative Middles," p. 386.

6. See Bruce Kawin's study of repetition in film and literature, *Telling It Again and Again* (Ithaca, N.Y.: Cornell University Press, 1972), p. 34.

7. Quoted by Siegel in *Val Lewton*, p. 31.

8. Jackson, *Fantasy*, p. 158. The link Jackson makes between Todorov's theory that fantasy is essentially an experience of limits and the idea that an epistemological desire is involved in this experience speaks directly to the workings of the Lewton films as well as to the perspective advanced by Hillman.

9. René Girard, *Violence and the Sacred*, trans. Patrick Gregory (Baltimore: Johns Hopkins University Press, 1977), p. 160.

10. René Girard, "Differentiation and Undifferentiation in Lévi-Strauss and Current Critical Theory," *Directions for Criticism*, ed. Murray Krieger and L. S. Dembo (Madison: University of Wisconsin Press, 1977), p. 135.

11. We should note that the term Palladist etymologically contains this notion of a privileged wisdom. It suggests one who is devoted to or worships Pallas—or Athena—the Greek goddess of wisdom.

12. Girard, *Violence and the Sacred*, p. 276.

13. Ibid., p. 187.

14. In a background essay on the recent remake of the original *Cat People*, Val Lewton, Jr., describes this same nursery rhyme, noting that his father "used to listen while my mother sang me a little lullaby about cathedral bells, the last line of which went: 'Here comes a candle to light you to bed and here comes the chopper to chop off your head.'" Stalking the Original 'Cat People,'" *The Washington Post*, 11 Apr. 1982, H5. This childhood reminiscence obviously reaffirms the notion that Lewton wielded a strong creative hand in his productions and also underscores the attention to detail which characterizes all of the films in the series.

15. Stephen Heath, "The Question of Oshima," in *Questions of Cinema* (Bloomington: Indiana University Press, 1981), p. 156.

Notes to "The Specter of *The Ghost Ship*"

1. Miller, "Ariachne's Broken Woof," pp. 59–60. Just as in Miller's conception of narrative, the Lewton films consistently develop a "shadow" reality which is gradually revealed to be the only reality and the deep foundation upon which we base our artificial, monological conception of the world.

2. Hillman, *The Dream and the Underworld*, p. 125.

3. Review of *The Ghost Ship*, *New York Times*, 25 Dec. 1943, p. 19, col. 4.

4. Farber, "Val Lewton: Unorthodox Artistry at RKO," in *Kings of the B's*, ed. McCarthy and Flynn, p. 107.

5. Despite the film's obvious indebtedness to this naturalistic tradition and to such popular works, it was the target of a plagiarism suit, brought by two men who had submitted manuscripts to Lewton's office on broadly similar seafaring material. According to Lewton, the manuscripts had been returned unread, as was the usual policy with unsolicited material. In the judgment of Joel Siegel, both Lewton's original story and the final script written by Donald Henderson Clark "had nothing in common with the submitted material" other than "those essentials which all stories in that genre share." In truth, the film apparently took much of its shape from the usual studio exigencies under which the Lewton unit worked, namely the need to fashion a story around a large ship set left standing from a previous film and to create a suitable role for Richard Dix who was finishing his contractual obligations to RKO. Surprisingly, though, the courts ruled against RKO and *The Ghost Ship* was withdrawn from circulation. For further details on the suit, see Siegel's *Val Lewton*, p. 53.

6. Farber, "Val Lewton: Unorthodox Artistry at RKO," p. 107.

7. See Peary's interview, "Mark Robson Remembers," p. 37.

8. Frank Kermode, "Secrets and Narrative Sequence," *Critical Inquiry* 7 (Autumn 1980), 87. I employ Kermode's terms here to emphasize the complex relationship between structure and theme that seems to mark so many of the Lewton films, as the former typically casts an informing shadow on the latter, which hints at some "secret" which awaits our discovery.

9. See Miller's "Narrative Middles," p. 386. His definition of irony is particularly telling in light of *The Ghost Ship*'s lack of a clear narrative center or single perspective; irony, Miller contends, "is the confounding,

the point by point deconstruction, of any narrative order or determinable meaning. It does this by the abolishing of any identifiable controlling center."

10. Quoted in Siegel's *Val Lewton*, p. 83.

11. Peary, "Mark Robson Remembers," p. 36.

12. See Hillman, *The Dream and the Underworld*, p. 1. While he takes the phrase *via regia* from Freud, Hillman does so in order to invest it with a new and quite different meaning, in effect, to cast a new perspective on Freud's work.

13. Hillman, *Re-Visioning Psychology*, p. 33.

Notes to "Fantasy as Reality, Reality as Fantasy: *Curse of the Cat People*"

1. See *Agee on Film* (New York: Grosset & Dunlap, 1969), 1:137.

2. David Riesman, *The Lonely Crowd* (New Haven, Conn.: Yale University Press, 1950).

3. Hillman, *Re-Visioning Psychology*, p. 23.

4. Quoted from James's letter to Dr. Waldstein, in *The Letters of Henry James*, ed. Percy Lubbock (New York: Scribner's, 1920), 1:297.

5. Review of *Youth Runs Wild*, *New York Times*, 2 Sept. 1944, p. 17, cols. 2–3.

6. Bruno Bettelheim, *The Uses of Enchantment* (New York: Alfred A. Knopf, 1976), p. 7.

7. For a more detailed discussion of Lewton's early years, see Siegel's *Val Lewton*, pp. 8ff.

8. Of course the character Alice is also a holdover from the earlier *Cat People*, where she describes herself to the troubled Oliver as "the new kind of other woman." The subtly seductive danger—or attraction—implied in this self-description has here been brought under control with Alice's marriage to Oliver. However, even in this situation Alice, like most of the female characters in the Lewton films, seems to have a far greater sense of the complexity and dark possibilities of her world than does her "good plain Americano" husband. Because of characters like Alice and the large number of central female figures, the Lewton films easily and profitably open up to a feminist critique of American culture in the 1940s.

9. See Freud, *Beyond the Pleasure Principle*. Freud's discussion of children's game playing seems especially pertinent to the activity engaged in by the child characters in the Lewton films, although it also

points up the marked difference between the archetypal approach of
Jung and Hillman and Freud's primary concern with what we have here
termed the dayworld. Such playing, Freud believed, is essentially a repetition of real experience by children whereby "they abreact the strength
of the impression and, as one might put it, make themselves master of
the situation" (p. 11).

10. Bettelheim, *The Uses of Enchantment*, p. 119.

11. Ibid., p. 130. Bettelheim further notes that while parents may
fear "that a child's mind may become so overfed by fairy-tale fantasies
as to neglect learning to cope with reality," in fact "the opposite is true";
a "faulty development" occurs in the psyche if that imaginative component of the child's personality is repressed or denied (p. 118), as occurs
in the case of Amy Reed.

12. Ibid., p. 52.

13. As Hillman notes in *Re-Visioning Psychology*, the experience of
fantasy fashions a perspective that "cracks the normative cement of our
daily realities into new shapes" (p. 109).

14. Bettelheim, *The Uses of Enchantment*, pp. 69–70.

15. Todorov, *The Fantastic*, pp. 33, 41. With this suspension of judgment, Todorov argues, the fantastic affords us a significant "experience
of limits" (p. 93), not just of what we normally conceive reality to be,
but of our human capacity to explain or make sense of that world we
inhabit. It is in this sense especially that all of the films produced by the
Lewton unit might be termed fantasies.

16. Hillman, *Re-Visioning Psychology*, p. 91.

Notes to "The Mythic Path to the *Isle of the Dead*"

1. Hillman, *The Dream and the Underworld*, pp. 48, 27.

2. Hillman, *Re-Visioning Psychology*, p. 206.

3. The use of this painting further underscores the thematic unity of
the various Lewton films, for it shows up in *I Walked with a Zombie* on
the wall of Betsy's room. Its reappearance suggests a continuing concern
with the dead and death not as a source of fright or for gratuitous shock
effect, after the fashion of most horror films, but as a necessary epistemological encounter. The excursion into darkness, into the realm usually
inhabited by the dead, zombies, or vorvolakas, as films like *Zombie*, *Isle
of the Dead*, and *The Body Snatcher* particularly imply, is needed to gain
a proper perspective on life itself. The recurrent use of artwork as back-

ground material also points up a particular stylistic impulse operating in these films. Both Mark Robson and Robert Wise have remarked on Lewton's reliance on period paintings in researching the proper look and atmosphere for his films, and it is a point which Lewton himself spoke to in a press release for the nonfantasy film *Mademoiselle Fifi*, quoted in Siegel's *Val Lewton:* "A painting is so much superior to a photograph for it does more than reproduce a street or an inn. It gives you an attitude, a feeling about the place" (pp. 65–66).

4. Quoted in Siegel's *Val Lewton*, p. 74.

5. See Lévi-Strauss's famous essay, "The Structural Study of Myth," in *Structural Anthropology*, trans. Claire Jacobson and Brooke Schoepf (Garden City, N.Y.: Doubleday, 1967), p. 226, and the "Overture" to his *The Raw and the Cooked*, trans. John and Doreen Weightman (New York: Harper & Row, 1969), p. 16. The term "mythic thinking," which I employ here, is also taken from Lévi-Strauss as he articulates it in *The Savage Mind* (Chicago: University of Chicago Prss, 1966), p. 22. In this work he also reminds us that mythic activity can never be satisfactorily rendered into "intelligible dimensions" by modern thought, since its fundamental elements "lie halfway between percepts and concepts" (p. 18) and thus occupy a sort of middle ground between our rational and irrational responses to the world around us.

6. As Hillman explains in *The Dream and the Underworld*, the archetypal experience in dream or fantasy "does not complete ego-consciousness, but voids it" (p. 112).

7. Joseph Campbell, *The Hero with a Thousand Faces* (New York: Meridian Books, 1956), p. 4.

8. We might note that Greece did indeed fight a victorious war in 1912, the first of the Balkan wars against Turkey in which the Greeks won back Macedonia and Crete. However, the peace after this war was short-lived, a second Balkan war breaking out early in 1913. Of course, this fighting was then superceded by the World War in 1914; as historian W. A. Heurtley notes, "The outbreak of the European war in August 1914 was for the Greeks, as for their Balkan neighbors, only the intensification of a crisis which had begun two years earlier" (*A Short History of Greece* [London: Cambridge University Press, 1965], p. 113). In this continuing cycle of violence, we should be able to discern the paradigm for the film's situation, especially General Pherides's worries that his victories will "mean nothing" if the plague—the symbolic extension of that human violence—is allowed to spread.

9. We might compare the unconscious mythic resonances of this open-ing to similar scenes in other films of the series, all of which work to reveal the characters' unconsciousness of how deeply their actions are pervaded by the archetypal. The famous scene in *Cat People* wherein Oliver attempts to fend off his panther-wife with a ship designer's T-square offers probably the clearest comparison. As he brandishes this "weapon," Oliver cries out, "In the name of God, leave us in peace," and we see his silhouette as he appears to be using a crucifix to ward off some evil. Although Oliver unconsciously evokes that mythic force, it is no less effective, and it serves as a pointed reminder to the audience of the great power which the mythic wields.

10. Girard's thesis is outlined in his *Violence and the Sacred.* For his discussion of the necessary relationship between the community and its myths and rituals, see pp. 266 – 68 especially.

11. In "The Plague in Literature and Myth," *Texas Studies in Litera-ture and Langauge* 15 (1974), 833 –34, Girard notes the plague's recur-rence in a "whole range of literary and even non-literary genres, from pure fantasy to the most positive and scientific accounts. It is older than literature—much older, really, since it is present in myth and ritual in the entire world." Throughout these many appearances he identifies "a strange uniformity," suggesting a correlation "between the plague and social disorder" that underlies my interpretation of the plague in *Isle of the Dead* as emblematic of a larger, cultural problem.

12. The name Oliver Davis clearly echoes that of Oliver Reed of *Cat People* and *Curse of the Cat People*. It seems a preeminently common-place name, in keeping with the recurrent emphasis on mundane male protagonists who, like both Davis and Reed, are more bystanders in the important events of the films than active forces helping to effect some resolution. It is a name, moreover, that suggests two levels of commen-tary. While it was probably chosen simply to underscore the ordinariness of these characters—an ordinariness, we might suppose, implicit in the olive which is one possible source of the name—it also holds out a potential for ironic commentary in keeping with the typical strategy of these films. The name is, after all, that of the legendary hero of medieval romance (Roland); and another possible derivation, as the *American Her-itage Dictionary* offers, is a Germanic equivalent for the Old English "Ælfhere" or "elf army," which might be read ironically, as implying an essential littleness bound into a larger, and questionably stronger, body or group.

13. Hillman, *Re-Visioning Psychology,* p. 186.

14. Ibid., p. x.

15. Kawin, *Telling It Again and Again,* p. 34.

Notes to "Dealing with Death: *The Body Snatcher*"

1. Hillman, *The Dream and the Underworld,* p. 27.

2. Hillman, *Re-Visioning Psychology,* p. 140.

3. According to Siegel, Lewton was required to take credit for the screenplay, since so much of what finally appeared on the screen was his own creation, as was the case also with the last film of the RKO series, *Bedlam.* Lewton's associates have contended, however, that this result was hardly unusual, since he "rewrote everything that his writers turned in; the last draft [of each script] was always his." See Siegel's *Val Lewton,* pp. 24–25.

4. Quoted from one of Lewton's letters in ibid., p. 154.

5. In light of the wartime restrictions, which put an arbitrary ceiling of $5,000 worth of new material for set constructions on each film, this decision to limit the narrative scope of the film suggests a happy marriage of aesthetic and economic considerations. Then, too, it is precisely the sort of dual concern which a producer who was also a film's scriptwriter would necessarily have. For further information on such wartime restrictions, see Perry Ferguson's "More Realism from 'Rationed' Sets?" *American Cinematographer* (Sept. 1942), 390–91, 430.

6. Quoted in McBride's "Val Lewton, Director's Producer," p. 12.

7. Robert Louis Stevenson, "The Body Snatcher," in *The Complete Short Stories of Robert Louis Stevenson,* ed. Charles Neider (Garden City, N.Y.: Doubleday, 1969), p. 426. All subsequent references are cited in the text.

8. Siegel, *Val Lewton,* p. 155.

9. "Robert Wise," in *Directors at Work,* ed. Bernard R. Kantor, Irwin R. Blacker, and Anne Kramer (New York: Funk & Wagnalls, 1970), p. 396.

10. Farber, "Val Lewton: Unorthodox Artistry at RKO," in *Kings of the B's,* ed. McCarthy and Flynn, p. 108.

11. See the *Directors at Work* interview, p. 396.

12. Hillman, *Re-Visioning Psychology,* p. x.

13. Ibid., p. 207. In his *The Dream and the Underworld,* Hillman urges that we interpret all images of "this realm of death, whether they be fantasies of decay, images of sickness in dreams, repetitive compul-

sions, or suicidal impulses, as movements towards a more psychological perspective," and thus important steps in that larger process of "soul-making" (p. 47).

14. We might note that the lamp as a symbol of clear vision shows up frequently in the Lewton series, most notably in *Isle of the Dead*. After surveying the battlefield, General Pherides and Oliver Davis embark for the island cemetery where the plague eventually strikes. "I'll leave this here to guide us back," Drossos comments, as he places his lamp on the dock; by the time they reach the island, however, their beacon has ominously disappeared, thus suggesting the difficulty they will have in ever returning to this world, as well as the inadequacy of the "light" of reason in this dark, myth-haunted realm.

Notes to "*Bedlam*'s Walls and the Age of Reason"

1. Hillman, *Re-Visioning Psychology*, p. xiii.

2. Hillman, *The Dream and the Underworld*, p. 52.

3. *Agee on Film*, 1:192.

4. Review of *Bedlam*, *New York Times*, 20 Apr. 1946, p. 16, col. 4.

5. Robson, director of five of the Lewton films, sees a particular link between the recurrence of insanity or deranged characters in these works and the specific narrative formula which the unit typically employed. He suggests that when "dealing with melodrama, these mental aberrations or mental defects lend themselves very well to the situation." See his comments in Peary, "Mark Robson Remembers RKO," p. 37.

6. Cawelti, *Adventure, Mystery, and Romance*, pp. 45, 262.

7. Robson claims that the idea for *Bedlam* and the use of the Hogarth prints originated with him, following a chance encounter with an article on the asylum. See his interview in *The Celluloid Muse*, ed. Higham and Greenburg, p. 211. Most people connected with the production, however, credit Lewton and note his almost "encyclopedic knowledge" of painters, including Hogarth. See, for instance, McBride's "Val Lewton, Director's Producer," p. 14.

8. McConnell, *Storytelling and Mythmaking*, pp. 13–14, 172.

9. See Campbell's *Hero with a Thousand Faces* for a full discussion of this pattern. Campbell asserts that the normal human world and the "other" realm which the hero must explore "are actually one," but the latter "is a forgotten dimension of the world we know." His later comment, that "the exploration of that dimension, either willingly or unwillingly, is the whole sense of the deed of the hero," thus takes on an added

importance, for it underscores that the hero's task is less to gain a specific boon or prize for man than to discover—and perhaps repair—a fundamental rift in the world we inhabit (pp. 217ff.). This seems precisely the task which *Bedlam*'s narrative describes.

10. Michel Foucault, *Madness and Civilization*, trans. Richard Howard (New York: Random House, 1965), pp. 46, 40.

11. Ibid., p. 84.

12. Ibid., p. 259.

13. Hillman, *Re-Visioning Psychology*, p. xi.

14. James Hillman, *The Myth of Analysis* (New York: Harper & Row, 1978), p. 146. In fact, Hillman believes that such a freezing or hard and fast categorizing of experience is one of the chief afflictions of the process of mental analysis itself, and thus one of the major problems facing the treatment of many mental problems today.

15. Campbell, *Hero with a Thousand Faces*, pp. 35, 77.

16. We should note that Richard Sheridan's famous play *The Rivals* includes no charater named Aurora; in fact, since it first appeared in 1775, the play is clearly an anachronism for the 1761 period indicated by the opening title. The character's name, Aurora, however, is consistent with the light imagery associated with Nell Bowen throughout the film, and the play's title affirms Nell's position in an ongoing struggle of opposites, seen here most obviously in the contention between Whigs and Tories, and metaphorically in the opposition between the worlds of reason and unreason. The theme of rivalry, moreover, recurs throughout the Lewton films as a natural development of the doubling motif which occurs in every narrative.

17. This imagistic connection of scenes is another example of the short-hand style of narrative which marks most of the Lewton works, and which we noted earlier in *The Leopard Man* and *The Body Snatcher*.

18. Campbell, *Hero with a Thousand Faces*, p. 60.

19. Hillman, *The Dream and the Underworld*, p. 52.

20. Campbell, *Hero with a Thousand Faces*, p. 190.

21. McConnell, *Storytelling and Mythmaking*, pp. 156–57.

22. Campbell, *Hero with a Thousand Faces*, p. 19.

Notes to "The Redemption of Nonphysical Reality"

1. Hillman, *The Myth of Analysis*, p. 190.

2. Hillman, "A Note on Story," in *Loose Ends*, p. 3.

3. Jackson, *Fantasy*, p. 48.

4. Ibid., p. 102.

5. Jung's approach is summarized by Hillman in his essay)n the father of arcl ypal psychology, "Archetypal Theory: C. G. Jung," in *Loose Ends,* p. 174.

6. Hillman, *Re-Visioning Psychology,* p. 209.

7. Owen Barfield, *Saving the Appearances* (New York: Harcourt, Brace and Jovanovich, 1965), p. 107. For a more detailed account of Barfield's theories and particularly of their pertinence to the work of the horror film, see my article, "Faith and Idolatry in the Horror Film," *Literature/Film Quarterly* 8, no. 3 (1980), 143–55.

8. Barfield, *Saving the Appearances,* p. 142.

9. Ibid., p. 179.

10. John McCarty, "The Parallel Worlds of Jacques Tourneur," *Cinefantastique* 2, no. 4 (1973), 26.

11. Hillman, *Re-Visioning Psychology,* p. 179.

Bibliography

Agee, James. *Agee on Film.* Vol. 1. New York: Grosset & Dunlap, 1969.

Austin, Bruce. "An Interview with Robert Wise." *Literature/Film Quarterly* 6 (Fall 1978), 294–313.

Baffer, Christopher. "In Defense of *Isle of the Dead.*" *Classic Film Collector* no. 39 (Summer 1973), 37, 44.

Barfield, Owen. *Saving the Appearances: A Study in Idolatry.* New York: Harcourt, Brace and Jovanovich, 1965.

Bazin, André. *What is Cinema?* Vol. 1, trans. Hugh Gray. Berkeley: University of California Press, 1967.

Bergman, Andrew. *We're in the Money: Depression America and Its Films.* New York: Harper & Row, 1972.

Bettelheim, Bruno. *The Uses of Enchantment: The Meaning and Importance of Fairy Tales.* New York: Alfred A. Knopf, 1976.

Bodeen, DeWitt. *More from Hollywood: The Careers of Fifteen Great American Stars.* New York: A. S. Barnes, 1977.

Bonitzer, Pascal. "Partial Vision: Film and the Labyrinth," trans. Fabrice Ziolkowski. *Wide Angle* 4 (1981), 56–63.

Bordwell, David. "The Art Cinema as a Mode of Film Practice." *Film Criticism* 4 (Fall 1979), 56–64.

Campbell, Joseph. *The Hero with a Thousand Faces.* New York: Meridian Books, 1956.

Cawelti, John G. *Adventure, Mystery, and Romance: Formula Stories as Art and Popular Culture.* Chicago: University of Chicago Press, 1976.

Clarens, Carlos. *An Illustrated History of the Horror Film.* New York: Capricorn Books, 1967.

Cornford, F. M., ed. and trans. *Plato's Theory of Knowledge.* London: Routledge & Kegan Paul, 1935.

Craig, Robert, and Carrol L. Fry. "'Even a Girl Who is Pure at Heart': Patterns of Symbolism in Val Lewton's *Cat People.*" *Illinois Quarterly* 42 (Fall 1979), 5–12.

Culler, Jonathan. *The Pursuit of Signs: Semiotics, Literature, Deconstruction.* Ithaca, N.Y.: Cornell University Press, 1981.

Derrida, Jacques. "The Law of Genre," trans. Avital Ronell. *Critical Inquiry* 7 (Autumn 1980), 55–81.

―――. *Speech and Phenomena and Other Essays on Husserl's Theory of Signs*, trans. David B. Allison. Evanston, Ill.: Northwestern University Press, 1973.

Dillard, R. H. W. *Horror Films.* New York: Monarch Press, 1976.

Ellison, Harlan. "Three Faces of Fear." *Cinema* (California) 3 (Mar. 1966), 4–8, 13–14.

Everson, William K. *Classics of the Horror Film.* Secaucus, N.J.: Citadel Press, 1974.

Ferguson, Perry. "More Realism from 'Rationed' Sets?" *American Cinematographer* (Sept. 1942), 390–91, 430.

Foucault, Michel. *Madness and Civilization: A History of Insanity in the Age of Reason*, trans. Richard Howard. New York: Random House, 1965.

―――. *Power/Knowledge*, ed. Colin Gordon. New York: Pantheon Books, 1980.

―――. "What is an Author?" *Textual Strategies*, ed. Josué Harari, pp. 41–60. Ithaca, N.Y.: Cornell University Press, 1979.

Freud, Sigmund. *Beyond the Pleasure Principle*, trans. James Strachey. New York: Liveright, 1961.

―――. *Civilization and Its Discontents*, trans. James Strachey. New York: W. W. Norton, 1961.

Girard, René. *Deceit, Desire, and the Novel*, trans. Yvonne Freccero. Baltimore: Johns Hopkins University Press, 1965.

―――. "Differentiation and Undifferentiation in Lévi-Strauss and Current Critical Theory." *Directions for Criticism*, ed. Murray Krieger and L. S. Dembo, pp. 111–36. Madison: University of Wisconsin Press, 1977.

―――. "The Plague in Literature and Myth." *Texas Studies in Literature and Language* 15 (1974), 833–50.

―――. *Violence and the Sacred*, trans. Patrick Gregory. Baltimore: Johns Hopkins University Press, 1977.

Hammond, Paul. *Marvellous Méliès.* London: Gordon Fraser, 1974.

Harrington, Curtis. "Ghoulies and Ghosties." *The Quarterly of Film, Radio and Television* 7 (1952–53), 191–202.

Haver, Ron. "The RKO Years: Orson Welles and Howard Hughes." *American Film* 3, no. 3 (1978), 28–34.

Heath, Stephen. *Questions of Cinema.* Bloomington: Indiana University Press, 1981.

Higham, Charles, and Joel Greenberg, eds. *The Celluloid Muse: Hollywood Directors Speak.* Chicago: Henry Regnery Co., 1971.

————. *Hollywood in the Forties.* New York: A. S. Barnes, 1968.

Hillman, James. *The Dream and the Underworld.* New York: Harper & Row, 1979.

————, ed. *Facing the Gods.* Irving, Tex.: Spring Publications, 1980.

————. *Loose Ends: Primary Papers in Archetypal Psychology.* Irving, Tex.: Spring Publications, 1978.

————. *The Myth of Analysis.* New York: Harper & Row, 1972.

————. *Re-Visioning Psychology.* New York: Harper & Row, 1975.

Houseman, John. *Front and Center.* New York: Simon and Schuster, 1979.

————. *Run-Through: A Memoir.* New York: Simon and Schuster, 1972.

Huss, Roy, and T. J. Ross, eds. *Focus on the Horror Film.* Englewood Cliffs, N.J.: Prentice-Hall, 1972.

Jackson, Rosemary. *Fantasy: The Literature of Subversion.* London: Methuen, 1981.

Johnston, Claire, and Paul Willemen, eds. *Jacques Tourneur.* Edinburgh: Edinburgh Film Festival, 1975.

Jung, Carl G., ed. *Man and His Symbols.* New York: Dell, 1968.

————. *Modern Man in Search of a Soul,* trans. W. S. Dell and Cary F. Baynes. New York: Harcourt, Brace & World, 1953.

Kaminsky, Stuart M. *American Film Genres.* New York: Dell, 1974.

Kantor, Bernard R., Irwin R. Blacker, and Anne Kramer, eds. *Directors at Work: Interviews with American Film-Makers.* New York: Funk and Wagnalls, 1970.

Kaufmann, Stanley, and Bruce Henstell, eds. *American Film Criticism: From the Beginnings to* Citizen Kane. New York: Liveright, 1972.

Kawin, Bruce F. *Mindscreen: Bergman, Godard, and First-Person Film.* Princeton, N.J.: Princeton University Press, 1978.

————. *Telling It Again and Again: Repetition in Literature and Film.* Ithaca, N.Y.: Cornell University Press, 1972.

Kermode, Frank. "Secrets and Narrative Sequence." *Critical Inquiry* 7 (Autumn 1980), 83–101.

Kierkegaard, Søren. *Fear and Trembling* and *The Sickness unto Death,* trans. Walter Lowrie. Garden City, N.Y.: Doubleday, 1954.

Kracauer, Siegfried. *Theory of Film: The Redemption of Physical Reality.* New York: Oxford University Press, 1960.

Lévi-Strauss, Claude. *The Raw and the Cooked,* trans. John and Doreen Weightman. New York: Harper & Row, 1969.

———. *The Savage Mind.* Chicago: University of Chicago Press, 1966.

———. *Structural Anthropology,* trans. Claire Jacobson and Brooke Schoepf. Garden City, N.Y.: Doubleday, 1967.

Lewton, Val, Jr. "Stalking the Original *Cat People.*" *Washington Post,* 11 Apr. 1982, H-5, cols. 2–6.

McBride, Joseph. "Val Lewton, Director's Producer." *Action* 11 (Jan.– Feb. 1976), 11–16.

McCarthy, Todd, and Charles Flynn, eds. *Kings of the B's: Working within the Hollywood System.* New York: E. P. Dutton, 1975.

McCarty, John. "The Parallel Worlds of Jacques Tourneur." *Cinefantastique* 2, no. 4 (1973), 20–23, 26–29.

McConnell, Frank D. *Storytelling and Mythmaking.* New York: Oxford University Press, 1979.

Miller, J. Hillis. "Ariachne's Broken Woof." *Georgia Review* 31 (Spring 1977), 44–60.

———. "Ariadne's Thread: Repetition and the Narrative Line." *Critical Inquiry* 3 (Autumn 1976), 57–77.

———. "The Critic as Host." *Critical Inquiry* 3 (Spring 1977), 439– 47.

———. "Narrative Middles: A Preliminary Outline." *Genre* 9 (Fall 1978), 375–87.

Naremore, James. *The Magic World of Orson Welles.* New York: Oxford University Press, 1978.

Nash, Mark. "*Vampyr* and the Fantastic." *Screen* 17 (Autumn 1976), 29– 67.

Nogueira, Rui. "Robert Wise at RKO." *Focus on Film* no. 12 (Summer 1972), 43–49; "Robert Wise at Fox," no. 14 (Spring 1973), 47– 49; "Robert Wise Continued," no. 16 (Autumn 1973), 49–54; "Robert Wise to Date," no. 19 (Autumn 1974), 52–59.

Onosko, Tim. "RKO Radio: An Overview." *Velvet Light Trap* no. 10 (Fall 1973), 2–5.

Peary, Dannis. "Mark Robson Remembers RKO, Welles, and Val Lewton." *Velvet Light Trap* no. 10 (Fall 1973), 32–37.

Prawer, S. S. *Caligari's Children: The Film as Tale of Terror.* New York: Oxford University Press, 1980.

Rabkin, Eric S. *The Fantastic in Literature*. Princeton, N.J.: Princeton University Press, 1976.

Riesman, David. *The Lonely Crowd: A Study of the Changing American Character*. New Haven, Conn.: Yale University Press, 1950.

Sartre, Jean-Paul. *Literary and Philosophical Essays*, trans. Annette Michelson. New York: Philosophical Library, 1957.

Siegel, Joel. "Tourneur Remembers." *Cinefantastique* 2, no. 4 (1973), 24–25.

———. "Val Lewton." *The American Film Heritage*, ed. Kathleen Karr. Washington, D.C.: Acropolis Books, 1972.

———. *Val Lewton: The Reality of Terror*. New York: Viking Press, 1973.

Stevenson, Robert Louis. *The Complete Short Stories of Robert Louis Stevenson*, ed. Charles Neider. Garden City, N.Y.: Doubleday, 1969.

Thomson, David. *America in the Dark: Hollywood and the Gift of Unreality*. New York: William Morrow, 1977.

Todorov, Tzvetan. *The Fantastic: A Structural Approach to a Literary Genre*, trans. Richard Howard. Ithaca, N.Y.: Cornell University Press, 1975.

Tourneur, Jacques. "Taste Without Clichés." *Films and Filming* no. 9 (Nov. 1956), 9–11.

Turner, George. "Val Lewton's *Cat People*." *Cinefantastique* 12, no. 4 (1982), 22–27.

White, D. L. "The Poetics of Horror: More Than Meets the Eye." *Film Genre: Theory and Criticism*, ed. Barry K. Grant. Metuchen, N.J.: Scarecrow Press, 1977.

Wise, Robert. "Dialogue on Film: Robert Wise." *American Film* 1 (Nov. 1975), 33–48.

Wood, Robin. "Return of the Repressed." *Film Comment* 14 (July–Aug. 1978), 25–32.

———. "The Shadow Worlds of Jacques Tourneur." *Film Comment* 8, no. 2 (1972), 64–70.

Index

A Note on the Author

J. P. Telotte is an associate professor of English at Georgia Institute of Technology, where he has taught since 1979. He received his B.S. from Loyola University of the South, an M.A. from the University of New Orleans, and the Ph.D. from the University of Florida. A member of the editorial boards of *Film Criticism, Literature/Film Quarterly,* and *Post Script,* he has previously published in such journals as *Film Quarterly, Genre, South Atlantic Review, Journal of Popular Film and Television,* and *Southern Quarterly.*